D1606348

LITERACY AND THE SOCIAL ORDER

LITERACY AND THE SOCIAL ORDER

Reading and writing in Tudor and Stuart England

DAVID CRESSY

CAMBRIDGE UNIVERSITY PRESS

CAMBRIDGE

LONDON   NEW YORK   NEW ROCHELLE

MELBOURNE   SYDNEY

Published by the Press Syndicate of the University of Cambridge
The Pitt Building, Trumpington Street, Cambridge CB2 1RP
32 East 57th Street, New York, NY 10022, USA
296 Beaconsfield Parade, Middle Park, Melbourne 3206, Australia

First published 1980

Printed in The United States of America

Typeset by Ward Partnership, Widdington, England
Printed and bound by Vail-Ballou Press, Inc., Binghamton, New York

British Library Cataloguing in Publication Data
Cressy, David
Literacy and the social order.
1. Illiteracy — Social aspects — England
2. Illiteracy — England — History
I. Title
301.2'1   LC156.G7   79-41767
ISBN 0 521 22514 0

Contents

Illustrations

Tables

Note. The sources for the maps, tables and graphs are given in the text and relevant notes.

Preface

This book is a study of the dimensions and value of literacy in pre-industrial England. It grew from a larger interest in social structure and cultural change in the sixteenth and seventeenth centuries and supplies one line of attack on a vexed and important question. What were the limits of participation in the main stream of early modern society? To what extent could people at different social levels share in the political, religious, literary and cultural episodes for which their age is famous? How vital was the ability to read and write, and how widely distributed were those skills? If we can reconstruct the profile of literacy in pre-industrial England and examine the uses to which it was put we may better understand the pattern of communications and its importance for social cohesion and change.

The approach adopted here involves a combination of humanist and social science methods. Traditional archival and literary research into education, religion, social commentary and law is blended with a quantitative investigation of social structure and cultural attainment. I have tried to expose with candour the formidable problems of evidence and analysis with which this undertaking is encumbered, while providing the reader with reliable information about the penetration and significance of literacy. Attention is drawn to gaps in the evidence as well as to firm conclusions, and there is an implicit invitation to inter-disciplinary collaboration and further research.

Almost a decade of data-gathering, thinking and writing has gone into this book, although the pace of research has not been at all constant. Some of that time has been spent pondering Tudor palaeography or seventeenth-century bibliography and several months were spent tending the terminal of a DEC-10 computer. In the course of this study I have incurred many debts which cannot be discharged by a simple list of acknowledgements.

Professor G. R. Elton of Clare College, Cambridge, taught me to love documents but not to trust them. Peter Laslett of Trinity College, Cambridge, has been constantly encouraging and has stimulated and challenged my thinking about social structure.

Richard Wall and others at the SSRC/Cambridge Group for the History of Population and Social Structure offered criticism and advice over coffee and biscuits and drew my attention to theses and articles which I would otherwise have missed. Margaret Spufford has been my closest critic and although she will not agree with everything in this book she may recognize her influence in several chapters. Above all I am grateful to Roger Schofield, without whose help this book could not have been written. The basic research design is his and he has generously allowed me access to the data he collected for his own unpublished study of illiteracy. The argument of this book and the statistics which support it would both be much weaker without his contribution, although the figures here and the conclusions drawn from them are my own.

Librarians and archivists everywhere have been helpful but special thanks are due to the staff of the Cambridge University Library, Guildhall Library, London, and the Huntington Library, San Marino, California, who always made me want to return. Thanks are due to the students at Pitzer College, Claremont, California, who unveiled the mysteries of computer programming and data management, especially Houston P. Lowry, Richard Lee and E. Berkeley Shands, who were so patient with my demands. Various stages of this research were supported by grants from the American Council of Learned Societies, the National Endowment for the Humanities, and the Pitzer College Research and Development Committee. In 1978 I was a Fellow of the John Simon Guggenheim Memorial Foundation, studying 'literacy and the character of English migration to early America', and some of the material examined at that time has found its way into this book.

I

Reading, writing and the margins of literacy

The value of literacy was widely proclaimed by religious and secular authors in early modern England. From the reformation to the industrial revolution there was a constant clamour among men of God and men of letters to the effect that reading and writing brought enormous benefits to whoever possessed those skills. Spiritual benefits and worldly advantages would reward those people who learned to read and write and who made proper use of their literacy. Horrors and difficulties were forecast for the unfortunates who failed to embrace literacy, and pity was extended to the illiterates who were unable to remedy their condition. Literacy was highly desirable, at least in the minds of those who already had it.

The case for literacy was persuasive. A person who could read was better equipped to prepare for salvation than his illiterate fellow Christians and was more likely, in the view of protestant divines, to lead a life of duty and godliness. Without the equipment of literacy he could not fully meet the obligations or reap the rewards of the protestant Christian experience. Practical and intellectual advantages were also at stake. One who could read was more likely to be at ease in a world which was increasingly dominated by written instruments and instructions, documented decisions, correspondence, record-keeping and the printed book. Reading gave one access to information and ideas, diversion and stimulation, controversy and entertainment, which lay beyond the immediate reach of the totally illiterate. A person who could write possessed even more advantages. He could set down his ideas, his accounts, his reports or his instructions and communicate them over distance and time. In matters of business and pleasure alike a person who was fully literate could engage in a broader range of affairs and cope better with the complexities of the world than his contemporaries who were unable to read or write.

Yet it is possible that the writers who proclaimed the advantages of literacy overestimated its value to ordinary men and women. People who were not unduly troubled about salvation, who were content within their horizons of knowledge and experience, and

1

whose daily or seasonal routine required no mastery of print or script, had no pressing need of literacy and could hardly be persuaded to seek it. Those who campaigned for literacy were often faced with an uphill struggle, especially when faced by a population for whom the skills were superfluous. Evidence from the seventeenth century, which will be examined in detail in later chapters, shows that England was massively illiterate despite an epoch of educational expansion and a barrage of sermons. More than two-thirds of the men and nine-tenths of the women were so illiterate at the time of the civil war that they could not even write their own names. This fact of illiteracy underlies all the rhetoric and commentary which will be discussed in this chapter.

Religious conservatives of the mid-Tudor period saw little reason for people to trouble themselves with literacy, and viewed with disdain the early protestant effort to spread the vernacular Bible. Thomas More, for example, denied that 'the having of the scripture in English be a thing so requisite of precise necessity that the people's souls should needs perish but if they have it translated into their own tongue', since the illiterate multitude would not be able to benefit from it. In any case, religious literacy was beside the point. 'Many . . . shall with God's grace, though they never read word of scripture, come as well to heaven.'[1] Most people could not read, but the sacraments secured their salvation and images and emblems reminded them of their faith. Popular illiteracy caused little harm.

Stephen Gardiner would have agreed with More. In a letter of 1547, provoked by some excessive protestant iconoclasm at Portsmouth, Gardiner argued that images, both secular and religious, adequately supplied the place of writing.

For the destruction of images containeth an enterprise to subvert religion and the state of the world with it . . . The pursuivant carrieth not on his breast the king's names written in such letters as few can spell, but such as all can read be they never so rude, being great known letters in images of three lions and three fleurs de lis, and other beasts holding those arms. And he that cannot read the scripture written about the king's great seal, either because he cannot read at all or because the wax doth not express it, yet he can read Saint George on horseback on the one side and the king sitting in his majesty on the other side . . . And if the cross be a truth, and if it be true that Christ suffered, why may we not have a writing thereof such as all can read, that is to say an image?[2]

Images suffered badly with the reformation, being rooted out in church after church down to the very 'stones, foundations, or other places, frames or tabernacles, devised' to display them.[3] The conservative position was being eclipsed in the mid sixteenth century and a new tradition emerged which placed heavy emphasis on holy texts and which held literacy dear. Visual information continued to be important, as it still is today, but few would justify it as an alternative to reading and writing. In a church purged of images the eye would be caught by newly painted and enscribed tables of the Ten Commandments and the Lord's Prayer, words which were worth a thousand pictures.[4] Whether the congregation could actually read them is another matter.

Writers of protestant devotional and inspirational works in the sixteenth and seventeenth centuries commonly urged literacy on their countrymen as a means to advance religion. Literacy was singled out as a tool for godliness, a weapon against anti-Christ, an essential component in leading a proper Christian life. Bibles, prayer books, psalters, homilies and other religious books were available in churches with the intention that parishioners should read them. Clergy were instructed to

comfort, exhort, and admonish every man to read the Bible in Latin or English, as the very word of God and the spiritual food of man's soul, whereby they may the better know their duties to God, to their sovereign lord the king, and their neighbour.[5]

By the end of the sixteenth century there was increasing encouragement to read the Bible at home as well. Church attendance was to be supplemented by private study of the scriptures, since Christian devotions were incomplete without regular reading in the Bible. Nicholas Bownde, a Puritan writing in the 1590s, recommended, 'so many as can read, let them do it upon the Lord's day, and they that cannot, let them see the want of it to be so great in themselves that they bring up their children unto it'. Englishmen, like their protestant co-religionists throughout northern Europe, were expected to 'learn to read and see with their own eyes what God bids and commands in his holy word'.[6]

The idea that literacy formed a crucial part of a Christian's armour echoes in sermons and tracts throughout the seventeenth century. For Puritans in England as in New England, 'literacy was a universal prerequisite to spiritual preparedness, the central duty of the covenant'.[7] Preachers and teachers pressured and cajoled, and warned of the consequences of failure to learn.

Illiteracy created problems for this world and the next. As George Swinnock lamented in 1663,

some for want of reading their neck-verse have lost their lives, but ah, how many for want of reading have lost their precious souls . . . alas, the people perish for want of knowledge. And how can they know God's will that cannot read it?

Piety and devotion alone were not enough. Even faith was insufficient without literacy to guide it. Swinnock advised parents,

> I tell thee, didst thou but know of what concernment reading is to the soul of thy child, thou wouldst rather beg of every person in thy parish and the next too, rather than let them go without it.[8]

The point was made again by Richard Baxter, who summarized the evangelical tradition in his massive *Christian directory* of 1673. 'By all means let children be taught to read, if you are never so poor and whatever shift you make, or else you deprive them of a singular help to their instruction and salvation.'[9] Yet salvation was not the only issue, since that was in the hands of God rather than man. Civility and Christian neighbourly behaviour also suffered, or so the preachers believed, when people lacked training in literacy. The author of *The office of Christian parents* (1616) argued that without literacy to guide them in godliness children would become 'idle . . . vile and abject persons, liars, thieves, evil beasts, slow bellies and good for nothing'. William Gouge in 1622 warned that 'rudeness, licentiousness, profaneness, superstition, and any wickedness' would follow from the inability to write and read. Reading and writing he referred to as 'the groundwork of all callings', and added that 'many that have not been taught them at first would give much for them afterwards'. Baxter feared that without literacy there would be barbarity, 'a generation of barbarians in a Christian happy land'.[10]

If the fruits of illiteracy brought misery, its banishment promised happiness and delight. 'Civil and moral comeliness in behaviour', as well as 'the knowledge of Christ', was associated with learning to read and write. 'The surest guides to duty and happiness' were available to the literate through 'study of the sacred scriptures'. Sermonists spoke repeatedly of the 'mercy' and 'profit' involved in being able to read.[11]

Since literacy was so vital the Christian had a duty to help those around him learn to read God's word. Parents should teach children, masters should teach servants, those who could read and write were to assist their associates who could not, while philanthropists and governors should cooperate in the provision of public education. With his characteristic blend of good sense and high ideals, Richard Baxter advised that

> if you have servants that cannot read let them learn yet (at spare hours) if they be of any capacity and willingness. For it is a very great mercy to be able to read the holy scriptures for themselves, and a very great misery to know nothing but what they hear from others.[12]

The benefits of literacy were compelling. Being able to read led one directly to the word of God, and it freed one from dependence on the availability and reading ability of others. John Ball argued in his much reprinted *Short treatise* that 'private reading maketh the public ministry more profitable'. The ability to read 'enableth us better to judge of the doctrines taught . . . thereby we are better fitted for the combat . . . and many evils are prevented'.[13] Baxter was equally convinced that only through literacy, and a discriminating religious literacy at that, could a Christian sufficiently arm himself for this world and the next. Baxter's own religious awakening, like that of his father before him, was attributed to the private reading of books, and books could bring about a similar transformation in others. His eloquent commentary on the importance of books in a Christian's continuing education was not just because he wrote so many himself.[14]

The writings of divines are nothing else but a preaching the gospel to the eye as the voice preacheth it to the ear. Vocal preaching hath the pre-eminence in moving the affections, and being diversified according to the state of the congregations which attend it. This way the milk cometh warmest from the breast. But books have the advantage in many other respects. You may be able to read an able preacher when you have but a mean one to hear. Every congregation cannot hear the most judicious or powerful preachers, but every single person may read the books of the most powerful and judicious. Preachers may be silenced or banished, when books may be at hand. Books may be kept at a smaller charge than preachers. We may choose books which treat of that very subject which we desire to hear of, but we cannot choose what subject the preacher shall treat of. Books we may have at hand every day and hour, when we can have sermons but seldom and at set times. If sermons be forgotten they are gone, but a book we may read over and over till we remember it, and if we forget it may again peruse it at our pleasure or at our leisure. So that good books are a very great mercy to the world . . . Books are, if well chosen, domestic, present, constant, judicious, pertinent, yea and powerful sermons, and always of very great use to your salvation.[15]

It was one thing to listen and be inspired, but an altogether more satisfactory activity to read and review, to go back over difficult passages, compare texts and glosses, and find one's own way about the scriptures. Without literacy this dimension of the Christian experience was closed. Nor should the Christian fear that private reading would lead to error. To forbear reading for fear of erring makes sense, according to Baxter, 'no more than that men must forbear eating for fear of poison, or that subjects must be kept ignorant of the laws of the king for fear of misunderstanding or abusing them'. Only 'papists' took such an attitude to literacy.[16]

The Christian could also benefit through being able to write. Sermons made good listening in church but they could be savoured afresh from notes made during the service. Writing permitted one the extra pleasure of committing remarks from the pulpit to paper and sending the substance of a sermon to somebody else. Oliver Heywood, for example, accompanied his mother to hear dozens of preachers and served as her amanuensis by recording their main points for the aid of her memory. When he went up to Cambridge in 1647 his father instructed him to 'take short notes of every sermon and write some fair over for your loving mother'. Grammar-school boys were often required to take notes on the sermons they attended, although this may have been to enforce their attention and practise their handwriting, as much as to stimulate their piety. Among religious enthusiasts a longhand summary of a sermon or debate could serve much the same function as Baxter's books after the speaker had departed.[17]

Writing allowed one to interact with the holy word, not merely to absorb it. One who possessed that skill could make marginal remarks on his Bible or any other work in print, and could collect together choice verses or comments in a commonplace book. William Cecil advised his son to procure expositions of the New and Old Testament 'to be bound in parchment and to note the same books with your pen'. Oliver Heywood was advised by his father to 'labour to get every day some sanctified thoughts. . . and write them in a book'.[18] Exhortations to pious writing were by no means unusual. The most accomplished literate Christian might maintain a spiritual diary or list of objectives, write letters of comfort to his brethren, and even compose devout writings of his own. Such high attainments were not the normal requirements of a godly life, but if God had given you the ability to write then it should be used, like all other talents, to his glory and in his service. Writing was never so important as reading, but the ability to set down words on paper could refine and enhance the active Christian experience.

Literacy was said to benefit civil society as well as the kingdom of God. Educational writers from Roger Ascham in the sixteenth century to Christopher Wase in the seventeenth argued that 'misorders' and 'disobedience' would diminish if young people were properly educated and learned, through literacy, their duties to man as well as to God. The entire commonwealth could profit since literacy was associated with such desirable features as 'policy and civility' and 'justice and discipline'. Literacy was good for you, good for your soul, and good for everyone else.[19]

A world of information and entertainment was opened for people who could read. Literacy was the gateway to grammar and all humane learning as well as an avenue to godliness. Most pedagogues saw elementary reading and writing as but stepping stones to classical literature and it was taken for granted that anyone wishing to be familiar with the finest thoughts of antiquity, or who merely wished to mix well with the educated clergy and gentry, would quickly master basic literacy and pass on to higher things.

Tudor and Stuart humanists had little to say about simple literacy but the ability to read and write English could have immediate and useful applications for people who never aspired to grammar. Works of practical wisdom and volumes of literary diversion poured off the printing presses along with Bibles and other religious texts. Not everyone stayed focused on sin and salvation. Almanacs and prognostications, jest books and chap books, travellers' tales and histories, and advice for farming or housekeeping, were all available from London booksellers and their provincial agents. Works on husbandry which reported successes in soil improvement, lawbooks for the layman with abridgements of the statutes and model instruments for legal actions, tables of tides and calendrical, medical and meteorological advice of the sort found in almanacs, all put valuable information into the hands of people who could profit from it.[20]

Although we cannot yet trace their circulation or pinpoint their market it is thought that such materials had a popular appeal at least comparable to that of the Bible, especially after the expansion of printing in the later seventeenth century. Thomas Tryon in the mid seventeenth century recognized that 'the vast usefulness of reading' extended beyond its spiritual benefits and could help one comprehend the world. His own literacy took him to commercial success as well as religious awakening.[21] Literacy offered the curious reader a feast of discoveries and adventures, histories both natural and political, and delights like *A strange and wonderful relation of the burying alive of Joan Bridges* (1646), none of which was directly accessible to the illiterate.

Literacy could keep you politically alert, telling of recent and current events and advising on future developments. If you could read you were more likely to know what was going on, although traditional oral communication was also effective in spreading information. A literate villager and his illiterate neighbour might both set their names to petitions or declarations in the civil war period, by signature or mark, but the one who could read might better appreciate the significance of the action. Through literacy you might get your information earlier and you might also get it right. Checking a text or reading a broadsheet for oneself was more reliable than tracing a rumour or trusting in village demagogy. Information may or may not be power but at least it gives you some contact with the doings and wishes of the powerful.

Popular political literacy was not necessarily in the best interests of the ruling elite, but it was an increasing force to be reckoned with throughout the seventeenth century. Political activists and political commentators took to print to justify their actions and vilify their opponents. Handbills, advertisements, proclamations and packets of news made the ability to read such things politically significant, and spread political information away from the centres of political action. The role of popular literacy in the political crises of the period, and the degree to which ordinary people participated in them, is a subject deserving of much greater study. Literacy was not essential to political consciousness but it surely enhanced political sophistication. Richard Overton, the leveller, regarded reading and writing as part of the suppressed birthright of Englishmen, and in this he was not alone.[22]

If reading could bring enrichment and advantage it could also imperil the soul, damage the mind and subvert the moral bases of society. Printing was powerful, like gunpowder, in the acerbic view of the royalist James Howell.[23] Concerned preachers repeatedly warned their congregations against the dangers of 'wicked books' and 'the loose and immoral writings which swarm in the present day'. Horror stories and ballads, 'playbooks and romances and idle tales' kept printers in business and preachers close to apoplexy. Many of those who could read were drawn to material which was unabashedly escapist fun, and in this respect the early modern period was, perhaps, little different from the present. Phillip Stubbes argued that 'books and pamphlets of scurrility and bawdry are better esteemed and more vendible than the sagest books that be', and he lamented the resulting infection and corruption.[24]

Literacy was evidently a double-edged tool, which could lead to depravity as well as to godliness, to dissipation as well as to practical improvement. Elizabethan and later puritans railed against these seductive timewasters. Stubbes believed that 'toys, fantasies and bableries' from the popular press went so far as to 'corrupt men's minds, pervert good wits, allure to bawdry, induce to whoredom, suppress virtue and erect vice'. Nicholas Bownde protested that the circulation of printed ballads threatened to 'drive away the singing of psalms'. Richard Baxter was outraged by the 'tempting books' that were 'the very poison of youth'.[25]

The attack from the pulpit was testimony to the attractiveness of popular printed entertainment. Some of the critics had themselves succumbed in early days to the temptations of literary poison and this, perhaps, added to the urgency and passion of their condemnation. John Bunyan had been led astray in his youth by cheap peddled literature 'that teaches curious arts, that tells of old fables', and Richard Baxter also confessed to an early bewitchment and corruption by popular romances and fables.[26] The advocates of educational expansion were in a difficult bind. On the one hand, they wanted everyone to learn to read in order to know their religious duty; on the other, they knew that reading, if not rigidly controlled, might do more damage than good. It would be ironic if the activists who pressed so hard for protestant education held back from a wholehearted literacy campaign for fear that popular literacy would be profane. The only comfort — dubious comfort — was that most people in pre-industrial England still lacked the ability to read these materials, and were kept from sin by their ignorance.

Writing was important to the promoters of literacy for its practical secular utility as well as for its contribution to the maintenance of civilization. 'The art of writing', wrote Martin Billingsley, 'is so excellent and of such necessary use, that none ought to be without knowledge therein'. Through writing, according to David Brown,

all high matters of whatsoever nature or importance are both intended and prosecuted, secret matters are secretly kept, friends that be a thousand miles distant are conferred with and (after a sort) visited; the excellent works of godly men, the grave sentences of wise men, and the profitable arts of learned men, who died a thousand years ago, are yet extant for our daily use and imitation; all the estates, kingdoms, cities and countries of the world are governed, laws and printing maintained, justice and discipline administered, youth bred in piety, virtue, manners and learning at schools and universities, and that which is most and best, all the churches of God from the beginning established and always unto this day edified.

Writing served as a cultural cement, a social lubricant, 'the key', in Billingsley's words, 'to the descrying and finding out of innumerable treasures'.[27] Billingsley and Brown, of course, were professional writing men who taught calligraphy and orthography in Stuart London and who had a commercial interest in promoting literacy, but it is hard to disagree with their encomium.

The extent to which literacy was valued as a career asset is difficult to discern. Conventional opinion in Tudor and Stuart England generally frowned on personal advantage and private advancement since these qualities were thought to challenge the much stronger ideal of order and balance in the commonwealth. Arguments in favour of literacy tended to stress its general usefulness to the community, for the service of God and the betterment of society, rather than its utility for individual ambition. But occasionally a voice was heard which subordinated traditional considerations. David Brown frankly explained how the ability to write could bring social and business advantages to his pupils and clients.

> Not to write at all is both shame and scathe. Shame for two causes: first, because whosoever seeth that thou canst not write knoweth thee to be ignorant of all kinds of learning; and why? because writing is the key or beginning of all learning . . . And secondly, it is shame both to employ a notar to subscribe for thee in any security, and to want that good token of education which perhaps thine inferior hath, for wheresoever any man of honest rank resorteth who cannot write, chiefly where he is not known, he is incontinent esteemed either to be base born or to have been basely brought up in a base or moorland desert, that is, far from any city where there be schools of learning, discipline, policy and civility.

The scathe or injury lay in having to rely on a scrivener or notary who might take advantage of your illiteracy and betray you. Through illiteracy you might 'lose some good design', which the simple ability to write might otherwise obtain for you.[28]

The implication was clear. Anyone who wished to make headway in the world should learn to read and write, and the professional penman was only too willing to teach them. 'If thou be such a one, whether the negligence hath been in thy parents, friends or in they self . . . whether thou canst read or not', David Brown was ready to take on customers.[29]

We must be careful not to read a universal attitude to literacy in the salesmanship of the writing masters. There may have been, as Billingsley claimed, 'a multitude of inconveniences'[30] attendant on not being able to write, but the value of full literacy was tempered by its context and use. The sophisticated market economy of Stuart London may have created a unique environment where anxieties about writing would thrive and where literacy was sought as an aid to ambition, but a much more relaxed attitude to literacy was likely in other parts of England. It is difficult to discover anyone who actually felt shamed by his inability to write or who feared damage to his reputation or frustration of his designs. For the ordinary Englishman writing indeed facilitated a great range of activities, but it was not absolutely essential for any of them.

The skill of writing made possible a more complex set of interactions with one's neighbours, loved ones, enemies and associates. A man who could write might make a more useful community servant, as churchwarden, constable or overseer, although literacy was never a prerequisite of these duties. Hundreds of parochial officials were unable to sign their names but the tasks of record-keeping and rendering of accounts must have been easier for the others who were literate. Literate and illiterate alike appeared before the manor courts as tenants, before the church and secular courts as witnesses or plaintiffs, and dealt with landlords, creditors and others who used writing to regulate and endorse their activities. Knowing how to read and write must have helped in these affairs, but the verbal process of the courts and the availability of professional scribes enabled people without those skills to manage.

Credit transactions which passed with a handshake were more secure, and less likely to be forgotten, when the details were preserved in writing. Desperate debts might stand some chance of recovery by heirs and executors if the amounts and obligations were written. Travel arrangements, assignations and matters concerned with employment could also be handled more efficiently, and messages, introductions and letters of recommendation could be better communicated if writing was no obstacle. Full literacy made possible the keeping of accounts and journals, the writing of letters, even authorship and creative writing. If the skill was there then needs would supply it with activity.

Needs, of course, varied with one's situation. People involved in trade, specialized manufacturing and farming for the market increasingly found themselves confronted by print or script, and more and more of them maintained written records of their transactions. In a world growing more familiar with bills and reckonings, acquittances and memoranda, the ability to read such instruments could be turned to personal advantage, even if there was a specialist on hand to write them. Nicholas Breton ennumerated the ordinary tasks for which literacy was useful, in a dialogue of 1618. The speaker is a 'countryman' whom one takes to be a yeoman despite his having a courtier for a cousin.

This is all we go to school for: to read common prayers at church and set down common prices at markets, write a letter and make a bond, set down the day of our births, our marriage day, and make our wills when we are sick for the disposing of our goods when we are dead. These are the chief matters that we meddle with and we find enough to trouble our heads withal.[31]

Literacy here was not primarily a key to salvation or even a device for entertainment, but merely a useful adjunct to the rural routine. The yeoman who could jot down market prices and compare them from week to week or season to season would have an obvious advantage over his illiterate competitor who relied on his memory. One who could write his own letters and dispose of his own affairs in writing would be free of the awkwardness, expense and possible untrustworthiness of the scrivener or writing-man. The very fact of his literacy, confidently displayed, might give him some credit in the eyes of officials, associates and subordinates. Reading skills could serve the same mundane purposes, steering clear of both spiritual elevation and romantic corruption. The yeoman might find profit in one of Markham's texts on husbandry, while the practical information in handbills and almanacs might alert him to opportunities about which his illiterate counterpart was ignorant.

A good example of active practical literacy is found in the almanac notebook of the innkeeper at the Three Cranes in Doncaster. This man had a simple almanac for the years 1652–8, interleaved with blank pages on which he made laconic jottings about his family and commercial business. Many of the pages remained blank, but others announce the terms of a lease, the dimensions of an orchard, an agreement for discharging a bond, and such remarks as

all beere taylied. . . 2 kilderkins of small bere came in. . . Anne Bastard ½ a yeare wages due 25th day [March] 1. 10. 0. . . my wife took her journy. . . in Stepny pulpit one Powel a Welsh minister ingaged his credit on it that Antichrist should be destroyed anno 1656. . . Samuels rent is due for his chamber. . . lent to Robert for a paire of stockings 3s. . . 2 kilderkins of strong beere brought in. . . to be at Ferribridge.[32]

The document, script on print, is hardly a diary of the journal sort but it evidently served its first owner as an occasional engagement book and a place to enter brief memoranda and records of transactions. By writing down specific terms, amounts and dates the landlord could fix these things for future reference and protect his interests in the event of dispute. Without full literacy there could be no such control of one's affairs. The landlord of the Three Cranes expressed some wonderment at the prophecy of the Welsh minister, but there is not another religious reference in the entire six-year record. Literacy in his case was a commercial asset, a tool for dealing with suppliers and customers and for regulating a miscellany of arrangements. The tradesman was using his skill, not for the improvement of his soul but for the improvement of his profits.

Innkeepers, like yeomen, moved in circles where literacy was useful. At other levels of society the skill was dispensable. The countryman, according to Nicholas Breton, could be perfectly content without any book-learning and could probably make do without being able to read or write.

We can learn to plough and harrow, sow and reap, plant and prune, thresh and fan, winnow and grind, brew and bake, and all without book. These are our chief business in the country, except we be jurymen to hang a thief or speak truth in a man's right, which conscience and experience will teach us with a little learning.[33]

The rural routine and the demands of most crafts saw little need for literacy. Of course, it could be useful, as Breton's countryman acknowledged, but folk who had managed for years without being able to read or write could continue in their ways and feel no disadvantage. Even given the opportunity and capacity, people might normally acquire no more literacy than they needed.

Although the importance of literacy was widely proclaimed by religious and secular propagandists the majority of the population remained illiterate, at least to the extent that they could not write. The leaders of society might agree that reading and writing were desirable skills, especially if dedicated to approved purposes, but they could not, through argument alone, achieve a literate society. Countrymen, artisans and the labouring poor could live illiterate lives without regretting their condition. Only if they were stung by a radical religious awakening, a rare enough experience even in the seventeenth century, might they take steps to learn to read and to write, and then they might learn from their minister or their fellow enthusiasts and seek similar instruction for their children. The religious push into literacy was often unheeded, while the pull of economic and social utility seems to have been felt by only a fraction of the population.

There were, of course, exceptions, which have attracted the attention of historians even more than of contemporaries. Acts of philanthropy, self-improvement, self-sacrifice, pious motivation and energetic ambition turned illiterates into readers and readers into writers, and demonstrate the power of the written and printed word.[34] But for the most part the demand for literacy was sluggish. The incentives and rewards repeatedly publicized by authors and preachers were not sufficiently strong to break people from their deep-rooted and quite comfortable illiteracy. Illiteracy was a problem only for those who were forced to deal with print and script, and in any case there were ways to alleviate the difficulties.

People could cope with illiteracy and might have no sense of its being a handicap. The praise of books by authors like Baxter and Brown would have little meaning for the thousands of people whose world did not hinge on reading and writing. Who needed to read and write if he could mend a fence, tell the weather, cure a sick animal and perform the seasonal tasks enumerated by Breton? The oral culture, on the other hand, with its traditions and tales, its proverbs and jokes, customs and ceremonies, offered enough in the way of entertainment and enrichment to sustain a satisfactory alternative. Face-to-face communication, the sharing of stories and songs, the re-telling of news and the spreading of gossip may have provided a sufficient range of information and diversion for the ordinary illiterate Englishman. We must be careful neither to dismiss nor to romanticize the folk life of the 'world we have lost', but it is important to acknowledge its vitality.

Illiteracy could, no doubt, lead to insularity and ignorance, but the man without reading and writing was not necessarily cut off from the world of higher affairs. We may smile at the story that skirmishers clearing the field at Edgehill before the battle between king and parliament were asked by a baffled countryman, 'Have they two fallen out?'[35] But this should not be taken as typical. Important national news travelled swiftly, and every villager had in his parish clergyman as well as in his literate neighbours a bridge to events and ideas beyond his immediate horizon. At church, inn and market there were men who could read who might share their skill with others. The extent to which this bridging took place is impossible to gauge, but it must have varied with the heat of the news and the urgency or interest of the ideas. The means existed to mobilize and alert the nation, but in normal circumstances most people were probably indifferent to matters beyond their horizons. Such complacency was shattered by the civil war; it would be interesting to know the breadth and intensity of political discussion on the margins of literacy in the rest of the seventeenth century.

From the tracts and texts of the reformation to the pamphlets and chapbooks of the later Stuart period there was a spillover from the literate to the illiterate. The world of print and the oral culture were not entirely separate, and in fact there was a constant feeding from the one to the other. The English New Testament drew illiterate auditors in the 1530s, just as printed ballads, newssheets and chapmen's wares were read aloud later in the sixteenth and seventeenth centuries. Some folk performers broadened their repertoire with songs and stories which had first appeared in print, and many of the things that people said or heard had formerly been printed or written.[36] Illiterate people could participate, at some distance, in the increasingly dominant literate culture, but they still could not participate directly.

Even in religion there were ways to alleviate illiteracy. Despite the evangelical insistence on reading, the church continued to stress the oral elements in liturgical worship and catechetical instruction. Easter communicants and intending marriage partners were supposed to 'say by heart' the crucial prayers and precepts, and were not expected to read them. In the Province of York the table of degrees of affinity and consanguinity forbidding marriage was to be read out loud to the parishioners 'every year twice at the least', despite having the text prominently displayed on the wall.[37] Psalms could be learned and sermons could be digested without requiring a formal education.

The protestant revolution notwithstanding, it was not necessary to be literate to be devout, and entry to the kingdom of heaven was not conditional on being able to read. Thomas More had recognized this in the 1530s, and protestant pastors acknowledged its truth a century and more later. Richard Steele, whose sermons of the Restoration period were printed and went through several editions (for the use of fellow-preachers), acknowledged the illiteracy of his country congregation:

Though you cannot read a letter in the book, yet you can by true assurance read your name in the Book of Life, your scholarship will serve. . . if you cannot write a word, yet see you transcribe the fair copy of a godly, righteous and sober life, and you have done well.[38]

It was enough to listen and pray.

Just as being unable to read could be mitigated by having someone else read for you, so being unable to write, on the rare occasions when writing was called for, could be overcome by having access to another person's writing ability. Breton's countryman puts it well. 'Now, if we cannot write we have the clerk of the church or the schoolmaster of the town to help us, who for our plain matters will serve our turns well enough.'[39] Indeed, there are numerous examples of village literati acting as informal scriveners. Schoolmasters and clergymen were often brought in to help draw up wills, set down agreements and arrange complicated business in writing. Thomas Salter, a schoolmaster of Upminster, Essex, in 1585 was a witness in a case concerning tithes when an indenture he had prepared came into question. Another Essex schoolmaster, William Smith of Lucton, had to testify in 1589 about someone's will he had written, while Hugh Luscombe, a teacher at Totton, Devon, gave evidence in 1617 about one of his wills which was now in dispute. In Cambridgeshire the scribes of village wills included gentlemen and clergy, churchwardens and schoolmasters, shopkeepers, yeomen and husbandmen who possessed the necessary skills and who were willing to write for their neighbours. Margaret Spufford has shown how these scribes could even shape the religious testament of the dying man.[40]

There is ample evidence to show that professional men and others who were known to be handy with a pen were constantly pressed into service to help out their illiterate neighbours. There was always someone who could write, who would do your business for a small fee or favour, although as David Brown pointed out it was not always wise to entrust your intimate affairs to anyone else. Roger Lowe, a provincial shopkeeper in the 1660s, kept a diary which wonderfully illustrates the activity of the informal scrivener. In 1663 he records several occasions when he wrote letters, composed wills and cast accounts for people in his vicinity. On 5 February 1663, 'I was much troubled at a business that befell about writing a letter for Ellen Ashton to her son Charles. She related that I writ to have her son come down, that she knew not of, which was a false lie.' On 29 October, 'John Hasleden . . . told me that he loved a wench in Ireland, and so the day after I writ a love letter for him into Ireland.' Being an amanuensis had its pleasures as well as its problems, and could also bring in a supplementary income. Roger Lowe referred in April 1663 to '£3 that I had gotten with writing'.[41]

In addition to the amateurs and para-professionals like Lowe and the schoolmasters, there were also full-time scriveners who made their living through their pens. Most towns of any substance would be served by scriveners or writing-men who knew the formulae for acquittances, bills and wills and other legal and commercial instruments. They performed a variety of services, including the commercial teaching of writing for individuals and schools, but the full range of their activities awaits investigation. London was said to be swarming with them, many of them 'botchers' according to Billingsley, 'not one of them almost worthy to carry a penman's ink-horn after him, much less to bear the name of a good penman'. The charge, of course, was directed at their poor calligraphy rather than their ethics or their actual ability to write.[42]

One more practical aspect of literacy remains to be considered, the one already alluded to by George Swinnock when he wrote of those who lost their lives 'for want of reading their neck verse'. It involves special circumstances and a peculiar test of literacy and so should be kept separate from the general discussion. In medieval England, when literacy was virtually a clerical monopoly and criminous clerks were judged more leniently than lay felons, the ability to read a set text of the Bible was regarded as a competent proof of clerkship. The criminal had only to ask for the book and read the standard verse, the 'neck verse', to escape the gallows. The first verse of the fifty-first psalm was usually chosen for this purpose, its acknowledgement of transgressions and its appeal to God for mercy being particularly appropriate for the occasion. Literacy could have very real benefits.[43]

Although various statutes created an increasing number of exemptions and restrictions, the opportunity remained in Tudor and Stuart England for the literate felon to claim 'benefit of clergy' and escape the full severity of the law. As William Lambarde explains, 'if he can read he may at any time desire of the judge the allowance of his book'. If successful his thumb would be branded and his future entitlement to benefit of clergy would be revoked. 'Where clergy lieth it is grantable but once to one person, except he be within holy orders, for such a one may have it often'.[44]

Stone has suggested that '47% of the criminal classes of Jacobean London could read', since they successfully pleaded benefit of clergy. The Middlesex records in fact show 32% of the capital felons in the reign of Elizabeth and 39% in the reign of James successfully claiming clergy, a somewhat lower percentage than cited by Stone.[45]

We do not know how many criminals faked their literacy by learning in rote fashion the required verse, nor do we know enough about the procedures of the courts and their attitude to this particular dispensation. In an interesting case after the Restoration the judge denied clergy to 'an old thief' who would have been granted it by the court official responsible for administering the book.

He delivered the book to him and I perceived the prisoner never looked upon the book at all, and yet the bishop's clerk, upon the demand of *legit* or *non legit*, answered *legit*. . . and so I caused the prisoner to be brought near and delivered him the book, and then the prisoner confessed he could not read.

The lax official was fined five marks and the prisoner was sent to the gallows.[46]

Benefit of clergy may have been, as Stone argues, one of the 'two powerful incentives to encourage the poor to learn to read', the other being the attraction of the Bible.[47] But it seems unlikely that anticipation of a future death sentence would weigh heavily in the decision of most people to embrace literacy. In any case, most people learned to read and write, if they learned at all, while they were quite young, so any study of motivation should look first to their parents.

Literacy had a variety of uses, but was not absolutely essential for happiness or success. Despite the promotion of reading and writing for religious and secular purposes, England remained only a partially literate society. Many people lived on the margins of literacy and were either not convinced of its value or had little opportunity to test it. Opportunities to learn reading and writing were constrained by social, economic and domestic circumstances while facilities for the dissemination of basic literacy were underdeveloped. The central part of this book will examine which sectors of society actually mastered basic literacy; but first we must review the ways in which people were taught to read and write.

2

The acquisition of literacy

Although the curriculum and practice of the sixteenth- and seventeenth-century grammar schools has been extensively explored in the works of Baldwin, Charlton, Simon, Vincent, Watson and others, the elementary curriculum which laid the foundations for all subsequent learning and which brought children into possession of basic literacy has received relatively little attention.[1] Too often it is taken for granted, as if learning to read and write were of little consequence, or were skills that were naturally acquired in childhood without much conscious effort.[2] On the contrary, the acquisition of literacy involved discipline and practice, and success was unlikely without strong motivation on the part of the child and his parents and patience and skill on the part of his instructor.

It will be shown in this chapter that a considerable body of expertise was developed in pre-industrial England relating to the teaching of literacy, but obstacles of many kinds stood between pedagogic theory and popular practice. Professional educators worked to devise and prosecute a successful elementary programme, and thousands of children benefited from their efforts. Many more, however, were handicapped by inadequate teachers, lack of support or the problem of access to qualified instruction. The eighty years before the English civil war may indeed have been a period of 'educational revolution', but for the majority of English children it was a revolution which passed them by.[3]

Elementary education did not command the resources or attract the prestige associated with grammar schooling. Teaching children to read and to write was a difficult art, attended by frustration and failure as much as by success, and those engaged in it were mostly poorly rewarded. Many petty teachers were little more than child-minders, but the best of them were conscientious and a few took to print to explain their procedures and to promote their techniques. Some grammar teachers wrote on the elementary curriculum in the hope that their remarks would improve the dismal level of basic education and ease their own work with entering pupils. By the early seventeenth century there was a growing body of literature to which teachers of reading and writing could turn, and most of it was based on actual classroom experience. A review of this literature will help us to trace the path to literacy, at least in so far as it was followed in the classroom.

Sixteenth-century educators developed a method for teaching children to read and to write which continued with minor modifications at least into the nineteenth century. William Kempe, writing in 1588, described its essential components as '*Prosodia*, in pronouncing of letters, syllables and words with the mouth, and *Orthographia*, in writing of them with the hand'.[4] The distinction was at the heart of Tudor and Stuart pedagogy and would be followed in endowed foundations and informal schools alike. Reading was taught before writing and separate strategies were employed at different stages in the curriculum to impart the two skills. John Hart, in a publication of 1570, advised the unlettered 'first to learn to read before they should learn to write, for that is far more ready and easy'.[5] There was really little alternative. Basic literacy was a compound product, where fluency in reading might be acquired independently of facility in writing. Unlike the modern child whose work with a pencil reinforces his progress in reading from the very beginning, the schoolboy in pre-industrial England tackled reading and writing separately and in sequence. Only in the hands of an unusually demanding schoolmaster would a pupil tackle writing while still learning to read.

Learning to read was an oral process, a matter of associating sounds with shapes and figures. A child could say aloud letters and combinations of letters long before he could reproduce them on slate or paper. The early work with the alphabet and the elements of spelling in the horn book was entirely an exercise for voice and memory. According to Kempe,

the scholar shall learn perfectly, namely, to know the letters by their figures, to sound them aright by their proper names, and to join them together, the vowels with the vowels in diphthongs and the consonants with vowels in other syllables.

Edmund Coote, whose popular manual first appeared in 1596, advised that 'when your scholar hath perfectly learned his letters teach him to know his vowels; and after two or three days when he is skilfull in them teach him to call all the other letters consonants'. Francis Clement followed the same method of recitation: 'Let the child learn the vowels perfectly without the book so that he can readily rehearse them. . . beware he missound not'.[6]

Similar methods were used in the seventeenth century. Writing in the mid seventeenth century, Charles Hoole reported that the usual way to begin with a child when he is first brought to school is to teach him to know his letters in the horn book, where he is made to run over all the letters in the alphabet or Christ cross row, both forwards and backwards, until he can tell any one of them which is pointed at.

The child was then subjected to a drilling in letter combinations and syllables and entered into the elements of spelling, before being declared ready for reading.

The ordinary way to teach children to read is, after they have got some knowledge of their letters and a smattering of some syllables and words in the horn book, to turn them into the ABC or primer and therein to make them name the letters and spell the words till by often use they can pronounce at least the shortest words at the first sight.[7]

Hoole, to his credit, recognized that this was a grim regime for most children and wished to make lessons more cheerful, but he could not alter the universal framework of instruction.

Learning continued by interrogation and response, a secular catechism which paralleled the child's education in godliness. Progress in literacy was demonstrated by sounding and saying, aimed, according to Coote, at 'distinct reading', spelling from memory and 'the true framing of your voice'. Coote gives an example of his classroom practice whereby pupils were encouraged to test each other, which clearly shows the absence of writing from the first stage of becoming literate.

John: How write you *people*?
Robert: I cannot write.
John: I mean not so, but when I say write I mean spell, for in my meaning they are both one.
Robert: Then I answer you, p,e,o,p,l,e.[8]

The word was 'written' out loud, not set down for inspection on paper. The child was supposed to master the constituents of English spelling and grammar without writing any of it down.

Having entered so far into literacy, the pupil would proceed to practise his spelling and reading in such books as the primer and catechism. Nowell's *Catechism*, which was required reading in every school after 1571, contained a useful reservoir of spelling examples as well as a thorough review of the Christian religion.[9] Fluency in reading would come by practice, with the psalms and the testament for text.

When he can read any whit readily let him begin the Bible and read over the book of Genesis and other remarkable histories in other places of scripture which are most likely to delight him, by a chapter at a time.

Secular material was also permissible, added Hoole, 'so the matter of it be but honest'.[10]

Having progressed so far the master wished to impress on his pupil a love of books and a discriminating taste in reading. Literacy should, after all, benefit both its possessor and the commonwealth at large. Francis Clement was aware of the various uses of literacy and its possible consequences. Readers were warned against 'lovebooks' and encouraged to 'booklove'. Lovebooks, by which were meant romances and idle tales, 'be the enemies of virtue, nurses of vice, furtherers of ignorance, and hinderers of all good learning'. Booklove, by contrast, the love of good learning, 'embraceth virtue, abandoneth vice, expelleth ignorance, and nourisheth wisdom and learning'.[11] The teachers of reading were delivering a double-edged instrument.

Reading was taught before writing but the separation of the two skills was not necessarily so strict as has been suggested. Richard Mulcaster, that most philosophical of Elizabethan schoolmasters, argued that reading depended on writing, as chickens did on eggs.

I handle specially. . . the right writing of our English tongue, a very necessary point out of force to be handled ere the child be taught to read, which reading is the first principle of the whole elementary. For can reading be right before writing be righted, seeing we read nothing else but what we see written?

Mulcaster's concern was that English orthography was so irregular that it demanded the urgent attention of all who were engaged in teaching reading. In principle, writing should be considered before reading, 'as the matter of the one is the maker of the other', but in classroom practice, of course, the conventional arrangement prevailed.[12]

Much of the elementary curriculum was planned with an eye to its utility in writing as well as reading. The strong emphasis on correct spelling while learning to read would be useful later in writing, since the child with that skill could make words as well as decipher them. Meticulous pronunciation aloud enabled the learner to make sense of a sentence and also prepared him for the time when he would write his own. As Francis Clement advised, 'it is necessary for him that should write truly to know at the least rightly to pronounce his word and to give to every syllable his just sound according to the vowel thereof'.[13] The construction method of reading a letter or syllable at a time was also applicable to writing, and the professional pedagogues expected their pupils to progress to at least that stage.

Although reading was given earlier and stronger emphasis, the secondary skill of writing was by no means ignored. The elementary curriculum was incomplete without writing and some teachers recommended its early introduction. William Kempe would start teaching writing while the pupil was reading the catechism,

for the better confirming of all these things in memory ... for orthography, which teacheth with what letters every syllable and word must be written and with what points the sentence and parts thereof must be distinguished, is a practice of the same knowledge, but expressed by the hand as the former is by the tongue ... seeing it hath singular use and commodity in the exercise of grammar the master shall teach his scholar to write.[14]

William Bullokar, another Elizabethan educator, also taught writing along with reading. His pupil would be 'learning to read and to spell all words truly, while he learneth to write his letters for change of exercise, without grief to the learner or pain to the teacher'. But since Bullokar was more concerned to promote his novel alphabet, with thirty-seven letters, eight vowels and seven diphthongs, than to describe standard classroom procedures, his testimony may be suspect.[15]

The child who had mastered the elements of reading was expected to begin to write, and advanced work with the primer and all subsequent instruction in reading might be accompanied by exercises in writing. Much may have depended on the energy and diligence of the teacher. David Brown, an early Stuart teacher of considerable energy, boasted of his pupils that 'immediately after they have learned somewhat to read, they have begun also to write, and then in short time have known how to read other men's writ by the like letters of their own writ'.[16] Other teachers may never have gone much beyond the horn book. Reading 'writ' or handwriting was distinguished from the easier reading of print. Thenceforth, if all went well, the two elements of literacy, Kempe's *prosodia* and *orthographia*, could be developed in harness.

Writing, however, continued to be a subordinate part of the elementary curriculum. School days were long, at least in regulated institutions, and Kempe advised that 'in this exercise of writing the scholar shall spend but two or three hours in a day at the most, employing the rest of the time in reading, until he be about seven years old'. Brinsley recommended daily practice in writing 'for an hour's space or near', adding, with the voice of experience, 'and that about one of the clock, for then commonly their hands are warmest and nimblest'. This was to recognize that writing was, and still is, as much a matter of dexterity and fine motor skills as of intellect and memory. Even practising for just one hour a day a child should have been able to develop a useful facility with a pen, although, as Clement observed, 'without longer use and due continuance to write well will hardly be had'.[17]

Writing was a discipline for the hand and eye, as much as reading was a task for the eye and voice. Kempe regarded the 'skill of the hand' in writing as belonging 'properly to the art of painting and not unto grammar, so that the best grammarian is not always the best penman'.[18] The business of teaching writing was much more complicated than teaching to read and involved the making and mastery of special equipment. Brinsley reviewed 'all the necessaries belonging thereunto, as pen, ink, paper, ruler, plummet, ruling-pen, penknife, etc.', and described in detail how every pupil should make and prepare his pen.[19] One wonders if the mess and nuisance involved was a disincentive to teaching this skill. It was surely much easier to hear the alphabet or catechism than to cope with the debris of ink, blottings, penknives and goose feathers.

Once the pens were made they had to be mastered, no easy matter for unpractised hands. Peter Bales offered useful advice in 1590.

First, hold your pen between your two forefingers and your thumb; let your thumb be highest, your forefinger next and your middle finger lowest. Next hold your pen softly in your hand, with no more strength than is needful. . . lean softly upon your pen, for by overhard leaning thereon you shall mar your pen and the letter both at once . . . hold not your pen too upright in your hand, nor too much aslope . . . nor bear your thumb too stiff.[20]

Similar advice was given by Francis Clement on how to obtain 'the variable direction of the pen' and how to form strokes of different size by varying the pressure.[21]

Hints like these were commonplace in the works of Tudor and Stuart schoolmasters. They sound so rudimentary as to be super-fluous, but it should be remembered that most people in the past grew up with no access to writing materials of any kind and had none of the practice of doodling, scribbling or sketching that children enjoy today. Simple penmanship, a prerequisite for writing, was an underdeveloped skill.[22]

Writing was first taught as a supplementary skill in order to consolidate what had already been learned through reading. The beginning writer would work his way through the letters, diph-thongs, syllables and words that he had already learned to recog-nize and pronounce. According to Kempe,

the master shall teach his scholar to write by precepts, of forming the letters in due proportion, of joining them aptly together; by practice, of drawing the pen upon the figures of shadowed letters, then of writing without shadowed letters by imitating a copy, lastly of writing without a copy.[23]

One of the first things a modern child learns to write is his or her own name, not only for the utility of a signature but for the sense of identity and achievement it brings, and considerable effort is put into practising it. But none of the educators of pre-industrial England recommended children to learn to write their own names. Indeed, the writing of personal names in school exercises may actually have been discouraged, since they did not conform to the rules of spelling which the teachers were trying to instil. Edmund Coote complained that 'our English proper names are written as it pleaseth the painter, or as men have received them by tradition', while, as John Hart observed, 'by our present disorder . . . many a man doth scantly know how the writing of his own name should be sounded'.[24] Instead of teaching a standard orthography for personal names and encouraging their writing at school, Coote and the others concentrated on writing with a more universal application. Children who were just learning to write might have more success writing 'people' than their own individual signature.

Considerable effort and ingenuity went into perfecting the teaching of basic literacy in Elizabethan and Stuart England. Whether the methods described here were widely adopted in village schools and by semi-professional teachers is not known, but no alternative programme of instruction was in evidence. The modern emphasis on words rather than letters, and the integration of writing with reading, seems not to have been practised. Educational theorists may judge whether the techniques pioneered by the Elizabethan pedagogues were more conducive to early learning than those in use today, or whether they created unnecessary difficulties which frustrated educational progress. The brightest pupils learned to read and write, as they learn today, with or despite the methods employed by their teachers, but marginal children may have suffered without the encouragement of a more sensitive and flexible curriculum. If schoolboys had trouble with prosody and orthography, how much more difficult must it have been for the underprivileged masses who never went to school at all?

The time taken to learn reading and writing varied, of course, with the ability and application of the child, the motivation and concern of his parents, the skill and experience of the teacher and other intervening circumstances. Richard Mulcaster put it wisely: 'ripeness in children is not tied to one time . . . some be hastings and will on, some be hardings and draw back'.[25] He might have added that some were free to attend a regular course of instruction,

while others had to patch their education together in the gaps
between drudgery and idleness.

Most of the schoolmasters who wrote about elementary education considered a year or two sufficient to teach reading and
writing, and some claimed success with innovations which greatly
accelerated the process. Few liked to acknowledge that the
acquisition of literacy could be a prolonged and much-interrupted
endeavour. William Kempe would have his pupils writing as well
as reading by the age of seven, at which point they were ready to
take on Latin. Charles Hoole also thought seven or eight was a
fit time to begin the grammar curriculum, after 'two or three
years' of 'learning to read English perfectly'. Others were less
conservative, promising wonders. John Hart offered to teach 'any
natural English reasonable creature to read English in one quarter
of the time that ever any other hath heretofore been taught to
read by any former manner'. William Bullokar claimed that 'all
learners may read and write English in a quarter of the time'
using his revolutionary alphabet with thirty-seven letters, 'all
which may be learned in six weeks by a child of five years of
age'.[26]

Writing-masters sometimes offered spectacular results. William
Pank claimed to have

devised such plain, easy and exact rules for fair writing as one of ordinary
years and capacity . . . though they never handled pen, may in a short space,
at idle times not hindering their other business and by their own private
practice, attain to write both the secretary and the Roman hand.[27]

Even more confident claims were made by David Brown, who

teacheth those that can read and be capable and careful to write any hand
well in six hours which they never wrote before . . . and those that cannot
write at all, or not well or not true English, neither can read written hand,
write without rule nor keep accounts, he teacheth to attain all these better
in one month, an hour only in a day.[28]

The writing-masters appealed to a mixed-age clientele. Their
methods were applicable to adults who had missed the opportunity
to become fully literate as well as to children who were just
beginning. Brown in particular addressed the mature student who
could find the teacher's fees in his own pocket. He worked 'for
redeeming the time and renewing the occasion of learning to all,
but chiefly those of middle age who have wanted, lost or neglected
either in their youth and cannot now spare long time to learn'.
He claimed to be 'moved by the earnest entreaty of some virtuous
minded men who now in their age do far more sensibly feel the

want, neglect or loss of time in their youth', and had a remedy to hand. 'For it may be that many hundreds who are both past the date of going to schools and much employed about other business will yet spare some convenient time to learn alone by the help of this little book.'[29] David Brown was an educational entrepreneur, thriving in Stuart London. His private practice evidently prospered, as new migrants to the metropolis came to appreciate the usefulness of literacy, but the service he offered may not have existed in more traditional parts of the country. In most places the opportunity lost in childhood was lost forever.

Some writers hoped that adults would seek to remedy their illiteracy if their children were at school. The enthusiasm of children learning to read and write was supposed to spill over to infect the elders, as if literacy could slip back through the generations by contagion. White Kennett, for example, praising the effects of the charity schools at the end of the Stuart period, alleged that

some parents have been regenerated and born anew by the influence of their own flesh and blood. To see their children between the school hours delighting in their books and lessons at home, this by degrees has turned the hearts of the parents the same way; they have recovered their lost reading and have been restored to the knowledge and practice of morality and religion.[30]

Such results must have warmed the hearts of philanthropists but they are unlikely to have been statistically significant. In any case, Kennett's sermon was as much an advertisement as Brown's book on writing, a promotion rather than reliable testimony.

The age at which educators recommended a start to schooling and the age at which children actually began varied considerably. William Kempe thought a child should meet his first schoolmaster when he was 'about five years old', while Francis Clement would have the boy discerning vowels from consonants 'though he be but four years of age'. John Brinsley advised 'that the child, if he be of any ordinary towardness and capacity, should begin at five years old'. However, he recognized that country children with fewer opportunities would not normally start before they were seven or eight. 'Six is very soon.' As Charles Hoole wrote, 'it is usual in cities and greater towns to put children to school about four or five years of age, and in country villages because of further distance, not till about six or seven'.[31] The schoolmasters were unanimous in urging an early start to formal education.

Family circumstances as well as geography influenced the time of starting school. *The office of Christian parents* advised the 'poorer sort' of parents that 'once their child entreth into the eight year of his age they should assuredly provide, if it be possible, that they may be furnished with the knowledge of reading and writing'. For more fortunate children 'it will be found most meet to make them very perfect to read and write their own vulgar tongue' before seven years of age.[32] The age range for elementary schooling that emerges from the educational literature of the early modern period – from four to eight – is remarkably similar to the age at which children begin to read at school today.

Some attempt has to be made to find out what progress ordinary children made towards literacy. When we move away from the urgings of divines, the advertisements of promoters and the self-congratulation of schoolmasters, a less cheerful picture emerges. Many children never went to school and others said their lessons intermittently, but even those who were placed with a school-master did not necessarily learn much. John Brinsley reported pupils who took two or three years to learn to read English and others who were still in difficulty after six or seven years of ineffective teaching. Charles Hoole found children, often 'the most and best . . . learning a whole year together, and though they have been much chid and beaten too for want of heed could scarce tell six of their letters at twelve months end'.[33]

Thousands of children must have been discouraged by their lack of progress and failed to become literate, even if social and economic circumstances conspired to send them to school. Sitting still and dissecting sentences does not come naturally to boys of seven or eight, and the discipline that kept them to it may have soured them on learning for life. It was easy to sympathize with the character in Thomas Nashe's masque who said: 'nouns and pronouns, I pronounce you as traitors to boys' buttocks . . . I'll never be a goosequill while I live'.[34] Seventeenth-century auto-biographies are rich in cautionary tales of youngsters who squandered their chances to become literate as schoolboys and who later grew to regret it. Some of them report severe difficulties with inadequate teachers or poor motivation, but we learn only of the few who overcame them. Others may have gone on into life illiterate with their wasted schooldays behind them.

Exposure to formal education was irregular and intermittent for many children, fluctuating with the demands of the agri-cultural season, the needs of the family and community and the relationship which developed between child, teacher and parents. Some schooling was free, supported by charitable endowments, but more often a quarterly fee was required. Even the so-called free schools exacted an array of petty payments for such things as candles, firing and educational materials, so the stretch of a family budget could determine how long a child was sent to school. A domestic catastrophe such as the loss of a breadwinner could completely curtail a child's beginning education if guardians or friends were not prepared to continue the outlay. Rather than imagining the acquisition of literacy to have happened everywhere at a standard stage in the life cycle we should conceive of a shifting tide of youngsters in touch with schooling for greater and lesser periods, with a great many barely exposed to it at all.

Most seventeenth-century autobiographers began their schooling at the age of six, although some began as early as four and others much later. Six seems to have been a common age to embark on elementary education, and seven or eight the usual time to stop.[35] Autobiographers, however, were special people, sometimes precocious and often exceptionally gifted, and their experiences do not necessarily form a reliable guide to the common experience. Actual records of elementary school attendance in the seventeenth century are hard to find, but an eighteenth-century register from Witham, Essex, finds boys entering the day school with a mean age of 6.1 and leaving a year and a half later, aged 7.6.[36] This was probably long enough to learn the rudiments of both reading and writing, although the retention and development of these skills was at risk without further encouragement. Delays and interruptions were commonplace and play havoc with any attempt to describe a typical educational experience. Some people were still emerging into literacy in their late teens while many of their contemporaries made no progress at all.

Henry Facy, a schoolboy at Crediton, Devon, was fourteen when he died in 1667. We can learn something of his educational progress because, exceptionally for a minor, he made a will which was challenged in the ecclesiastical courts for three years and his teacher was called to testify to Henry's literacy. According to Edward Bidwell, the schoolmaster, Henry Facy 'was able to write a good hand after a copy and could read in the Bible'. He had been learning to write for five or six months at the time of his death and had only recently achieved full literacy. Nobody expressed surprise that a teenager should still be learning to write, the only unusual thing about Henry being his will and his early death. The teacher continued:

The said Henry did learn what was taught him very well, as well as could be expected from a boy of his age, about thirteen or fourteen years old as this deponent believes, and as well as most other boys being in the school of his age and time of learning, this deponent then having about forty scholars.[37]

Henry Facy was no more typical than anyone else, but his case reminds us that while some people could read and write at seven others were still mastering the elementary curriculum at twice that age.

Another glimpse of the age at which literacy was acquired is provided by the register of the Great Yarmouth Children's Hospital at the end of the Stuart period. Boys and girls aged five to fifteen were received into the hospital when they were orphaned or when their families became incapable of maintaining them. The register makes it clear that most of the children came from respectable working families, with fathers in such occupations as sailmaker or blacksmith, shoemaker or mariner. The hospital was neither for foundlings nor the sick, but served as a charitable workhouse which fed, clothed and sheltered the needy youth of the community, and prepared them for apprenticeships.[38]

One of its responsibilities was to educate the children in its care. By his contract with the trustees, Abraham Bayly, who became master of the hospital in 1696, was

> to be allowed for teaching every child, viz., twenty shillings when it can read well in the Bible, twenty shillings more when it can write well, twenty shillings when it can cypher well to the rule of three inclusive, and twenty shillings when each girl can sew plain work well.

So as to spread the incentives between teacher and taught the children were to be given two shillings and sixpence each when they passed these educational milestones.[39] The sequence of reading before writing was made clear in these arrangements, although the aim was for children to master both skills. The hospital administrators evidently knew the value of literacy as well as the efficacy of payment by results, and attempted to supply the burghers of Yarmouth with literate apprentices. Bayly's arrangement also gave rise to some unique documentation, since he had to show that he was earning his money.

In addition to conventional biographical and administrative details, the hospital register under Bayly records the level of literacy of each entering child. Further remarks about educational attainments were usually added a few years later when the child left to become an apprentice. For example, 'Benjamin, son of Samuel Woolsey, mariner, 10 years old, was taken into the workhouse by order of the committee, August 14, 1697. In his horn book.' Five years later, 'Benjamin Woolsey, son of Samuel and Lydia, was bound apprentice to Benjamin Jolly, baker of this town, and Frances his wife, this 4th day of March, 1703. Reads in the Bible and cyphers indifferently.' Bayly's regime evidently had some effect, although the fifteen-year-old **Benjamin** was not claimed as being able to write.[40]

The register allows us to build a profile of literacy by age among the entrants to the hospital and in some cases to see how children improved there. Table 2.1 shows the literacy attainments by age of boys admitted to the Great Yarmouth Children's Hospital between 1698 and 1715. Of 132 male entrants in this period 12 were marked 'knows not his letters' and another 55 were marked 'cannot read' or 'reads not' or 'cannot read at all'. Just over half the entrants were completely illiterate and they ranged in age from six to fourteen. Another 7 boys were at the very beginning of the elementary curriculum and were marked 'in his horn book' or 'knows his letters', while a further 17 had progressed beyond the simple material of the alphabet and the horn book and were now on the primer. Only 36 of the entering boys, little more than a quarter of the total, could read with any fluency, with 23 on the testament and 13 able to read the Bible. Most of them were well behind the children described in the educational literature and less accomplished than the boys who grew up to become auto-biographers. The numbers are too small to discern any pattern of attainment related to age, although the older children had usually made more progress towards literacy. Only 16% of the boys aged six to eight were fully able to read, compared to 37% among those aged nine and above.

The girls entering the hospital, as shown in Table 2.2, were less accomplished than the boys. Forty-five of the entrants, a little more than half the total, did not know their letters or could not read at all, while only 11 had reached the stage where they could read the testament or the Bible. The girls had only half the reading rate of the boys and did not share their association of literacy and age.

The register of the children's hospital records the progress of some of the inmates towards full literacy. Although there is not enough information for a statistical treatment it appears that the most accomplished products of the workhouse were those who had already made some beginnings with literacy before they were admitted. It was noted that Francis Mileham, when he was apprenticed to a keelman in 1705, 'reads well in the Bible and cyphers well in arithmetic to the rule of three', but he could already read the Bible when admitted at the age of seven in 1700. Joseph Fawk, apprenticed to a carter in 1710, 'reads well in the Bible, writes very well, and cyphers in reduction', but he too was already reading the testament at the age of seven in 1704. Others owed

Table 2.1   *Literacy of boys entering Great Yarmouth Children's Hospital, 1698–1715*

Age	'knows not his letters'	'cannot read'	'in his horn book'	'in the primer'	'reads Testament'	'reads Bible'	Unknown	Total
6		3			2		1	6
7	2	10		6	2	1		21
8	2	10	2	6	2	1	1	24
9	1	6	4		5	1		17
10	4	13			9	5	2	33
11		5		1	1	1	1	9
12		3	1	2	2	4		12
13		3		2				5
14		1						1
Unknown	3	1						4
	12	55	7	17	23	13	5	132

Table 2.2 *Literacy of girls entering Great Yarmouth Children's Hospital, 1698–1715*

Age	'knows not her letters'	'cannot read'	'in her horn book'	'in the primer'	'reads Testament'	'reads Bible'	Unknown	Total
5		1						1
6	1							1
7		2	1	2	1		1	7
8		8	2	2	2	1	3	18
9	4	7	1	2		1	3	18
10		7	1	1	1	2	1	13
11		4		4		1		9
12	2	6				1		9
13		1		1				2
14		1	1			1		3
15				1				1
Unknown		1		1			1	3
	7	38	6	14	4	7	9	85

their literacy to their workhouse schoolmaster. Simon Moore could not read at the age of ten, but five years later when apprenticed to a seaman he 'reads in his Bible and cyphers pretty well'. The master recorded that Mary Clark 'can't read at all' at the age of nine in 1700, but after four years of instruction 'she reads in her testament but indifferently and hath gone through her sampler'.

In some cases the schoolmaster successfully taught writing as well as reading. Only a handful was noted as achieving this secondary skill. Phillip Clark could 'read well, write indifferently' when he was apprenticed at the age of sixteen. John Foster was returned to his father at the age of eight able to read in the Bible 'and in writing makes letters'. Hugh Douglas 'writes joining very well' at the age of fifteen, and a few more boys departed with some writing ability. In each case the schoolmaster was building on previously established foundations, for even young John Foster could read in the psalter when admitted at the age of six. Nobody was credited with being able to write his name. All sorts of minor accomplishments were recorded so the absence of any reference to a signature suggests that no special value was attached to writing one's name and no particular coaching was provided for it. Being able to write one's name was an unremarked by-product of being able to write. None of the girls reached the stage of writing. Their highest achievement was to sew well and to read in the testament or Bible, but few left the workhouse with fluency in reading. A large number stuck at the elements of literacy, at that stage where the letters are familiar but where they do not quite make sense.

It would be unwise to draw any general conclusion about the acquisition of literacy from these children at Yarmouth, except perhaps to say that there was no set pattern. All the evidence we have assembled suggests that opportunity, capacity, motivation and talent varied, as did the quality of the results. By the end of the Stuart period there were children from humble and unfortunate families who had learned to read and write, along with a great many who had not. Literacy did not occur as a natural development at a particular stage of childhood, but depended on successful contact with a teacher, contact which for many children was frustrating, fleeting, or never happened at all.

The children's hospital was an exceptional institution. Most children who learned to read and write acquired their literacy from local schoolmasters or freelance teachers with, perhaps, some help at home. However, as will be argued, domestic instruction was less important than formal education.

Children from the most privileged families were attended by a private tutor from an early age and had their education at the hands of expensive specialists. Others were fortunate enough to attend a common or public school where professional school-masters taught literacy in English as a preparation for literacy in Latin. At some schools the ushers or under-masters, or even senior students, taught basic reading and writing to pupils who were not prepared to grapple with grammar. Despite their constant grumbling that elementary education was not their business the grammar schools were regularly 'toiled amongst such little petties' and 'troubled with teaching ABC'.[41]

A scattering of endowed and well-constituted schools existed solely to teach the elementary curriculum. At Willingham in Cambridgeshire an English school was founded by community subscription, with detailed provisions for its funding and organiz-ation. Another English school was founded at Chigwell in Essex, with an endowment of £25 a year for a master to teach children 'to read, write, cypher, cast account, and to learn their ac-cidence'.[42] Elementary schools like these never had the prestige of the grammar schools, but they continued, from generation to generation, to help local children towards literacy.

Still more children went to school in places where no formally endowed or organized institution ever existed. Charters and charitable instruments alone did not determine where education took place, nor was the holding of classes contingent on the existence of a schoolhouse. Legal and architectural arrangements were in fact subordinate, and served only to ensure continuity and recognition. The crucial element was the presence of a competent teacher, whose school would operate for as long as he was available and which might fade from memory with his death or migration. Some freelance teachers were extraordinarily mobile, as they travelled in search of preferment or a better-paid position, or responded to offers from different parts of the country. Others served their community for years, sometimes combining their work as a teacher with service as parish clerk, or engaging in trade.

Recent graduates in search of a career and curates who needed the money were among those who turned to teaching and offered their services wherever they were in demand.[43] Occasionally such teachers would prepare a boy for a superior grammar school or even for the university, but the bulk of their work lay in teaching village children their letters. The lessons would be held in private houses, in rented rooms or in the parish church. The school might operate for several years and then disappear, or it might be replaced by a similar arrangement with another freelance teacher in charge. All these teachers were supposed to be licensed, regardless of their institutional affiliations, and it is often possible to trace their activities in ecclesiastical licensing and visitation records.

Parish clergy also taught some children to read and to write, although they did not normally compete with professional pedagogues. Many vicars and rectors held licences to teach which dated from earlier in their own careers, and some of them still operated small schools to assist the promising youth of the parish. In the diocese of Norwich in the seventeenth century as many as 11% of the licensed schoolmasters were in holy orders. At Maidenhead, Berkshire, Mr Dawson, the chaplain, 'demanded but 3d a week for every scholar that learned English only, and for such as learned to write and read or to cypher or learn grammar 4d weekly'.[44] The more radical ministers strongly believed that all their parishioners should acquire literacy, but most of them were too busy teaching the word to find time also to teach letters. Parish priests, for the most part, were supporters of schoolmasters, not substitutes for them.

Formal instruction of a sort could also be obtained in some places from literate neighbours or from shopkeepers and craftsmen who found teaching a few petties to be a profitable diversion. At Eccleshall, Staffordshire, in the seventeenth century, Robert Walker, a skinner by trade, had done duty as a schoolmaster. He was succeeded by his son Edward, a glover, who was noted in Bishop Lloyd's survey in the 1690s: 'He reads for hire and teaches school, an honest poor man, he keeps the overseers' accounts.' Towns like Eccleshall might offer a choice of semi-professional private teachers, especially with the quickening economy of the late seventeenth century.[45] The quality of such instruction varied enormously, as did the number of pupils in their care. With diligence and good fortune a literate layman could pass on his skills to young children, but some petty teachers were so bad that they delayed or even prevented their charges acquiring literacy.

Francis Clement was upset that

children, as we see, almost everywhere are first taught either in private by men and women altogether rude and utterly ignorant of the due composing and just spelling of words, or else in common schools most commonly by boys, very seldom or never by any of sufficient skill.[46]

The ecclesiastical records of the seventeenth century throw some light on the murky world of elementary education and show that Clement's observations had some truth. Although many petty schoolmasters were upright and competent, there were others like John Bagford of London, 'a teacher of little children to spell and read English . . . a very sickly, weak and impotent person, by reason whereof altogether uncapable to follow any other employment'. Too often we find invalids, paupers and others in reduced circumstances warding off total destitution by casual subsistence teaching. William Pledger of Barking, Essex, was 'an honest and peaceable man and an honest painstaker whilst his strength and years permit . . . but growing old and being past his labour he betook himself to teach an English school'. Another unfortunate who turned late to teaching was Richard Roach, a mariner who had broken his back and 'was forced to betake himself to keep a small school'.[47] We find no sense of 'calling' in these unhappy instances, but rather the sense that teaching petties was a last resort. The rewards were small, but teachers like these could always find clients who wished for someone to teach their children to read instead of undertaking the task themselves.

Schoolmistresses probably did no more damage than the men, but their activities are difficult to trace. Dorothy Gardiner remarked on their 'insignificant number and subordinate position' in Elizabethan England. The ecclesiastical licensing system which was supposed to embrace petty teachers as well as grammar masters seems, in practice, not to have concerned itself with women. Few ecclesiastical visitors took note of them so they rarely appear in the records unless they had offended someone. Mistress Foster of Chislet, Kent, 'doth teach school, namely to write and read', and William Watts, a licensed schoolmaster of the neighbouring parish of St Nicholas-at-Wade, resented her encroachment on his monopoly and petitioned 'that she may be inhibited from teaching'. Elsewhere we find the wives or daughters of schoolmasters assisting with the family business, teaching the horn book and teaching to read.[48]

Schoolmistresses or dames could be of very dubious quality. The dame of a village school in Sussex in 1699 had her children making clothes in school, and contracted for reading and writing lessons from visiting or near-by schoolmasters. The dames to whom poor children were assigned in early-seventeenth-century Norwich were to mind, supervise and control the unruly youngsters, and had no responsibility for teaching them literacy.[49] Perhaps it was just as well. Sarah Unwin of Hadstock, Essex, was reprimanded by the archdeacon of Colchester because the children in her care 'pronounce their words untruly, and those that could recite their catechism before she had them have now forgotten it'. Even worse was Elizabeth Snell of Watford, Hertfordshire. It was claimed in the court of the archdeacon of St Albans in 1579 that 'she teacheth scholars to read and she herself cannot read'. To test this amazing accusation the judge 'did openly make trial whether she could read or not, and laying before her the book of common prayer in a very fair and broad print, she could read nothing'.[50]

A part-time or irregular teacher was not necessarily incompetent. Any educated person with enough time and patience could teach literacy to amenable children so long as he followed a suitable method. The problem lay in devising a way for untrained teachers to guide children through their initial steps in literacy. Techniques and procedures for teaching reading and writing proliferated in Elizabethan England as successful schoolmasters offered to share their methods with the world. Some were models to be emulated in the ordered classroom but others were also pitched to the amateur or para-professional.

John Hart published *A method or comfortable beginning for all unlearned whereby they may be taught to read English in a very short time* in 1570. He had sufficient confidence in his model curriculum that

some one such in a house as now can read our present manner may be able to teach it to all the rest of the house, even the whiles their hands may be otherwise well occupied in working for their living, or otherwise being idle or sitting by the fire, without any further let or cost.[51]

Francis Clement urged children to attend the parish clerk, the tailor's shop, the weaver's loom or the local seamstress, where his own version of the elementary curriculum was presumably in use.[52]

Edmund Coote, one of the most celebrated schoolmasters of his age, offered his teaching methods to the public in a work that went through forty-eight editions between 1596 and 1696. Coote also believed that laymen could successfully teach the rudiments of literacy. 'Tailors, weavers, shopkeepers, seamsters . . . mayst sit on thy shop board, at thy looms, or at thy needle, and never hinder thy work to hear thy scholars, after thou hast once made this little book familiar unto thee.' Coote's little book was a valuable manual with rules for reading and spelling, but it probably had more appeal to learned schoolmasters than to well-intentioned artisans. John Brinsley recommended it as 'profitable' but Charles Hoole thought it too rigid, remarking that 'Mr Coote's *English schoolmaster* seems rather to be fitted for one that is a master indeed, than for a scholar'.[53]

It is remarkable that pedagogues like Hart, Clement and Coote should recommend the services of weavers and tailors without credentials at a time when other professions were trying to eradicate their competitors. While William Kempe told the burghers of

Plymouth that 'the charge of teaching appertaineth but only to a few of the learneder sort, namely to schoolmasters', other Elizabethan teachers were relatively unconcerned about their professional exclusiveness.[54]

John Brinsley argued that 'any poor man who will employ his pains may learn to teach children to read well in a short time, though this may seem unbefitting our profession'. Employing laymen as irregular elementary teachers would enable professional schoolmasters to concentrate on grammar, and had the additional advantage that 'it would help some poor man or woman who knew not how to live otherwise'.[55] Neighbours who doubled as part-time teachers were adjuncts to the profession, not threats, so long as children actually learned from them.

The sedentary indoor workers who undertook the teaching of reading as a by-employment were supposed to be able to do it without diverting their hands or their eyes from their work. If true, this suggests that their role was limited to the hearing of memorized lessons and the most elementary work with the alphabet and primer. They could not teach writing, since that required both equipment and attention that was beyond them, and they were unable to offer the kind of supervision that would advance a child rapidly in reading. A textiles workshop was unlikely to afford the discipline, systematic application and supply of teaching materials that was associated with an organized school. Just how many tailors and weavers were themselves literate enough to serve as teachers and profit from Coote's advice is difficult to assess, but the evidence suggests that few took on this burden.[56]

Village artisans and irregular teachers undoubtedly taught some people to read, but without more information about their frustratingly shadowy activities we cannot gauge their importance in the dissemination of literacy. A few of the autobiographers who discuss their early education report some contact with informal instruction, but nearly everyone had been to school. Even the extraordinary Thomas Tryon, who came late to literacy and learned his reading from shepherds and his writing from 'a lame young man who taught poor people's children', had been put to school for a while at the age of five and had there 'learnt to distinguish my letters'.[57] Irregular ways of acquiring literacy abounded but it was preferable and probably more common to rely on a schoolmaster.

Some children learned their literacy informally at home. It has been suggested that the spread of literacy in the early modern period actually owes more to casual contact with the culture of print than to the activities of specialist schoolmasters. People are said to have absorbed literacy as part of their environment, at home, at church and at work, and to have had little need for formal teachers of English. Laqueur, for example, argues the importance of domestic and neighbourhood networks among the cultural origins of popular literacy. 'Literacy was transmitted in much the same way as were the more traditional occupational skills. Most children learned to read and perhaps to write from their parents or from neighbours, unlicensed and untrained.' He reminds us, however, that 'the historical record for all this is murky'.[58]

It was, of course, possible to pick up the skills of reading and writing from one's parents or master, from one's elder siblings or from friends, but it is unlikely that many people acquired their literacy quite casually in this way with no experience of formal schooling. Reading and writing were not simple skills to transmit, like sewing a cushion or milking a cow. Nor, in many families, were they so eminently useful. Only those parents who saw the spiritual, social or economic benefits that literacy might bring would press it on their children, and even these would normally find someone else to do the teaching. The domestic circle did have a role to play, but they must have been unusual parents and friends who were educated enough, dedicated enough and blessed with enough time and talent to pass on the elements of literacy. Parents may have encouraged their children to learn to read and write, but there are few reports of mothers and fathers actually doing the teaching.

Most writers on childhood in the seventeenth century assigned parents the responsibility of having their children educated but assumed that a schoolmaster of sorts would be found to take on the burden. According to Brinsley, 'it much concerneth every parent to see their children to have the best education and instruction, which is the chief patrimony and greatest comfort and hope both of the parents and children', but the main parental responsibility was to find a suitable teacher. 'Parents who have any learning', a minority in Brinsley's view, were invited to hasten or supplement their children's earliest lessons, 'playing with them at dinners and suppers or as they sit by the fire', but they were never expected to substitute for the teacher.[59]

The office of Christian parents calls for children to 'be furnished with the knowledge of reading and writing', but nowhere asks that parents provide such instruction themselves. Rather, 'if the parents be able, the child will call for a schoolmaster'. William Gouge referred encouragingly to the 'small charge' involved in teaching literacy, adding that 'schoolmasters commonly cast the first seed into the hearts of children'. Richard Baxter eagerly sought literacy for English Christians, but parents had no direct role in achieving this aim. Much was made of 'the pious education of mothers', referring to their moral and religious training, but mothers were not to be drawn in as auxiliaries to teach literacy.[60]

The truth is that most mothers were useless for the transmission of literacy because most of them were themselves unable to write. Some could read who could not write, but even these could hardly have taken their children much beyond the ABC. Close to 90% of the women in seventeenth-century England could not even write their names, so few of them could have made satisfactory teachers.[61] Fathers were, perhaps, better equipped to transmit literary skills, but it was not regarded as part of their paternal role. Reading and writing, if wanted at all, were skills that were sought out and purchased from professionals.

Young people in service were no more likely to acquire literacy than children at home unless they were unusually fortunate in their choice of master. Heads of households were sometimes advised to teach their servants to read, and in colonial New England they were charged with this responsibility by law, but it is impossible to say how often this advice became practice. Richard Baxter recommended that servants learn to read 'at spare hours', and George Swinnock helpfully suggested that 'time may be found mornings or evenings, or on wet days when thou canst not work, or on Lord's days, to teach them'. Reading would allow them to read the word of God, but neither Baxter nor Swinnock advised that servants should be taught to write.[62] Masters were generally no better equipped to teach literacy than parents, and, unless they were clergymen or enthusiasts of education, had even less motivation. Most people in pre-industrial England spent part of their adolescence or early adulthood in service, but it is unlikely that that experience was any kind of substitute for going to school.

Literary and documentary sources alike suggest that there were plenty of ways for young people to acquire literacy in pre-industrial England. Opportunities opened up around the age of seven or eight and closed again as people became fully occupied in work around fifteen. For those seven or eight years there was some chance of receiving an elementary education, but if the parents could not see the value in it, if the child was hostile or the teacher lacking in talent, if the schooling proved too expensive or was not locally available, then the opportunity might pass, never again to return.

3

The measurement of literacy

How can we measure the extent of literacy and illiteracy in Tudor and Stuart England? The approach adopted in this book regards the signatures and marks that men and women made on various documents as the best evidence of literate skills. For all its problems, this evidence when properly analysed is remarkably sensitive to changes in the distribution and progress of literacy. It also has the unique advantage of being 'universal, standard and direct'.[1] Other types of anecdotal or indirect evidence lend themselves to inferential judgements about literacy, but are less valuable to the sociological historian. The comments of contemporaries and other literary materials may be useful for purposes of corroboration and illustration, but taken alone they can be misleading. Some of the indirect evidence for the extent of literacy will be reviewed here before turning to the problem of marks and signatures.

According to certain protestant propagandists the common people of England were mired in illiteracy, to the grave peril of their souls and the distress of their more godly neighbours. A great effort of missionary education would be necessary to remove this burden. The Elizabethan preacher Nicholas Bownde believed 'there be too many' drifting from Godliness because of illiteracy, and called for a determined campaign of sermons, psalm-singing and sabbath observance to win to Christ those who 'cannot read themselves, nor any of theirs'.[2] Francis Inman in the early seventeenth century found

many poor servants and labourers, many that are of trades and manual sciences, many aged persons of weak and decayed memories; of these, some never learned so much as to read, some very little, and the most of them have or will have small leisure to learn long discourses, the world or other vanities taking up their thoughts and cares.[3]

Some Restoration ministers believed that illiteracy and atheism went hand in hand. 'Alas', wrote George Swinnock, 'the people perish for want of knowledge. And how can they know God's will that cannot read it?' Richard Baxter saw illiteracy as 'an unspeakable loss that befalls the church and the souls of men'. He described poor tenant farmers who 'cannot spare their children from work while they learn to read . . . so that poverty causeth a generation of barbarians in a Christian, happy land'.[4]

Remarks such as these, from the reign of Elizabeth to the reign of William and Mary, suggest that illiteracy was widespread among the poor and underprivileged of pre-industrial England. The dark corners of the land seemed to be crowding into the centre. Nor was this depressing vision confined to protestant divines who needed to contrast the glowing order that would arise through godly teaching and preaching. The conservative Stephen Gardiner observed in the sixteenth century that reading books was 'such as few can skill of, and not the hundredth part of the realm'.[5] For him, popular illiteracy was not a matter for lament, since images could take the place of books to provide a sufficient Christian education. Whether or not Gardiner and his puritan successors were accurate in their estimates of illiteracy, they none the less contributed to a tradition which saw the ability to read and write as limited to a small minority.

Secular writers also referred to popular illiteracy. Richard Overton, the leveller, was angered that 'the free men of England' might still be 'ignorant of reading and writing' because of insufficient schooling.[6] Educators, with a professional interest in redressing the situation, sometimes despaired at the pitiful quality of teaching that left so many people illiterate. Francis Clement remarked in 1587 on

how few be there under the age of seven or eight years that are towardly abled and praisably furnished for reading? And as many there be above those years that can neither readily spell nor rightly write even the common words of our English.

Almost a century later Thomas Lye, another pedagogue, lamented 'how few, how very few are there in comparison that, after all, can exactly read, spell and write true English, or indeed (*infandum dolorem*) but distinctly read a chapter'.[7] The alarmists paint a grim picture of illiteracy in England.

A much more optimistic view, more widely cited by historians, saw literacy expanding at all levels of society. There are scraps of evidence from as early as the reformation to suggest that literacy did extend beyond the elite, although how widely the skills were disseminated they do not tell. We hear of 'divers poor men in the town of Chelmsford' who were buying and reading the English New Testament, and there are reports of the servant of an Essex tailor, the maidens of an Essex village and a pointmaker of Cheapside who were also able to read.[8] Whether these people were typical or extraordinary is left unsaid.

The 1543 Act for the Advancement of True Religion (34 & 35 Henry VIII.c.1) is often cited as indirect evidence for widespread literacy. 'No women nor artificers, 'prentices, journeymen, serving-men of the degrees of yeomen or under, husbandmen nor labourers' were permitted to read the Bible in English. It is tempting to infer from this that many such people had indeed been reading the Bible for themselves and were sliding into doctrinal error. For Bennett the act points to a 'growing reading public, a body which was numerous and which covered many classes'. According to Adamson, it 'clearly regards reading in the vernacular as an art widely disseminated among the humblest social ranks irrespective of sex'. Altick also regards the act as 'evidence of the social distribution of literacy'.[9] The legislators may have been guided more by fear than by knowledge of the extent of literacy, but they give the impression that the ability to read was both widespread and dangerous.

Certain contemporary remarks also indicate a high level of literacy. John Rastell argued that since the reign of Henry VII 'the universal people of this realm had great pleasure and gave themself greatly to the reading of the vulgar English tongue'.[10] This is not to be taken too seriously, but the equally casual estimate of Thomas More has commanded much attention. More guessed 'far more than four parts of all the whole divided into ten could never read English yet', suggesting that possibly up to 60% of the population could read. The context of these remarks is easily forgotten. More was arguing that an English translation of the Bible was not essential for the salvation of souls. His point was that the ability to read was rare, not widespread, and from the standpoint of salvation this did not matter. 'Many . . . shall with God's grace, though they never read word of scripture, come as well to heaven.' His view on this essential matter was not much different from Gardiner's.[11] Their estimates of literacy, however, are a long way apart and, as Bennett points out, they cannot both be right. It is interesting that the opinion of the bishop has not been cited as often as the opinion of the saint.[12]

Another glimpse of literacy levels is given by reports of religious activity. An account of lay puritan Bible study in Cambridgeshire in the late sixteenth century is, for Margaret Spufford, 'the most conclusive and forceful argument for a widespread ability to read'. Bible-reading laymen were disputing the text with their preachers. The evidence for this, however, is not only qualitative and indirect but also suspect, since its source is an imprisoned Jesuit who

mixed scorn with ridicule in his description of popular protestantism.[13] Whether hostile or sympathetic, contemporary
observations about religious literacy have to be treated gingerly.
There is indeed evidence that some people, even poor people,
knew and read their Bibles, but we are far from knowing if such
ability was widespread.[14]

Remarks by seventeenth-century conservatives are also suggestive
of widespread popular literacy. The opinion flourished in some
circles that the advance of literacy was socially and politically
dangerous. As William Cavendish wrote to the exiled Charles II
in the 1650s, 'the Bible in English under every weaver and
chambermaid's arm hath done us much hurt'. About the same
time James Howell complained of 'people of all sorts though never
so mean and mechanical' who pursued literacy. 'It were to be
wished that there reigned not among the people of this land such
a general itching after book learning.'[15] Taken uncritically,
remarks such as these could lead to the impression that weavers,
chambermaids and the like could all read the Bible. It should be
remembered that Cavendish and Howell were frustrated royalists,
who were not alone in allowing their bitter opinions to colour
their reports.

From beginning to end the evidence of contemporary reportage
is contradictory, contaminated by the bias and interest of its
authors. Like much literary evidence, it can be quoted selectively
to illustrate an hypothesis or document an argument, as if the
citing of examples actually established a case. Unfortunately,
we have no clear picture of the condition of English literacy from
the indirect evidence cited above, but only a vague and confusing
blur. Baxter, More and the rest are easy to quote but hard to
evaluate. None of them was equipped to make more than a guess
at the extent of literacy, and in any case literacy was far from the
centre of their concerns. Their discussion of the reading public
was in most cases marginal to a larger argument about salvation,
godliness or the social order. None of them knew, or seriously
endeavoured to know, how many of their countrymen were
literate.

If the remarks of contemporaries are to be distrusted where
else can we turn? A well-tried and possibly more rewarding indirect
approach is one that examines the factors with which literacy is
thought to have been associated. It is reasonable to assume some
correlation between the level and progress of literacy, and book
production, book ownership and the history of education. The
connections are shown in the diagram on the next page.

The expansion or improvement of education increases literacy,

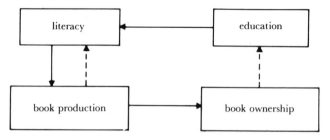

which in turn leads to a greater demand for books. The rising output of printed matter makes it possible for more people to own
books, and may itself stimulate the spread of literacy. The greater
circulation of books may create more opportunities for people to
learn to read them. The diagram fails to do justice to the full
range of feedback, cross-contact and chain reaction which this
system envisages, nor does it take account of other economic and
cultural factors which may have impinged on literacy; but the basic
connections are clear. By charting the output of the printing
presses, the number of books appearing in probate inventories and
the incidence and availability of schooling, it is hoped that more
light may be thrown, indirectly, on the problem of literacy.

The assumptions behind these connections are rarely laid bare.
Apart from the obvious difficulty in inferring the unknown from
the known or half-known, we are not sure exactly how literacy,
books and education were related to each other. Nor can we be
confident that we even have all the parts of the equation. Nevertheless, some progress has been made with this approach.

Adamson claimed that the character and circulation of printed
matter in the early sixteenth century 'argues a fairly large number
of persons already able to read'. Having established that books
were sold at provincial fairs, Bennett argues that 'the provision of
books on this scale postulates a considerable reading public'. For
the early seventeenth century he finds the *Short Title Catalogue*
'irrefutable . . . prima facie evidence that a wide range of readers
was being catered for'. Bridenbaugh goes further to claim 'the
surest testimony to the widespread literacy among the English
people of this era is the number and variety of the titles in the
Short Title Catalogue'. Stone also finds indirect evidence about
literacy in 'the insatiable market for the flood of pamphlets and
newspapers which poured from the English presses'.[16]

No doubt these conclusions are correct, at the most general
level. The problem with remarks of this kind, apart from their
maddening vagueness about 'fairly large', 'considerable' or 'widespread' literacy, lies in the assumption that book production was

directly associated with literacy. As Schofield has pointed out, changes in the volume of book production may have as much to do with the technology, economy and legal status of printing as with the ability of people to read.[17] Just because a book appears in the Stationers' Register or the *S.T.C.* does not mean that it sold, and even books that are known to have sold well did not necessarily extend to a new and popular reading public. Indeed, a relatively small number of regular book-buyers could absorb most of the output of the London press, and when output increased it is at least conceivable that the same people bought more.

The Stationers' Company registered about 150 titles a year in the late sixteenth and early seventeenth centuries. Some of these were never printed, while others appeared that had escaped registration. W. W. Greg estimated an average of 200 titles a year came off the press in the period 1576–1640.[18] Assuming 1,500 copies of an edition, a high estimate for this early period when print runs were often smaller, there would have been a maximum of 300,000 volumes to dispose of each year. Where did they go? Virtually the entire output of the London press could have been absorbed if a volume was purchased for every member of a gentle, clerical or professional household. Thirty thousand privileged people buying ten books or pamphlets a year could have cornered the market. This is not to suggest that only the upper class bought books or to pre-judge the book-buying behaviour of any social group, but rather to illustrate the scale of the problem. We simply do not know the market for popular print in the Elizabethan and early Stuart period.

The whole scale of the business was transformed in the second half of the seventeenth century. George Thomason was able to collect an average of 680 books and pamphlets a year between 1640 and 1660 including 1,966 in the crisis year of 1642. Analysis of the Wing Catalogue shows roughly 1,000 titles a year being published in normal periods, zooming to 2,000 or more in moments of political hysteria. Editions were often larger, running to 3,000 copies of hot religious properties like *Julian's arts to undermine christianity* (1683), and even more of popular almanacs. The figures point to a tenfold expansion of print, with two million or more volumes to be disposed of each year, including 400,000 twopenny almanacs. We still do not know who bought this enormous output, but a picture is emerging of efficient and widespread marketing through printers and publishers, hucksters and 'mercury women', chapmen, wholesalers and book-sellers.[19] Whether it signifies a broadening of literacy remains in doubt.

Some authorities would disagree. Neuberg insists 'that an increase in the sheer volume of popular literature argues for an increase in the size of the reading public at the lower end of the social scale', but this remains to be proved. Indeed, the correlation is very weak. At the very time that the popular press was expanding, in the late seventeenth century, the direct evidence of marks and signatures shows the literacy of the common people to have been stagnant or even deteriorating.[20] Other factors, such as the development or degeneration of literary taste, the surplus wealth available for spending on print, and the activities of the book trade, may also be involved. Margaret Spufford may well be right that 'the number of devotional works . . . argues a market for such works', but again other explanations are possible.[21] For this particular religious genre the missionary zeal of the protestant activists to spread their ideas and the desire of some clergy to see their words in print may be as much factors as authentic popular demand. Until we know more of the market for books, especially outside London, we should be hesitant about the bearings of the book business on literacy.

If the history of printing and publishing turns out to be an inadequate instrument for measuring literacy, the history of book ownership seems to promise more precision. Probate inventories in many parts of the country record the possession of books among the goods and chattels of the deceased, affording a glimpse of the penetration of literature into the provinces. Several collections of inventories have been examined and the proportion mentioning books ranges from less than one-twentieth to more than one-third. More books appear as the period progresses and more books are found in towns than in the country.[22] While the evidence permits no more than the most superficial judgements about the distribution of books, it has been enlisted as an indirect indicator of literacy.

Clark sees book ownership as 'part of the general advance in literacy'. Employing the direct evidence of marks and signatures as well as probate inventories, he finds in urban Kent 'some correlation . . . between high or low levels of literacy and book ownership'. The social structure of book ownership is said to reflect the social distribution of literacy, while changes over time in the proportion of books in inventories is taken to indicate changes in the ability to read them. For example, Dyer finds 'a striking proliferation of book ownership' in late-Elizabethan Worcester 'which would parallel the increasing literacy rate'.[23] If it were true that book ownership indeed matched or reflected the progress of literacy we could concentrate on probate inventories instead of marks and signatures. Unfortunately, this indirect approach is vitiated both by the problematic nature of the source material and by the difficulty of assessing its results.

Laslett has argued that probate inventories are 'unlikely to provide evidence of much importance' about book ownership, and sadly it seems he is correct. The limitations of this body of evidence are well known and defy most attempts to surmount them. Ecclesiastical law and custom referred the inventories of some men of substance to higher jurisdictions, so they might not appear in archidiaconal or diocesan collections. Men of little substance, on the other hand, rarely appear at all since they had little in the way of moveable property to distribute and the church was not interested in their estates. Inventories of the prosperous greatly outnumber inventories of the poor, and women are severely under-represented.[24] Although it is evident that the record is socially selective, there is no simple way to gauge the severity of the bias.

More serious than their social bias is the casual way in which books were treated in inventories. The titles of some books are given, but often the appraisers merely entered 'his books' or 'books and other lumber' or left them out altogether. There seems to have been no standard procedure, but well-bound volumes and religious works had a greater chance of being listed than popular romances and ephemera. It is common to find the inventories of professional men and others who are known to have possessed books not mentioning a single volume. Laslett finds the quantitative evidence from inventories hard to reconcile with the literary evidence about book-buying and book-handling, while Spufford concludes 'that books were not worth listing, even if they were there, and that Bibles would not necessarily be entered separately'.[25]

Probate inventories, then, are an incomplete guide to book ownership since so many volumes went unrecorded. Poorer people, who presumably owned few books, are under-represented, while the books of those for whom inventories were made are under-registered. The two biases may be said to cancel each other but little confidence can be placed in such an equation. As a measuring device the inventories are seriously flawed.

More fundamental is the question whether the ownership of books was even indirectly an indicator of literacy. Changes in the number of books in circulation could reflect changes in people's ability to buy them or the efforts of stationers to sell them, as well as changes in literacy. The greater proportion of books in urban areas may reflect the trade routes along which books and other commodities were distributed, and the more diversified

economy and culture of the towns, as well as the alleged superiority
of the urban readership.[26]

It should also be recognized that books could easily fall into the
hands of people who could not read them. Bibles in particular
were plentiful but their mere possession does not signify that
their owners could read. It is no surprise to find that Bibles
dominate the lists of known titles in probate inventories. Clark
notes 'the ubiquity of the Bible . . . often a fairly expensive item'.
Laqueur believes 'that substantial numbers of even the very poor
owned Bibles', and refers to their 'relatively low cost'. Bibles in
seventeenth-century probate inventories varied in value from four
to fourteen shillings depending on their condition and binding.[27]
Cheap or expensive, the Bible seems to have been everywhere and
may even have been, as William Cavendish alleged, 'under every
weaver and chambermaid's arm'. Some people had more than one.
A non-conformist widow in Cambridgeshire left three Bibles to
her son in 1670, while the inventory of a husbandman in the same
county in 1668 recorded four.[28] Perhaps there was safety in
numbers.

These books were not always purchased by their owners. They
might be the gift of a literate relative, an inheritance perhaps, or
result from the largess of a pious benefactor. Some puritan
ministers pressed Bibles on their flocks in the same way that John
Eliot distributed *Um Biblum God* to the illiterate Indians of
Massachusetts. It was not uncommon for Bibles and other religious
books to be given away as prizes or as a form of charity. Herbert
Palmer in the 1630s regularly presented Bibles to new communicants. Joshua Richardson 'bequeathed Bibles and some
copies of Richard Baxter's *A call to the unconverted* to be given to
certain poor people in the parish of Myddle'. Thomas Gouge gave
away Bibles and pious books in Wales while the indefatigable
Richard Baxter flooded Kidderminster with over 800 free books.
'Every family that was poor, and had not a Bible, I gave a Bible
to.'[29]

Baxter even devised a scheme for the pious wealthy to channel
texts to the bookless poor. In 'a request to the rich' prefacing one
of his many publications he urges all who are able to 'bestow one
book (either this or some fitter) upon as many poor families as
you well can'. The hope was that 'rich citizens, and ladies, and
rich women who cannot themselves go talk to poor families' would
send out books to do their missionary work by proxy. Scripture
was now essential to salvation, and the poor should not be lost
for the lack of a five-shilling Bible.[30] Given such means of acqui-

sition we must be careful not to assume that a Bible in an inventory testifies to the active religious literacy of its owner.

Those who gave away Bibles, Baxter included, knew that the recipients might not be able to read them. None the less, possession of the text might prove an inducement to literacy, a vehicle for identifying printed letters and spelling out words. Who knows how many children first learned to read with a charity Bible? A Bible in the home also permitted literate visitors to read to an illiterate household. It was recommended for reading aloud to family and servants as well as for private study, so illiterates could be exposed to its contents. Nicholas Bownde in the 1590s specifically urged those who could not read to

> get the Bibles into their houses, that when any come that can read they may have it in readiness and not lose the opportunity that is offered, even as they are contented to have many other things in their houses which, though they know not how to occupy themselves, yet some of their friends may when they come.[31]

A Bible could be an important household possession, even if none of the household residents could read it.

A Bible around the house could be useful in many other ways. Oaths could be sworn on it, while family births could be recorded on its fly leaves with the hour as well as the date, so that accurate horoscopes could be cast. Its mere presence, unopened and unread, could be enough to ward off evil spirits and keep the devil at bay. With a key placed between its pages it was used in divination to uncover thieves and other guilty parties; the book was supposed to wag when the name of the criminal was stuffed in the barrel of the key.[32] The leaves of the Bible might be used to fan the face of a sick person, as if the magical power of the holy page was sufficient to effect a cure. In the same way a restless child might be soothed by laying the Bible on his brow. There are even reports of maidens sleeping with the Bible beneath their pillows, with a sixpence inserted in the Book of Ruth, to conjure dreams of future lovers. Scraps of evidence of this sort, from post-reformation and pre-industrial England, suggest that the Bible was not always used as the preachers intended. Baxter reports the marvel of soldiers' Bibles stopping bullets in the civil war, as if an ordinary volume, a jest book perhaps, would not have had such miraculous efficacy.[33] The power of the Bible was enormous and did not need literacy to unlock it. Valued as a charm as well as a sacred volume, possessed of healing and protective qualities as well as scriptural wisdom, who would not seek to own one?

These observations on popular beliefs should serve as a corrective to the view that books were just for reading, or that their mere possession implies literacy. Many of us today own books which we have not read, and we know of families with encyclopedias or finely bound sets of literary classics which stand unopened from year to year. The same was true in the past. Petrarch in the fourteenth century owned a copy of Homer in Greek which he cherished but could not read.[34] Visitors to seventeenth-century libraries may have been impressed more by the bindings than by what lay between them. Books in any age can be kept for their status value and as ornaments, as well as for the wisdom and delight of their contents, and in some cases may be worth more as totems than as texts. Even if we could establish who owned books in the past we could not be sure that book ownership was a reliable guide to literacy.

The final indirect approach to literacy is through the study of education. Adamson believed that opportunities to learn to read were plentiful under the Tudors, while Bennett argues that the growth of educational facilities under the early Stuarts 'must have greatly increased the number of readers'. The 'educational revolution' of 1560—1640 is very well known and there is no shortage of studies attempting to tie changes in educational provision to changes in literacy.[35] Both qualitative and quantitative aspects of the history of education are brought to bear on the question. We may count the foundation of schools, chart the flow of educational philanthropy, trace the careers of licensed and unlicensed schoolmasters, and follow pupils who move on to the universities; we can also take account of the curriculum, the writings of pedagogues and benefactors, autobiographical reminiscences, and the political and cultural climate with which education engaged.

The links between educational history and the measurement of literacy are, however, indirect and imprecise. Most of the evidence concerns grammar schools and there is little to suggest that elementary education was similarly expanded. Where it is possible to trace the careers of petty schoolmasters they seem to have given fitful service. In East Anglia schoolmasters teaching reading and writing could be found in most large villages in the late Elizabethan period, but later in the seventeenth century they were mostly confined to the principal market towns. Reliable information about the extent of petty schooling and the teaching of literacy is woefully wanting.[36] Nor should we assume that the acquisition of literacy was exclusively the product of formal schooling. Family, friends and neighbours could share the task of teaching, but we have no way of calculating how often this happened or with what success.[37]

The progress of education in the sixteenth and seventeenth centuries was irregular rather than steady, and was affected by such things as fashion, the state of the economy, government and church policy. There was an over-all expansion of facilities, but it is arguable that the increase went mostly to benefit the middle and upper groups in society, who already possessed basic literacy, leaving the poor to the charity or despair of the clergy. Educational opportunity was highly stratified and did not always reflect the intentions of reformers and philanthropists.[38] Education was undoubtedly related to literacy but the two were not inextricably linked.

Objections can be raised against every type of indirect evidence, and none of them alone can reveal the dimensions of literacy. Taken together, however, the impressions generated by one body of evidence may reinforce those from another to build a compelling picture. Contemporary opinion, book production, book ownership and the history of education all point to an increasingly literate population in the late sixteenth and early seventeenth centuries. The cumulative impression is broad, vague and uncontroversial. Only through a study of the direct evidence of marks and signatures can this impression be tested, sharpened and substantiated.

Although we would like to know how many people read their Bibles and what proportion of the population could follow religious tracts or political pamphlets and otherwise participate in the literate world, there is no direct way to obtain this information. Unfortunately, reading leaves no record, so some of the most tantalizing and important questions about literacy in Tudor and Stuart England will have to remain unanswered. The indirect evidence discussed above may help us to guess the size and character of the reading public, but it does not enable us to measure it. Only one type of literacy is directly measurable – the ability or inability to write a signature; and that by itself may be the least interesting and least significant.

None the less, the evidence of signatures and marks possesses two major advantages over the sources discussed so far. First, the test of alphabetic literacy is a direct, authentic and personal indicator of one particular skill. Faced with an autograph signature or mark on a document we do not have to guess or make inferences about its relationship to literacy. The person either did or did not sign his name. Second, this measure of literacy is universal and standard as well as direct. As Schofield points out, the evidence of marks and signatures can be used to make comparative judgements between people, between social and economic groups, between regions and between historical periods. No other body of evidence is so valuable to the sociological historian of literacy, or is so susceptible to numerical analysis. Only by a careful study of large numbers of marks and signatures can we resolve whether literacy was widespread and trace its dimensions over society, space and time.[39]

What level of literacy does a signature represent? Schofield argues that the exact level is relatively unimportant so long as it is standard, since what is needed for historical study is simply 'an agreed body of comparative evidence'. This is strictly correct, but it is still important to discover where the ability to sign one's name fits in the hierarchy of skills associated with literacy. The Registrar General suggested in 1861 that

> if a man can write his own name, it may be presumed he can read it when written by another; still more that he will recognise that and other familiar words when he sees them in print; and it is even probable that he will spell his way through a paragraph in the newspaper.

This may err on the side of caution. Schofield's comparison of the Registrar General's marriage-register figures with nineteenth-century surveys of educational attainment indicates that the ability to sign was roughly commensurate with fluency in reading.[40]

Recent work on French literacy finds a close association between capacity to sign and the ability to both read and write. There are three sets of evidence from nineteenth-century France which can be cross-checked to discover the relationship of signing and marking to other levels of literacy. Furet and Ozouf have performed factorial analysis and correlation tests with the information on literacy in the 1866 census, tests given to military conscripts, and the direct evidence of brides and grooms signing at marriage. They report 'la proximité spectaculaire des variables "capacité à signer l'acte de mariage" et "sachant lire et écrire", aussi bien pour les hommes que pour les femmes'. There is a strong positive correlation (0.91) between making a signature and knowing how to read and write, and an equally strong negative correlation (−0.91) between signing and not being able to read and write. The statistics point to a strong connection between signature literacy and complete literacy, and a surprisingly weak correlation (−0.12) between signing and just knowing how to read. There were people who could write their names yet could not read or write much else, but their numbers were not significant. Similarly, there were not many people who had mastered only the art of reading compared to the number who could both read and write or who lacked both skills. Furet and Ozouf are able to conclude that 'la signature est donc un bon baromètre de l'alphabétisation'.[41]

Whether one can extrapolate from Second Empire France or Victorian England to the Tudor and Stuart period is an open question. We have no early modern tests or surveys to compare with the direct evidence of autographs. It is possible that some teacher or minister kept detailed records of his class or congregation — the archives are full of surprises — but so far nothing suitable is known. However, the sequence of instruction in primary education was so little changed from the sixteenth to the nineteenth century that we might suppose a similar relationship between reading and writing and the ability to sign.

It is probable that the level of literacy measured by counting signatures and marks overestimates the number able to write with ease, underestimates the number able to read with hesitation, and indicates with some accuracy the number who were functionally literate by the standards of the seventeenth century. If you could write your name it is very likely that you could write other things and could also read with fluency. If you could not even form a signature your literacy was incomplete, although you might be able to manage some reading. This conclusion is almost a paraphrase of Schofield's and suggests that the statistical study of literacy over the last decade has been on the right track.

The quantitative evidence in this book rests on the assumption that people who knew how to write their names wrote signatures when the need arose, while those who lacked this elementary skill made marks. We have to be alert, however, to the possibility of feigned marks veiling true literacy and precocious or artificial signatures masking the real illiteracy of their makers. Contradictory or ambiguous cases raise questions about the reliability of the measurement, so it would be well to review them.

In discussions of literacy it is often objected that a signature is easily learned, as a trick or for its own sake, and should not necessarily be taken to indicate an ability to read and write. There is no denying that such things happened, and the evidence from France and England shows that counting signatures somewhat exaggerates the number of persons who were fully literate. Illiterate signers were, however, exceptional, and by their very rarity may have claimed some attention.

One curious case is William Herbert, Earl of Pembroke, who died in 1570. John Aubrey remarked that 'he could neither write nor read, but had a stamp for his name', thus giving Herbert the reputation as the last illiterate courtier in English history. It is almost inconceivable that an executor of Henry VIII's will, a Privy Councillor under Edward and an officer under Mary and Elizabeth, should not have known how to write his name. Aubrey explains it by calling him 'a mad fighting young fellow' with obscure origins, whose use of a name stamp on state documents presumably spared him the indignity of making a mark.[42] However, the record shows that Aubrey was wrong. Several of Herbert's autograph signatures survive. He certainly could write his name, even if he did it poorly, with a mixture of unconnected capitals and lower-case letters.[43] He may have learned to sign his name, and no more, because it was an accomplishment expected of one so exalted, but it is probable that, like most people who signed, he was actually able to read and write.

At a much more humble level Richard Mathew of Kent, aged 38 in 1576,

> declared that he signed 'his name in great Roman letters' as a witness to a will, admitting that he could not read 'yet he can write and doth use to subscribe all such deeds and writings as he passes with such great Roman letters and more he cannot write'.[44]

We do not know why Richard Mathew learned to write his name but he may have believed that a signature, however clumsily executed, was more impressive on a formal document like a will. If so he was in small company. Tens of thousands of respectable and responsible men in Tudor and Stuart England were content to authenticate important documents with a mark.

Both the incentive and the opportunity to acquire a capacity to sign without other attributes of literacy were extremely slender in early modern society. As demonstrated in chapter 2, children were not taught to write before they had learned to read. The two skills were conventionally taught in sequence, not in tandem, and there is no mention in any of the teaching manuals or pedagogical guides of practising writing by learning to sign. When you embarked on writing, you first learned to hold and control a pen, and then practised with the letters and phrases you had long since learned to read. Personal names were so varied, and their spelling so idiosyncratic, that they were not considered suitable as teaching material.[45]

Writing-masters like David Brown, hoping to drum up business, may have argued that there was shame attached to being illiterate, but in practice there was no point in faking.[46] The inability to sign was so widespread – and included people of rank and prominence as well as the humble — that few eyebrows would have been raised at making a mark. In any case, a mark was perfectly satisfactory from the legal point of view, with as much authenticity and authority as a signature. There was simply no need to struggle to copy or trace a signature or painstakingly to practise writing one's name, and there was little time to reproduce those letters in the circumstances of court and commerce. If you were not familiar with penmanship, and were not well experienced in literacy, you would probably make a hash of it.

Examples abound of gentlemen, public officials and wealthy tradesmen not hesitating to sign with a mark. John Wilson, an esquire of Durham in 1567, John More, a gentleman of Essex in 1590, Roger Satlesbury of Norfolk in 1601, George White of Devonshire in 1665 and John Drinkwater of London in 1675 were among that one or two per cent of the gentry who appear in the records as illiterate.[47] These men were mostly of middle age, not wracked by senility or illness which could excuse their inability to sign. They subscribed with marks but their gentility was not thereby impugned. Of the 47 aldermen and common councillors of Great Yarmouth who endorsed a civic document in 1577, 10 did so with marks instead of signatures. A century later Thomas Mickleburgh and Thomas Whiteley, sheriff's officers in the city of Norwich, used marks to subscribe the Test Oath of 1673.[48] Roger Bradley, a governor of Bishop Auckland grammar school in county Durham, regularly left his mark in the minute book between 1605 and 1622 when the other 11 governors wrote signatures. Francis Leasie, a feoffee of Edward Latymer's school in Middlesex in 1627, was similarly unable to sign his name. If anyone had an incentive to learn a signature instead of an illiterate mark it was these men responsible for educational administration. William Shakespeare's father, John, a prominent businessman and alderman of Stratford, always used a mark. No signature by John Shakespeare has been found despite the anxious searching of Shakespearians.[49]

This brings us to another objection: that a mark does not really indicate an inability to write, and that people like John Shakespeare chose to employ marks instead of signatures for mysterious reasons of their own. The common mark in the form of a cross, it has been argued,

was not necessarily proof of illiteracy. When the cross was first placed upon legal documents it was a symbol of the Holy Cross and proof that the man who made it gave his assent religious sanctity. That is, it was the equivalent of an oath.

It is implied that those who made crosses let their piety override their literacy.[50] Similar claims are made for other types of mark. Five affeerors, adjudicators of fines, witnessed the record of a Leet court at Stratford in 1559, John Shakespeare among them, and only two actually signed. Of the others, we are told, 'Ap Williams' mark resembles a church-gable and possibly means Holy Church; Tyler's consists of two concentric circles quartered by a cross and may signify the Trinity'. Two quite ordinary marks are thus invested with religious allegorical significance. But the most ingenious interpretation is reserved for the father of the Bard.

There is strong tradition in Shakespearian biography that is reluctant to concede that the senior Shakespeare was illiterate.

John Shakespeare's sign-manual, it will be remembered, was his Glover's Compasses (used for ornamental cuttings on the back of the glove), with a single or double adjusting screw, signifying, we may believe, the devout thought 'God encompasseth us'.

John's other mark, which looks like a glover's stitching clamp, 'had some other, undeciphered allegorical significance'.[51] The mystery is best left to the cipher experts. We are not told why the other affeerors and associates of John Shakespeare irreverently signed their names, but a fair guess would be that they were the only ones who could write. People in Tudor and Stuart England used marks when they did not know how to write their names; it was a question of capacity, not of choice. The only exception was when people who had been fully literate grew senile or infirm and lost the ability to perform a signature, and in those cases we usually find a simple scrawl rather than a pictogram vibrating with symbolism.

Incapacity or failing health may explain the few but troublesome cases where people signed one document but marked another. Jenkinson remarked 'that a man not highly literate might use sometimes a signature, sometimes a mark', and gives the example of William Stallenge who signed an Exchequer account in 1609 but marked another in 1612. Sisson criticized Jenkinson's evidence and suggested that the later cross was not holograph. But supposing the mark of 1612 to be genuine, it is possible that Stallenge fell ill and lost the knack of manipulating a pen. Old Leonard Woolward of Cambridgeshire had once been able to write, 'yet that at the time of his will making [in 1578] he could not well write with ease or to his contentation, for that he was then very old and for that his sight then failed him much'.[52] People in his condition tended to make marks, even if they were formerly literate.

Blindness or injury could also be responsible for a mark. John

Stake of Westminster was excused from signing a Chancery deposition in 1599, '*non subscripsit quia cecus*', so we cannot evaluate his efforts. Quite remarkable is the device used by Peter Trumbel of Gateshead, Durham, when witnessing a legal document in 1678 and authenticating his will in 1687. He used a name stamp, carved from a piece of wood. One can only surmise that Trumbel, who was a butcher by trade, had lost or damaged his hand but was still determined to display a version of his complete signature.[53] Other handicapped persons, along with the genuinely illiterate, made do with marks.

Shakespeare makes the rebel Cade challenge a captured clergy-man, 'Dost thou use to write thy name, or hast thou a mark to thyself like an honest plain dealing man?' Most plain-dealing men in early modern England used marks because the majority of the population was illiterate. More than two-thirds of the men and more than four-fifths of the women in the seventeenth century could not write their names, as will be shown in later chapters.[54] Their marks ranged from the simple scrawl of someone who had never held a pen to the elaborate sketch or diagram of another whose dexterity was some compensation for his illiteracy. A few people could reproduce their initials as a personal mark, or attempt a couple of letters of their name, but failing a signature they are also classified as illiterate.

Working men often made marks which represented some implement of their trade. Andrew Favine, writing in the early seventeenth century, drew attention to the sub-heraldic devices of some common people which were akin to the arms of the nobility.

It was permitted to them to have only marks or notes of those trades and professions which they used, as a tailor to have his shears, a cutler a knife, a shearman his cloth shears, a mason his trowel and the compass or square.

Marks which depict these items and others are sprinkled through-out the archives of the sixteenth and seventeenth centuries. A brickmaker might draw his brick mould, a farmer a plough, a woolcomber a comb, a thatcher a thatching-rake, a baker his long wooden bread shovel. Anthony Farrard, a Kentish husbandman in 1598, deposed

that he is unlearned and never could nor can write or read but when he hath been sometimes called to set his hand to writings he hath made his mark, which he always made as near as he could the likeness of a hook such as carters use in the loading of their carts, called an owl hook.[55]

Characteristic marks are reproduced in the following diagram:

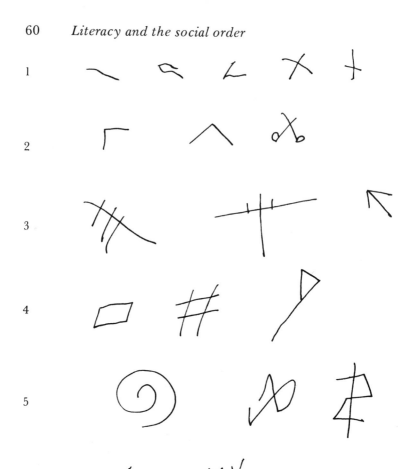

Personal marks made on depositions in the diocese of Norwich, 1580–1620
Row 1: simple scrawls and crosses; 2: mason, husbandman, tailor; 3: thatcher,
woolcomber, fletcher; 4: brickmaker, brickmaker, baker; 5: tailor, glazier,
worsted weaver; 6: mason, merchant, yeoman

The occasions on which ordinary people were called to write
their names or make their marks were few in pre-industrial
England. One might have to appear as a witness in a court case,
serve as a constable or churchwarden or be an appraiser of a
neighbour's goods for probate purposes; in times of great agitation
there might be loyalty declarations or petitions to endorse; and at

all times, if your life were that complex, there might be wills, marriage documents or business records which demanded a signature or mark of presence or approbation. Some people may have lived out their lives and never touched pen to paper, while others, literate or not, may have regularly been asked for an autograph. The record of these activities forms the only body of direct evidence for investigating the distribution of literacy in Tudor and Stuart England.

4
Literacy and loyalty

Signatures and marks are preserved by the hundreds of thousands in business and court records, probate documents and petitions of the sixteenth and seventeenth centuries. They were made whenever someone subscribed, endorsed or authenticated a statement or set his hand to an oath, a will or a deposition. By attempting to retrieve this scattered evidence and by subjecting it to numerical analysis it is possible to make reasonably confident estimates of the extent of literacy in pre-industrial England.

Direct evidence of the ability to sign one's name is abundant, but not all collections of signatures and marks are equally useful. Documents that were endorsed mostly by the prominent or prosperous, for example, are likely to yield a distorted profile of literacy, while records that were subscribed by criminals or charity recipients only, or by any other specific minority, are just as likely to be misleading. We may be interested to learn that a certain proportion of army officers could sign receipts or that a varying percentage of landholders could sign indentures, but such information tells us little about literacy in the population at large.[1] Records which are free from bias and which embrace a cross-section of the community are necessary in order to reconstruct the over-all distribution of literacy.

This chapter examines certain types of evidence which offer information about the literacy of whole communities at particular moments in time. Most of the sources discussed here stem from periods of political crisis in which the government felt urged to secure, or be assured of, the loyalty of the population.

From the sixteenth to the eighteenth century a series of oaths and declarations was promulgated in London and pressed on the inhabitants of England. They included the Succession Oath of 1534, the Protestation Oath of 1641 and the Association Oath of 1696. Each addressed a particular emergency and was intended to bind the nation, to alert and solidify opinion and to identify potential pockets of dissident opinion. The process was akin to an ideological mustering, and woe betide the man of tender conscience. Oath-takers were required to subscribe in writing so that their commitment became a matter of record, while the names of refusers were collected to be dealt with later.

The organizers were interested in propaganda and security, but the resulting subscriptions, signed and marked by masses of people, sometimes amounted to a census of literacy. The quality and survival of these records is uneven, but the best of them can be used to delineate the outlines of literacy.

The two principal difficulties with these lists of oath-takers concern their completeness and their authenticity. The results of a casual or voluntary subscription to an oath which was tendered to only part of the community are of limited interest, since they cannot be compared by time or place. Without knowing the circumstances in which each oath was prepared and the exact section of the population which was required to take it, the document will be of uncertain value for the study of literacy. It helps if there were standard conditions and explicit procedures, for only if we know how the document was presented in each locality and what pressures were exerted to ensure universal attestation can we decide whether the subscription list is complete. In most cases the entire adult male population was required to sign or mark, and the turnout can be checked against other evidence for the size of the particular community. Shortfalls and discrepancies can be explained by reference to short-term fluctuations, migration and the weaknesses of demographic data.[2]

The problem of authenticity is equally vexing. People were supposed to endorse the declaration by writing their signatures or making their marks in their own hand, and where this was done consistently it is a simple matter to calculate the proportion which was illiterate. But sometimes the official responsible for returning the document copied the names in his own hand and it is impossible to tell who could write and who could not. Even if the official was conscientious enough to show on his list who had subscribed with a mark, the fact that the autographs are not holograph vitiates the return for the study of literacy. Sometimes the document sports a sprinkling of original signatures and authentic marks but is spoiled by a sequence of names in a common hand, apparently entered by proxy. It was not uncommon for someone to subscribe for his neighbours, or for a literate member of a family to enter the names of his sons or brothers. We cannot determine whether these proxy signatures mask illiteracy or represent laziness, timidity or the lack of opportunity to use the pen for oneself. A local study which linked the subscribers with other pieces of evidence might make good use of these returns, but they have to be rejected here. Any list with signatures written by proxy or names written in a common hand, or which is in any way less than holograph, must be excluded from the statistical analysis of literacy. Only those returns which bear authentic signatures and marks and which appear to be complete can satisfy our criteria for acceptance.

The crisis of the reformation produced an oath which could be tendered to all subjects of full age. The oath, embodied in the Act for the Establishment of the King's Succession of 1534, asserted that the issue of Henry and queen Anne were true heirs to the throne. Those who took it associated themselves with Cromwell and the king against queen Katherine and the church of Rome, while refusers could find themselves in serious trouble. The oath was agreed in parliament on 30 March 1534 and in the following months was taken to the country by commissioners who were supposed to collect the names of all subscribers together with their marks and signatures.[3]

If the oath had been administered everywhere in accordance with instructions and if the records of this activity survived we might have been able to reconstruct English literacy in the early sixteenth century. Unfortunately all that we have is glimpses of the commissioners at work and some fragmentary and unreliable evidence about literacy.

Bishop Gardiner reported to Cromwell on 5 May 1534 that parishioners in his diocese of Winchester, 'menkind only, above the age of fourteen', were taking the oath of succession. He complained that this was 'a long work and will require a long tract of time . . . considering specially that every man's name must be written, as our commission purporteth and certifieth'. Archbishop Cranmer sought guidance on how to record the oaths of illiterates, explaining,

> I know not how I shall order them that cannot subscribe by writing. Hitherto I have caused one of my secretaries to subscribe for such persons, and made them to write their sheep mark or some other mark as they can scribble. Now would I know whether I shall instead of subscription take their seals.

Ordinary people had never before been asked to commit themselves in writing on such a sensitive matter of state and the officials were quite unprepared to handle popular illiteracy. One of the commissioners for Norwich seems to have been content if his oathtakers kissed the book.[4]

Whatever answer Cranmer received has been lost, along with all but one of the commissioners' returns. Only the return from Little Waldingfield in Suffolk survives to suggest the extent of illiteracy at the reformation. The oath at Little Waldingfield on 18 May

1534 was subscribed by 92 men; 12 wrote signatures, 34 made marks, and the rest were recorded but made neither mark nor signature. The document, therefore, is not entirely holograph and fails to meet the criterion of authenticity. Nevertheless, it is worth giving this return some consideration as a unique early record of literacy and loyalty.[5] The 46 men who failed to put pen to paper might have been absent, and leaving them out of the calculation leads to an illiteracy figure of 74%. It is more probable, however, that they were present but could not sign, in which case the figure should be revised to 89% illiterate. It would not be altogether surprising to find that almost 90% of the rural population was illiterate in the 1530s, but without other returns to the oath of succession we cannot say whether this was a typical level of illiteracy, or even whether the figure is accurate.

There were other oaths and tests in the sixteenth century but none of them was organized to produce written subscriptions on a large scale.[6] It is worth mentioning 'the instrument of an association for preservation of the queen's majesty's royal person' of October 1584. This was a widely circulated declaration of loyalty, mostly signed by 'the principal persons of the country', but it is more significant as a model for the Association Oath of 1696 than for any evidence about Elizabethan literacy that can be extracted from it.[7]

The revolutionary decade of the 1640s experienced a spate of oaths, covenants, remonstrances and petitions which were signed or marked by a large number of people. Some of these come close to providing a census of literacy. The Protestation Oath of 1641 is well known and has become a starting point for discussions of seventeenth-century literacy.[8] Equally fruitful material can be found among returns of the Vow and Covenant of 1643 and the Solemn League and Covenant of 1644. Some of the county petitions to the Long Parliament also have columns of marks and signatures arranged by parish, but most of them are so confused as to be almost useless. The sources are a genealogist's delight but the historian of literacy tangles with them at his peril.

The Protestation was drawn up in a mood of anger and fear and circulated to the country in a period of developing emergency. Invasion scares and rumours of plots buzzed around Westminster in the spring of 1641, as the attainder of Strafford approached its conclusion. Political observers were alarmed lest the king dissolve the parliament and take his revenge on its leaders. The House of Commons took the oath on 3 May 1641 and the Lords followed on 4 May, only a month after the discovery of a plot to throw the Irish army against England.[9]

Some of the tension in the atmosphere is caught by the preamble to the Protestation, which alleged that

there are still, even during the sitting in Parliament, endeavours to subvert the fundamental laws of England and Ireland, and to introduce the exercise of an arbitrary and tyrannical government, by most pernicious and wicked counsels, plots and conspiracies; and that the long intermission and unhappier breach of parliaments hath occasioned many illegal taxations, whereupon the subjects have been prosecuted and grieved; and that divers innovations and superstitions have been brought into the church, multitudes driven out of his majesty's dominions, jealousies raised and fomented between the king and people.

It was not necessary, however, to agree with this interpretation of recent events in order to endorse the Protestation. Those who took the oath made the quite unexceptional promise to defend 'the true, reformed and Protestant religion, expressed in the doctrine of the Church of England, against all popery and popish innovations'.[10] Only catholics and the most radical sectarians could object to this wording, since the oath was rather a show of solidarity and determination against danger than a document of division. However, the question of church *discipline* was left open and the document as a whole could be seen as an affront to the king.

On 6 May 1641 a bill was introduced to tender the Protestation throughout the realm, and on 30 July it was declared 'fit to be taken by every person that is well affected in religion and to the good of the commonwealth'. But it was not before January 1642 that the Protestation was printed and ready to be sent into the country. The crisis had now deepened and parliament was determined to obtain widespread support. The machinery for tendering the oath and collecting subscriptions was carefully organized at the county and local levels. Ministers, constables, churchwardens and overseers were to take it, since the opinions of community leaders were crucial. But the oath was also required of all 'the inhabitants of their several parishes, both householders and others, being of eighteen years of age and upwards'.[11]

More people were tendered the Protestation than were ever invited to vote in parliamentary elections. Every adult male throughout the kingdom was supposed to subscribe, and their names, together with details of any refusers, were to be returned to Westminster for inspection. In the characteristic style of the Long Parliament a committee was established to examine refusals to the Protestation, but it is unlikely that its members were especially busy.[12]

Most communities were eager to take the oath and demonstrate their loyalty. Some even swore the Protestation before it was formally required of them. As early as 30 May 1641 the parishioners of St Martin Orgar, London, took the oath 'for the maintenance of religion and the liberty of the subject', along with several other City parishes. Manuscript copies of the Protestation were circulating in the country by the summer of 1641 at the instigation of M.P.s and their agents. It was taken in Derbyshire at South Wingfield on 20 June and at Kedleston on 4 July. In Essex it was taken at Wanstead and Little Baddow on 27 June and at Hadleigh on 4 July. An irregular campaign to spread the Protestation continued for the rest of the year until parliament issued instructions for its nationwide circulation.[13] By March 1642 almost everyone in England who was a male aged eighteen or over had the opportunity to set his signature or mark to the Protestation.

Remarks introducing the names of subscribers often illuminate the way in which the oath was tendered. At St Katherine Cree, London,

the minister declared in the presence of the congregation, now because it would take up more time and indeed was impossible for everyone to express the same words, for more brevity the people expressed themselves after this manner as follows: I A.B. do in the presence of Almighty God freely and heartily promise, vow and protest the same which the leading person Mr George Rush did.

With 462 names to collect the minister is, perhaps, to be congratulated on this streamlined process. Unfortunately for our purposes he then copied all the names into the vestry minute book, where the document survives, so we cannot reconstruct the literacy of this important London congregation.[14]

Those taking the oath were supposed to swear it aloud and to write their names and marks in orderly columns. At Hayes, Middlesex, for example, the parishioners 'signified the taking of the Protestation either by their writing their names or by making their marks unto their names'. In parish after parish we are told that the Protestation was taken 'by us who have subscribed our hands or set our marks', and the page is adorned with a mixture of marks and scrawls and signatures of varying degrees of competence. The names of the parish priest and local officeholders are usually at the head of the list.[15]

The Protestation oath was an important event in many communities. It was, after all, very rare for parliament to ask the people at large to participate in so solemn a matter as the defence of religion against tyranny. At Harleston, Suffolk, the taking of the Protestation was accompanied by a public fast and a collection 'towards the distressed kingdom of Ireland'. At Great Greenford, Middlesex, 'there is no one in our parish forenamed that hath refused to take and to subscribe to the Protestation', while at Middleton, Essex, 'not one of the parish abovesaid refused to join in this act; as well women and youth of both sexes gave their full consent though they put not hereto their hands because they could not write'. Illiteracy did not inhibit the men of the community, however, since 12 of the 21 subscribers made marks.[16] Taking the Protestation together provided a moment of community cohesion as well as national solidarity with the defenders of protestantism.

Similar occasions were offered in the course of the civil war by the Vow and Covenant and the Solemn League and Covenant. Since subscriptions to these covenants contain important information about literacy it is essential to consider the circumstances of their adoption and the procedures employed for collecting signatures and marks.

The Vow and Covenant asserted that 'there hath been and now is in this kingdom a popish and traiterous plot for the subversion of the true Protestant reformed religion and liberty of the subject', and promised assistance to the forces of parliament. It was introduced in the Commons on 6 June 1643 and the next day 'recommended to the whole kingdom to take it'. Clear instructions were given on 27 June for organizing the Vow in the localities.

The constables of every town within the said several parishes shall bring unto the ministers the names fair written of all men above the age of fifteen residing within their several towns or villages, and the churchwardens of every parish shall before the said day so appointed provide a register book, in the beginning of which shall be the Vow and Covenant fair written, wherein every man, after he hath taken the said Vow and Covenant, shall write his name or make his mark, whereunto his name shall be written.[17]

The Vow and Covenant was a highly partisan declaration intended to rally a community at war. A public thanksgiving was proclaimed for the discovery of the plot and the menfolk turned out to subscribe wherever the vow was demanded. Anyone who refused faced sanctions. Soldiers were not to be paid until they subscribed while malignants were to be disarmed and have their names sent to London for further action. Under the circumstances it was hard to refuse, although some of the more cautious subscribers at Brantham Suffolk, annotated their vow, 'so far as lawfully I may'. The Vow and Covenant could, of course, be circulated only in areas under parliamentary control, and even there it was not pressed with the vigour of the Protestation.[18]

While signatures were still being collected for the Vow and Covenant another declaration was under discussion in London. The Solemn League and Covenant was agreed between the Scottish divines and the parliamentary committee on 14 September 1643, and a week later the ministers of the London area were instructed to 'exhort the people to the cheerful taking of it'. This declaration, 'for the reformation and defence of religion, the honour and happiness of the king, and the peace and safety of the three kingdoms', was strategically more important than the earlier Vow and Covenant since the Scottish alliance with which it was associated promised to help parliament win the war.[19]

By 30 January 1644 there was agreement on the instructions for taking the covenant throughout the nation. It was to be 'tendered to all men within the several parishes above the age of eighteen, as well lodgers as inhabitants', and they were all to 'subscribe their names in the book or roll with their neighbours'. The business was to be conducted in an appropriately solemn manner. The minister was to read the covenant from the pulpit

and at the end of this reading thereof all [were] to take it standing, lifting up their right hands bare, and then afterwards to subscribe it severally by writing their names, or their marks to which their names are to be added, in a parchment roll or book whereinto the covenant is to be inserted, purposely provided for that end and kept as a record in the parish.[20]

The procedure was likely to create complete and authentic sets of subscriptions, since there was no need to return a fair copy and only the names of refusers were reported to parliament.

The Solemn League and Covenant, with its introduction of presbyterianism, threatened rather to destroy the Church of England than to defend it, and had none of the unifying spirit of the Protestation. Despite this, or possibly because of it, the declaration was written out in full in several parish registers and subscribed by the adult males without apparent dissent. It was, in the words of an official responsible for its administration in Sussex, 'of special use for uniting of the minds and hearts of men to stand firm for the common cause'. Dissent was more likely to set in when the revolutionary era was over. At Prittlewell, Essex, the list of subscribers was gruffly annotated in a later hand, 'all roundhead villains', while it was common for the oaths and declarations of the civil war to be crossed out, obliterated, or even sliced off the page.[21]

Despite alarms and disruptions, the wartime covenants of 1643 and 1644 were administered locally in a manner similar to the earlier Protestation. London parishes were always the first to subscribe. At St Clement Eastcheap the Vow and Covenant was taken on 17 June 1643, 'every man subscribing his own name as follows'. On 8 October that year, months before parliament required it, they took the Solemn League and Covenant, each man 'having set hereto his own hand'. Mass involvement in public affairs was becoming habitual, and it was not confined to the metropolis. In Essex the Vow and Covenant was taken on 23 and 26 July 1643 'by all the inhabitants of Hadleigh whose names are underwritten'. The same parishioners received the Solemn League and Covenant on 10 and 17 March 1644, with as much enthusiasm as when they swore the Protestation oath in 1641.[22]

These three parliamentary declarations contain our best evidence for the extent of community literacy in the mid seventeenth century. They were administered in the parish church with the cooperation of local officials. The scrutiny was strict and sometimes the oaths were tendered again on successive Sundays to ensure the most complete attestation. But despite these precautions it is possible that a few men who should have subscribed avoided it or were never given the opportunity. Principled objectors should have been recorded but there may have been people on the village margins, men who rarely attended church and who were but slenderly attached to the community, whose absence was never noticed or not considered significant. Without community reconstitution and close demographic analysis it is impossible to tell whether such people were numerous and whether they were represented in the declarations. If, as seems likely, these marginal villagers were more illiterate than their more integrated neighbours, any figures derived from Protestations, Vows and Covenants which omit them will represent the upper limits of literacy. Levels of literacy may actually have been even lower than the figures collected here suggest.

Before turning to the figures that can be extracted from these three types of document it is worth considering some of the other records of the period which might complement them if analysed with care. The months before the outbreak of war in 1642 saw a stream of petitions to the House of Commons, praising God for the discovery of plots and giving encouragement to the work that was going forward. Thousands of signatures and marks were attached to these documents, as proof that literate and illiterate alike could be marshalled in support of the revolution at Westminster. Most of these petitions were modelled on the Protestation, subscribed parish by parish, and bundled up to make an impressive presentation. Over 13,000 names were attached to 'the humble petition of the knights, gentlemen, ministers and other inhabitants of the county of Essex', which was delivered on 20 January 1642. Similar petitions were handed in from Hertfordshire, Middlesex, Surrey, Kent, Suffolk and other counties in the next few weeks.[23]

Another document, similar in format but very different in tone, was the 'remonstrance or declaration of us the inhabitants of the county palatine of Chester whose names are subscribed, and of many more'. Dozens of sets of signatures and marks were attached to the declaration, and over 8,000 names were collected 'in maintenance of his majesty's royal and sacred person, honour and prerogative, and in preservation of the parliament and just privileges thereof, of our true and undoubted religion, laws, proprieties and liberties'. The subscribers were joined together against 'fostering and fomenting the unfortunate mistakes and fearful jealousies betwixt head and body, his majesty and his parliament'.[24] This may have been Cheshire's riposte to the Protestation, a well-organized demonstration of dissatisfaction with the drift of events in London. But despite the large number of marks and signatures the remonstrance cannot be trusted as a guide to literacy in the north west.

The main difficulty with petitions and remonstrances lies in our ignorance of the circumstances in which they were circulated. Unlike the declarations sponsored by parliament, which were sent out to be subscribed under strict supervision, the petitions were free of controls. The organizers wanted a large number of names in a hurry and may not have minded if the collection was casual or selective. We do not know whether the document was tendered to all the men in each community, or only to those who could be conveniently reached or who were thought most willing to subscribe. Although the total number of names collected in some communities suggests that there was a full turn-out we cannot be sure that the record is generally complete. The ordinary humble and poor, who were pressed into making their marks on the Protestation, do not appear to be fully represented, and this is reflected in the proportion of marks and signatures. Wherever rates of illiteracy can be recovered from the county petitions they are some 15% lower than in more reliable sources.[25]

Only subscriptions to the Protestation, the Vow and Covenant and the Solemn League and Covenant can be taken as acceptable guides to literacy in the 1640s, and these only when the returns are demonstrably authentic and complete. Most of the Protestation returns are in the House of Lords Record Office, having been sent to Westminster by the sheriffs in 1642, but others, including those made by local initiative in 1641, remain in the localities. All the subscriptions to the covenants have been found in local records, and more will no doubt come to light as parish registers, church-wardens' books and vestry minutes are further examined.[26] Table 4.1 shows the number of acceptable returns in each county, the total of subscribers, the number and percentage who were unable to write their names, and the range of illiteracy in each county. The county figures, which show the geography of illiteracy in mid-seventeenth-century England, are also given on Map 1, where percentages that are based on fewer than 500 subscribers are given in round brackets. (The figures for individual parishes are given in the appendix.)

The evidence for the literacy of the male population of England in the 1640s is based on the signatures and marks of more than 40,000 men from over 400 parishes in twenty-five counties. The vast size of the sample lends weight to the conclusion that 70% of the men who were tendered declarations in the decade of the civil war lacked the necessary skill to sign them. But before this figure is accepted as a summary of English illiteracy in the mid seventeenth century, it should be pointed out that the sample was not scientifically drawn, and that the parishioners who were counted were not necessarily representative of their countrymen at large. The parishes were selected for no other reason than that their declarations survived and passed the tests of completeness and authenticity. Most of the evidence comes from rural communities and many of them are in southern and south-west England. The returns from Cornwall are especially plentiful and may weight the over-all figures if Cornwall was particularly illiterate. On the other hand, there are very few returns from Yorkshire and the far north where literacy was probably just as poor, so the bias may not be too severe.

The figure of 70% is probably an accurate enough indication of the level of illiteracy in *rural* England, but it does not take full account of the sometimes superior level found in the towns. There is a scatter of evidence suggesting that townspeople could more often write their names than could country-dwellers. If only 22% of Londoners made marks (see Table 4.1), this suggests that the capital may have provided a uniquely literate environment. However, there are only four usable returns for London, and we cannot be sure that the parishioners of Holy Trinity the Less, St Clement Eastcheap, St Martin Orgar and St Mary Magdalen, Milk Street were typical inhabitants of the metropolis. Evidence from depositions and other sources, to be discussed later, confirms the precocious literacy of some Londoners, but it cannot be made to show the literacy of the city as a whole.[27] There may have been

Table 4.1   *Illiteracy in England, 1641—4*

County	Usable parishes	No. of subscribers	No. mark[1]	% mark	Illiteracy range (%)
Berkshire	12	725	535	74	93—57
Buckinghamshire	3	156	110	71	75—69
Chester city	5	736	385	52	82—30
Cornwall	116	15,868	11,426	72	92—47
Derbyshire	3	316	235	74	77—61
Devon	38	4,903	3,527	72	87—57
Dorset	9	573	400	70	77—47
Durham	2	247	183	74	77—68
Essex	16	1,081	681	63	85—36
Hertfordshire	1	85	63	74	
Huntingdonshire	28	1,933	1,299	67	80—7
Lincolnshire	48	3,152	2,304	73	94—50
London	4	609	132	22	33—9
Middlesex	3	392	242	62	77—41
Norfolk	4	146	105	72	89—56
Nottinghamshire	49	3,845	2,930	76	93—27
Oxfordshire	4	288	190	66	71—58
Shropshire	1	67	44	66	
Somerset	4	904	577	64	85—37
Staffordshire	3	312	201	64	71—63
Suffolk	6	294	131	45	58—36
Surrey	18	1,228	837	68	91—49
Sussex	28	1,797	1,272	71	82—59
Westmorland	7	797	591	74	94—62
Yorkshire	2	639	475	74	74—73
Total	414	41,093	28,875	70	94—7

1. 'No. mark' = number of persons making a mark (unable to sign their names), here and throughout the tables.

an underclass in the least fashionable parts of the city whose higher illiteracy went unrecorded.

A recent study of the population of London makes it possible to compare literacy and wealth in the reign of Charles I. Although we have literacy evidence for only four of the 110 London parishes it appears that there was a very close correspondence between the ability to sign and the proportion of substantial households. Holy Trinity the Less, where 33% of the men were illiterate, was a moderately poor community with less than 16% of the households qualifying as 'substantial'. St Mary Magdalen, Milk Street, at the other end of the scale with only 9% illiterate, was among the

Map 1   Illiteracy in England, 1641–4: percentages of men unable to sign
their names (bracketed percentages are based on fewer than 500 subscribers)

most prosperous parishes, with almost 69% substantial households.[28] Table 4.2 shows the figures for illiteracy and wealth in
the period 1638–44.

No usable returns survive for Norwich, Bristol or the other
leading towns of the seventeenth century, so we cannot gauge
their literacy from these sources. One Protestation has been found
in the parish records of St Stephen, Ipswich, where 36% of the 88

Table 4.2 *Literacy and prosperity in London, 1638–44*

Parish	No. of subscribers	% mark	No. of houses	% substantial households
Holy Trinity the Less	217	33	88	15.9
St Martin Orgar	152	21	101	32.7
St Clement Eastcheap	122	17	50	52.0
St Mary Magdalen, Milk Street	118	9	45	68.9

subscribers made marks. Usable returns survive for five parishes in the city of Chester, with 52% of the subscribers illiterate.[29] These performances were much better than the national average, and if similar levels could be assumed for other urban centres, the high figure of 70% illiterate might have to be modified. But before undertaking any calculations based on the relative size and literacy of the urban and rural populations, the weakness of the evidence for the superiority of the towns should be understood. Ipswich had a dozen more parishes besides St Stephen's, while the figures for Chester omit the parishes of St Bridget, St Oswald and St Peter. Without knowing the economic and social geography of towns with partial returns it would be extremely risky to generalize about their literacy.[30]

Smaller towns were not markedly different from the surrounding country. Bridgewater in Somerset, where 648 men subscribed the Protestation, was 67% illiterate, while Pontefract in Yorkshire, with 584 subscribers, had an illiteracy level of 74%.[31]

Illiteracy was generally higher in the north and in the far south-west, and lower in the midlands and south-east. Nottinghamshire had the worst illiteracy, with 76% unable to sign, while the northern counties of Yorkshire (74%), Derbyshire (74%), Westmorland (74%), Durham (74%) and Lincolnshire (73%) were almost as bad. Admittedly the figures for Derbyshire, Durham and Yorkshire are based on very few returns but they are not inconsistent with the much stronger evidence from the neighbouring counties of Nottinghamshire, Lincolnshire and Westmorland. On the basis of the surviving returns we may argue that the north of England was steeped in illiteracy, with three-quarters of the adult male population unable to write their names. Southern and midland England, by contrast, was better, with close to two-thirds illiterate. The Suffolk figure (44%), based on just 250 people in five parishes, seems too good to be true, but the returns from Middlesex (62%), Essex (63%), Oxfordshire and Somerset (66%),

Huntingdonshire (67%) and Surrey (68%) produce convincing figures for their regions.

This evidence fails to confirm Stone's suggestion, in his pioneer work on the Protestations, that regional variations in literacy were associated with the highland and lowland economic zones which divide the country diagonally.[32] The figures from Staffordshire (64%) and Shropshire (66%) tend to unsettle this hypothesis, but they are based on very few returns, and in any case those counties may have had more in common with the midlands than with the upland north. More serious is the appearance of high levels of illiteracy in the southern heartland, quite close to London. The Hertfordshire figure of 74% may be a freak, the product of a single unusual return, but Berkshire, with a dozen parishes in the mix, was also 74% illiterate, as backward as anywhere in the north. Nor does the evidence from Buckinghamshire and Sussex (71% each) or Norfolk and Devon (72% each) support the suggestion that literacy was superior in the lowland zone. The outer areas were moderately poor while even in the centre of southern England there were pockets of appalling illiteracy.

Stone's hypothesis, though suggestive of the economic variables which influenced literacy, is, then, too simple. The evidence at our disposal does not permit more than a hesitant sketch of the regional distribution of illiteracy. Where there is a large number of usable returns, as in Cornwall and Devon, Nottinghamshire and Lincolnshire, Huntingdonshire and Sussex, we may treat the county summaries with reasonable confidence. But elsewhere we must make the best of a sprinkling of returns from parishes which may or may not have been representative of their district. The north/south division may bear further investigation, but on the current evidence it is striking how small was the range of variation between all the different counties throughout the country. With the exception of Nottinghamshire on the high side and Suffolk, Middlesex, Essex and Staffordshire on the low side, the summary scores for all the counties for which we have evidence fall within five percentage points of the mean. There was no great variation from county to county but rather an over-all consistency. Our task may be to explain the similarities rather than focus on the differences.

The greatest differences were found at the local level. Far more striking than any regional pattern in the geography of illiteracy is the patchwork of variation from parish to parish. While the over-all performances of each county were close to the national average the summary figures mask an enormous range of differences within a small area. Illiteracy in Cornish parishes ranged from 47% to

92%, in Devon from 57% to 87% and in Nottinghamshire from 27% to 93%. Even neighbouring communities could have radically different literacy characteristics. In one village less than a third of the men were unable to sign their names, while in another village a short walk away the proportion of illiterates might have been higher than three-quarters.

Illiteracy in Nottinghamshire was worse than anywhere else, but at least nine of the 49 parishes for which we have evidence performed better than the national average. Middlesex and Essex were among the most literate counties, close to London in the rich and progressive south-east. But parish scores there ranged from 41% to 77% and 36% to 85% unable to sign. Despite the locational advantages which they supposedly enjoyed, Hayes in Middlesex and Little Oakley in Essex had illiteracy levels which might have shocked a north-country clergyman. Lesnewth in Cornwall and Hawton or Grove in Nottinghamshire, on the other hand, were outstandingly good despite being stuck in the darker corners of the land. Literacy varied wildly from place to place, displaying a bewildering array of irregularities within a short span of miles. Accounting for these variations poses a complex range of problems — which may be illustrated by the example of Essex.

Good evidence survives for the literacy of sixteen Essex parishes in the 1640s. Most of the declarations appear in the parish registers and five of them contain subscriptions to more than one oath. Hadleigh is unique in having usable returns to the Vow and Covenant and the Solemn League and Covenant as well as to the Protestation. For the purpose of calculating county statistics the returns with the greatest number of names have been preferred, but all of them will be considered in this local investigation. The Essex figures are shown in Table 4.3, together with the number of households recorded in the 1671 hearth tax and the number of communicants counted in 1676. These latter figures give some idea of the population of each parish in the later seventeenth century and also serve as a check on the completeness of the 1640s returns. Fyfield, for example, had 106 subscribers to the Vow and Covenant, 89 households according to hearth-tax records, and 210 people who were communicants in the Church of England. Using the least controversial multipliers suggested by historical demographers the three figures point to a Fyfield population of 339, 400 and 349 respectively, so there was no obvious short-fall in the number of men subscribing the covenant.[33] Similar calculations can be made for all the other parishes. Considering that the tax and communicant figures are from a later generation than the declarations, that rural Essex was as subject to migration

Table 4.3   *Subscribers, householders and communicants in
Essex parishes, 1641−76*

Parish	Declaration[1]	1640s subscribers	% mark	1671 householders	1676 communicants
Little Baddow	P	71	45	46	
Barnston	P	63	63	35	80
	V	49	63		
Boxted	V	131	61	121	250
Dengie	V	28	71	13	50
Fyfield	V	106	69	89	210
Hadleigh	P	50	82	25	30
	V	33	70		
	S	46	76		
East Hanningfield	P	67	67	50	200
Kelvedon Hatch	P	59	64	34	107
Middleton	P	21	57	21	57
Little Oakley	P	34	85	24	57
Great Parndon	S	73	58	74	
Prittlewell	V	155	65	77	200
	S	157	69		
Great Stambridge	P	26	69	28	
Marks Tey	P	29	52	30	
	S	36	56		
Wanstead	P	59	36	40	125
Wormingford	P	100	62	45	114
	V	76	64		

1. P = Protestation
   V = Vow and Covenant
   S = Solemn League and Covenant

and population change as anywhere else, and that the war may
have claimed some parishioners in the 1640s, the fit is remarkably
good.

Illiteracy figures in Essex, ranging from 36% at Wanstead to
85% at Little Oakley, are displayed on Map 2. Several parishes,
notably Barnston, Boxted, Kelveden Hatch and Wormingford,
scored close to the county average of 63%, but for others the
figures were significantly better or worse. The following discussion
attempts to make sense of these variations without pretending to
be either authoritative or definitive. Indeed, the discussion raises
more questions than it answers and argues the need for more
penetrating local research.

With what attributes or experiences was the literacy of a community associated in the seventeenth century? Were ideological

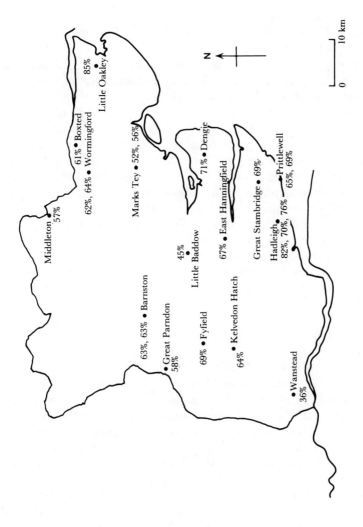

Map 2   Illiteracy in Essex, 1641—4: percentages for sixteen parishes of men unable to sign their names (to the Protestation, and to the Vow and Covenant, and Solemn League and Covenant, where applicable)

or economic factors more important? Was the literacy of a community rooted in its religious, political or educational background? Did the literacy of parliamentarian strongholds contrast with enclaves of royalist sympathies? Was the lord of the manor, the patron of the living, the principal landowner or the incumbent clergyman of deciding importance? Did the parishes which came under puritan influence enjoy higher standards of literacy than places which were more conservative in religion? Or were differences in literacy largely the result of different educational provision, with the presence and influence of schools and schoolmasters explaining the pattern? These matters concerning cultural exposure will be reviewed before turning to economic considerations.

Little is known about the persuasion and intensity of political activism in these sixteen Essex villages. Perhaps it was non-existent outside the circle of the squire and his friends, although some sparks and scuffles on the eve of the civil war suggest that our picture is incomplete.[34] Essex was penetrated by Laudians and supporters of the court as much as by puritans and opponents of 'thorough' and enjoyed a pluralist political culture until Warwick and his supporters took control of the county in 1642. It is not too difficult to uncover the political inclination of the leading men in the county, but there is no telling whether ordinary villagers were royalist or parliamentarian. They may have been strongly moved or utterly indifferent but most of their views are lost to history. We cannot pin political labels to the parishes on the map and then set about comparing their literacy. If local political attributes are to be correlated with literacy it might be better to examine the stability or otherwise of officeholding or the fractiousness or litigiousness of the community as expressed in court records, evidence which has not yet been collected for the parishes under consideration.

The names of principal landowners, manorial lords and patrons of livings come easily to hand, and a little effort will indicate the sympathies of most of them in the crisis of the 1640s. Robert Rich, the puritan Earl of Warwick who opposed the king on ship money and forest laws, and who gave generous support to puritans in East Anglia, held manors at Barnston, Fyfield, Hadleigh and Prittlewell and had the gift of the living in each of those parishes. The Mildmay family, just as strong in its opposition to king Charles, held land at Little Baddow, Dengie, East Hanningfield and Wanstead. Sir Henry Mildmay, the regicide, had his seat at Wanstead and was patron of the living. The king himself presented to the living of Little Baddow in 1632 during the wardship of the young lord of the manor, and was also patron at Marks Tey. The catholic

Countess of Rivers was patron at Little Oakley, where much of the land was controlled by the recusant Darceys. The other villages had lords and patrons of little renown, whose influence can be evaluated only after local studies. Two of them were linked to London institutions — Great Stambridge, where the advowson and one of the manors belonged to Charterhouse, and Great Parndon, where they were shared by Bridewell St Thomas' and Christ's hospitals.[35]

Whether these feudal arrangements had anything to do with literacy is doubtful. Little Oakley, attached to the Countess of Rivers, was the parish with the worst recorded literacy figures in Essex, while Wanstead, controlled by Sir Henry Mildmay, had the best, but apart from these extremes no general pattern can be seen. The other places ranged across the spectrum with no association between literacy and lordship. In any case the politics and religion of the principal landowner were probably of less importance for the cultural complexion of the community than his presence and power, and the degree of his dominance over local institutions; this too is a subject for future research.

The patron of a living could impress his views on a community, and possibly influence literacy, by his choice of clerical incumbent. The Earl of Warwick had twenty-two Essex livings in his gift and used them to promote puritan vicars and rectors. He usually sponsored godly ministers resistant to Laudianism, but there was no universal match between the views of the incumbent and his patron. Some parish clergy had held their benefices for many years and owed nothing to the ideological concerns of the present patron.

No matter when or how he obtained his benefice, the parish priest was likely to be a strong influence on the religious complexion of his community. He may also have borne some responsibility for its literacy. Given the renowned puritan enthusiasm for education, illustrated by the campaign for reading referred to in chapter 1, we might expect to find puritan parishes doing better than their more conservative neighbours when the Protestation and covenants came round to be signed. We can test this hypothesis by reviewing the religious history of each community.

Boxted, Dengie and Wormingford seem to have led quiet religious lives to the extent that their clergy did nothing to draw attention to themselves. They were served by neither scandalous cavaliers nor militant puritans and appear to have passed through the period without offending anyone. The literacy of Boxted and Wormingford was close to the county average, and Dengie was somewhat worse.

Other parishes had priests whose conservatism, Laudianism or outrageous behaviour led to their sequestration in the early years of the civil war. Alexander Read, rector of Fyfield since 1630, was a conforming high Anglican who bowed towards the altar and proclaimed the Book of Sports. It was claimed that he permitted games on the sabbath and encouraged people to cross themselves on the forehead when entering church. Puritans considered him a menace. More venial were the offences of William Frost of Middleton, who ran into trouble with Archbishop Laud as well as with his presbyterian successors. In 1636 he was found guilty of drunkenness and had to purge himself of charges of incest and adultery. He too enforced the altar and Book of Sports and was eventually ejected as an enemy to the proceedings of parliament.[36] Despite similarities in ministry and theology, the two parishes were very different in their level of literacy. Fyfield, with 69% illiterate, was among the most backward parishes in the immediate area while Middleton, with 57% unable to sign, was among the best in Essex.

Conservative religious leadership was associated with moderately high illiteracy at Great Stambridge. Anthony Andrews, rector from 1635 to 1641, was a pluralist who owed his second parish to the patronage of the king. His successor, Thomas Thorold, was no more acceptable to the radicals and suffered sequestration in 1643.[37]

Great Parndon and East Hanningfield shared the pluralist William Osboldston as rector. He was ejected from the first parish in 1643 but was allowed to continue at the latter. An old man by the time of the Protestation, he was usually non-resident and his rare sermons were notable for their preaching against frequent preaching. Like Read and Frost, he endorsed the Book of Sports and was condemned by strict Calvinists for his soft line on original sin. His parish of East Hanningfield had worse than average illiteracy although Great Parndon performed somewhat better. Can we attach blame or credit for these results to the rector? It may be significant that whereas Osboldston maintained his links with East Hanningfield, the administration of Great Parndon was left to curates, and they may have interested themselves in parochial literacy. In 1637 the curate at Great Parndon was Francis Onge, a puritan with a licence from the bishop to teach English and Latin.[38]

Other parishes were exposed to competing conservative and radical influences. Kelveden Hatch and Marks Tey each had Laudian rectors whose influence was countered by the presence of puritan ministers and laymen. The rector of Kelveden Hatch was Stephen Withers, a pluralist who also had the living at Sheering.

He was sequestered in 1643, charged with the usual range of malignancies — sexual offences, altar worship and contempt for the sabbath — which may or may not have been true. He had been rector at Kelveden Hatch since 1607 but was not the only spiritual leader in the community. His curate since 1637 was John Lavender, a supporter of parliament and enthusiastic endorser of the Protestation, and the puritan family of Luther was prominent among the parishioners.[39] Literacy at Kelveden Hatch was in the middle range.

At Marks Tey there was conflict over the appointment of a curate, which may have mobilized both conservative and radical factions. Nehemiah Rogers, the Laudian sinecure rector, was occupied elsewhere and his vicar, Henry Golding, enjoyed the patronage of the king. Robert Cooke purchased the tithes in 1635 and as lay rector of Marks Tey tried to have Golding removed. The attempt failed amid much acrimony and cost Cooke a spell in the Fleet prison. Although the details are unclear the struggle looks like the attempt of a puritan laity to install its own minister. It is hard to say what impact the episode had on the religious climate at Marks Tey, but since the parishioners were exceptionally literate they may have been deeply involved.[40]

Little Oakley, the most illiterate community recorded, was in the gift of the Earl and then the Countess of Rivers and it might be thought that a Romish priest would be installed. But John Malden was there from 1634 as curate, and the countess presented him to the living in 1641. This John Malden was still there in 1650, had ministered to a puritan classis, and seems to have found favour with the Westminster Assembly.[41] Little Oakley's illiteracy was not simply a product of pastoral neglect.

There remain five parishes whose leaders were unmistakably puritan. Little Baddow was a centre of vigorous puritan activity despite having a royal appointee as sinecure rector. John Newton was vicar from 1629 and he clashed regularly with the episcopal authorities over doctrine and discipline. Laud found him 'inconformable' in 1636, and 1637 he was reported for omitting the name of Jesus from the blessing. The informant was Richard Hooke, the royalist rector, who usually kept his distance from Little Baddow's religious radicalism.[42] More celebrated than Newton was his friend and neighbour Thomas Hooker. Hooker lived in Little Baddow and kept a school there with John Eliot, the future apostle to the Algonquin Indians. From 1626 to 1630 he was a Puritan lecturer in nearby Chelmsford and leader of the 'godly ministers' throughout Essex. Hooker's activities drew the wrath of the church courts and he was forced to flee, first to

Holland and eventually to New England. He was well away from Little Baddow by the time of the Protestation but the issues he had championed were kept fresh in memory by John Newton.[43] Continuing puritan activity, with lay support as well as godly preaching, was coupled with exceptionally low literacy at Little Baddow.

Barnston, where returns to both the Protestation and the Vow and Covenant show 63% illiterate, had a puritan minister who agitated in support of Hooker. John Beadle, rector since 1632, enjoyed the patronage of the Earl of Warwick. Even before his preferment he was 'not conformable in preaching nor practice' and in 1633 he received a canonical admonition from Archbishop Laud for non-conformity. With the change of regime in the 1640s Beadle could relax, and by 1648 the rector of Barnston was one of the best-respected puritan ministers in the county.[44]

The Earl of Warwick was also patron of Hadleigh and installed a succession of puritan ministers there. John Ward and then Nathaniel Ward were there in the 1630s, and William Wells was rector at the time of the declarations. It was he who entered the Protestation and the two covenants in the parish register and added a note to the Protestation that it did not extend to maintaining 'any form of worship, discipline or government or any rite or ceremony'.[45] The doctrine of the Elizabethan settlement might be acceptable to many puritans but they could not all bring themselves to support the church as governed by Juxon and Laud. The inhabitants of Hadleigh had such a puritan in the pulpit, but he made little impression on literacy. With between 70% and 82% of the men unable to write their names on the various declarations, the terrible illiteracy of Hadleigh was exceeded only by Little Oakley. To find a puritan tradition associated with high illiteracy is disturbing and throws doubt on the hypothesis linking religion and literacy.

The evidence from Prittlewell does nothing to restore support for the hypothesis. Prittlewell was another puritan parish not far along the Thames estuary from Hadleigh. There was a long tradition of non-conformity among its ministers, extending back through the reigns of James I and Elizabeth. Thomas Peck, who became vicar in 1633, was presented by the Earl of Warwick and maintained his dissenting activities until he was finally ejected after the Restoration. The puritan credentials of its clergy are complete but, none the less, 65% to 69% of the parishioners of Prittlewell could not sign their names when the covenants were tendered in the 1640s.[46]

Wanstead, like Prittlewell, had a long tradition of moderate puritan activity but a completely different level of literacy. From 1586 to 1615 it had in Peter Lawrence a 'diligent and sufficient preacher' and was blessed by godly ministers in the years that followed. Humphrey Maddison, who was rector at the time of the Protestation, was supported by Sir Henry Mildmay and became closely involved with Westminster presbyterianism.[47] Clerical and lay puritanism combined in a parish where literacy was outstanding.

Religion and literacy were evidently related in seventeenth-century Essex, but the association was imperfect and the connections unclear. Wanstead and Little Baddow were exemplary progressive centres with excellent literacy to match their puritan traditions. But Hadleigh and Prittlewell, which could also claim to be radical strongholds, were among the most illiterate parishes in Essex. The association between conservative parishes and high illiteracy is more persuasive, but again there were damaging exceptions. A case could be made that Fyfield, East Hanningfield and Great Stambridge were backward places, kept in ignorance by their malignant ministers. But Middleton, for all the outrages of the Reverend William Frost, escaped contamination and emerged remarkably literate.

The evidence so far assembled deals only with the stance of religious leaders in the period before the outbreak of war. It takes little account of religious impulses in earlier generations which might have shaped literacy in the 1640s and it does not allow for influences from outside the parish. More serious, it fails to review religion in the community at large. Further research might reveal the contours of popular religion and the penetration of progressive ideas among ordinary people. We need to know whether common lay puritans were more likely to be literate than their anglican or pagan neighbours, and by what margin. This question is beyond the scope of the present enquiry.

There was no more than an uncertain fit between religious leadership and popular literacy. Which was cause and which was consequence, or even whether there was a causal relationship, would be premature to adjudge. A backward community could be given the most radical minister to preach sermons at it, yet his concern for religious literacy might make a minimal impression. Similarly, a community of enlightened and well-educated laymen could suffer the incumbency of a minister who was lazy, indifferent or worse, without their own literacy being damaged. Religious zeal alone could not compel a congregation into literacy any more than religious lethargy could stunt it. The clergy could set a tone or establish a climate, but they were not solely responsible for their parishioners' performance. Other factors were involved in the pattern of illiteracy among the villages.

Literacy was probably linked most directly with education. Places with a school, schoolmasters or a tradition of elementary teaching might be expected to have displayed superior literacy, while places with no record of formal schooling were more illiterate. The hypothesis is appealing but the investigation swarms with problems.

The adult males whose signatures and marks are counted could have acquired their education elsewhere. Among them were migrants from different parts of Essex, East Anglia and beyond whose ability or inability to sign should be credited to a distant upbringing. Others were lifetime residents of the community in which they subscribed, but took their schooling outside the parish boundary. Not even at the peak of the educational revolution did every parish have a school or schoolmaster, but most places could find a licensed teacher within a few miles.[48] The local availability of a schoolmaster was more important than his exact address. This means that we should not confine our attention to the sixteen parishes with literacy figures but should also consider educational provision in the surrounding districts within walking distance; the investigation therefore grows in complexity.

A further problem concerns the sources from which we attempt to reconstruct the location of teachers in the past. Most of our information comes from the licensing and visitation records of the church, since education was considered to be 'of ecclesiastical cognisance'. Schoolteachers were supposed to be licensed and to show their papers at visitations. Unfortunately, the authorities varied in their view of what types of teacher required a licence and fluctuated in their efforts to trace them. While dozens of schoolmasters appear in the church records, there were others who entirely escaped episcopal supervision and are therefore invisible. Many of these were teachers of petties, exactly the group we need to locate in search of the roots of popular literacy. Schoolmistresses were especially elusive. As Margaret Spufford points out, the record of a teacher is positive evidence for educational activity, but absence from the records is not necessarily negative evidence.[49]

Even if a schoolmaster was present he was not necessarily available to everyone or interested in elementary instruction. His fees may have been too high, his school too exclusive or his curriculum too rigidly classical for everyone in the community to benefit. Some of the teachers who can be located had just a handful of pupils or drew their clients from a geographically wide but socially narrow area, and may not have been of much service to local children.[50] A further complication, already referred to in Chapter 2, is that some teachers were but casually or intermittently engaged in schooling, while others who were not considered schoolmasters at all took some of the responsibility for transmitting literacy. Informal education does not show up in the ecclesiastical records but it may have been important in the literacy of our parishes.

Suitably cautioned, we can begin to probe the local association between literacy and education. Half the parishes in our survey had no record of educational provision in the first half of the seventeenth century. Included are Little Oakley, Fyfield and Great Stambridge where illiteracy was high, as well as the more literate parishes of Wanstead, Marks Tey, Middleton, Barnston and Kelveden Hatch. Some of these places were close to well-established schools and may not have needed resident teachers. Wanstead was in the catchment area of Walthamstow, Ilford and Barking and is only a few miles from London. Marks Tey is just outside Colchester and could send its children there, while Middleton is just a short walk across the Stour from the important town of Sudbury in Suffolk. Even Little Oakley had formal schooling within reach. One had only to walk a mile or two across the fields to Ramsey or at most the four miles to Harwich to find a schoolmaster in the early seventeenth century.[51]

The other eight parishes had schoolmasters of their own from time to time, and some had a continuous history of educational provision. Little Baddow benefited from its village school in the 1620s and 1630s, where James Weeland in 1634 and one Jeckyne in 1637 were successors to the self-exiled puritan schoolmasters Hooker and Eliot. Great Parndon had a tradition of instruction by the curate, although there was no formally constituted school. Nicholas Kirby was curate and schoolmaster in 1619, and Francis Onge taught English and Latin from 1637.[52] Little Baddow and Great Parndon were among the most literate parishes.

Boxted and Wormingford, with average illiteracy in the 1640s, had schoolmasters in the early seventeenth century, although they are absent from the records after 1615. Prittlewell also had a Jacobean schoolmaster recognized by the church and may have continued to offer education in the 1620s. An entrant to Sidney Sussex College, Cambridge, in 1627 included Prittlewell among the places he had been schooled but did not indicate the name of the master.[53]

East Hanningfield had a teacher in 1605 but none thereafter, while no schoolmaster had been recorded at Dengie since 1589.

Neither community was in an area particularly well served by other schoolmasters so their poor literacy performance may be associated with a dearth of educational provision. Hadleigh, however, had no such easy excuse. Richard Bridges, who had been schoolmaster at Prittlewell, was recorded in Hadleigh in 1612 and reappeared in 1615 at nearby Leigh, where there was a sequence of schoolmasters from Elizabethan times to the civil war.[54] With its alarmingly high illiteracy, Hadleigh demonstrates that educational progress could not be achieved merely by the local presence of teachers. The cases of Little Baddow and Great Parndon suggest an association between parochial schooling and superior literacy but it is not reinforced by evidence from the rest of the county. The irregular distribution of literacy is not satisfactorily explained by the history of education so the hypothesis must be jettisoned or at least suspended until the geographical impact of schooling is better understood.

Were literacy levels more closely associated with economic conditions? Did the degree of literacy vary with the amount and distribution of wealth in a community or with the source of that wealth? How did industrial and agricultural districts compare, and were there variations with the type of farming? Were there detectable differences in social structure which might account for differences in literacy? Or were demographic variables more important? Was the sheer size of the community a determinant, with social concentration leading to improved performance? Did literacy vary with distance from London or a provincial centre, and was it affected by proximity to a main road or market town? It may not be possible to answer these questions but the material from Essex can at least provide some indications.

One of the most striking suggestions of recent work is that literacy may have varied with economic zones, in particular with the type of agriculture being conducted. There may have been strong ties between the geography of farming regions and the distribution of literacy. In her study of Cambridgeshire Margaret Spufford suggests that 'the tremendous variations from parish to parish of numbers of people able to sign their names can perhaps be accounted for by the type of agricultural and economic background concerned'.[55] Contrasting types of landscape and soil were particularly suited to different kinds of farming activity, and the varying systems of agricultural production led to variations in social structure, and hence to variations in literacy. Despite a strong element of determinism the hypothesis is highly engaging. But it cannot be established for certain whether it applies in Essex.

Seventeenth-century Essex was a county of mixed farming, strongly influenced by the appetite of London. Three different farming regions can be identified and we have some evidence for literacy in each of them. To the north and west lay an area of light clay soils especially suited to grain production. Here there was still a degree of open-field farming, and a mixed husbandry concentrating on corn. To the east and along the Thames estuary was marshland, where the economy was based on livestock. The marshland pastures fed dairy cattle, beef herds and sheep, and were renowned for their butter and cheese, but corn was also grown in this region. The central belt of Essex, running diagonally from the Stour valley to the Lea, was a wood–pasture region where large profits were made by stock fattening. The southern part of this region, close to London, was still well forested, while in the north there was a mixture of pasture farming and industry. The area around Colchester was one of the centres for the new draperies. These economic regions of seventeenth-century Essex are depicted on Map 3. The boundaries, of course, are only approximate, and each region included farmers whose activity would have been more characteristic somewhere else.[56]

The arable district of the north-west and the wood–pasture region of the centre were similar in their literacy. There may have been differences in agriculture, requiring different amounts of manpower and producing different rewards, but the literacy evidence is not sensitive to these economic variations. Although some parishes were worse than others the general performance of central and western Essex was better than the average. The marshland parishes of the east, however, were decidedly different, their inhabitants displaying a general inability to sign. The peninsular parishes of Little Oakley and Dengie and the estuarine communities of Hadleigh, Great Stambridge and Prittlewell had a pooled illiteracy of 73%, compared to 59% in the other eleven parishes. The figures point to a significant difference between coastal and inland Essex, which may reflect their different agricultural economies.

It may be that the mixed-farming regions of inland Essex, with industrial by-employments and commercial activities alongside agriculture, had a more complex social structure than the pastoral areas of the marshland. The yeomen and husbandmen, the butchers and tanners and craftsmen of mid-Essex, may have enjoyed a more diversified economy and culture than the shepherds and herdsmen of the littoral, and may have found a greater need for reading and writing. The evidence is suggestive, but only a detailed study of individual abilities in specific localities can confirm whether the economic environment was critical in shaping literacy levels.

Within the range of this small Essex sample there was no ap-

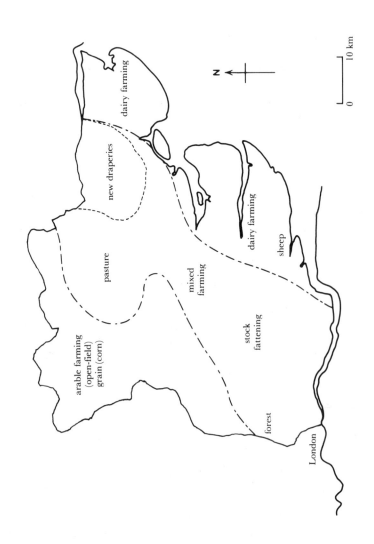

Map 3   Economic regions of Essex, c. 1640

parent correlation between the size of a community and its literacy. The ability to sign varied without any discernible pattern among places with from under 100 to more than 500 inhabitants. If the sample had included a market town, a major regional centre, the results might have been different. For it appears that the villages with the lowest illiteracy were all quite close to market towns and commercial centres. Wanstead was within easy reach of London, Little Baddow was close to Chelmsford and Maldon, Marks Tey was just outside Colchester, Middleton was near the Suffolk town of Sudbury, and Great Parndon was within the orbit of Harlow, Hertford and Ware. The association might be quite fortuitous, but it is likely that there was a connection between urbanization and literacy and that some of the economic and cultural richness of these towns reached out to the neighbouring villages. Indeed, the highest degree of literacy may not have been found in the towns themselves but in their satellite villages. Towns may have had extremes of literacy and illiteracy but were weighted down by their urban poor, while selected villages, like some modern suburbs, could enjoy the fruits of urban endeavour while avoiding the cultural costs of urban blight. By contrast, the most illiterate communities were far from towns in areas of thin settlement, like Little Oakley and Dengie in the Essex marshes.

Here as elsewhere the matter can be resolved only by further research which pays close attention to the geography of illiteracy and takes account of the interaction between communities, traffic networks, and the movement of people, goods and ideas.

If literacy were an economic asset we might expect to find a positive correlation between the ability to sign and the possession of wealth. The best way to test this would be to examine the fortunes and writing abilities of all the individuals who subscribed the declarations, a task which would require substantial documentation, careful record linkage, immense patience and resources which are not presently available. A surrogate test, lacking in sensitivity but simpler to apply, can be made by comparing the over-all prosperity of each community with its aggregate illiteracy. Ship-money assessments and hearth-tax returns have been examined to discover to what extent there was an association between literacy and wealth.

Essex was among the most recalcitrant counties in the 1630s, bridling both at the irregularity of the ship-money tax and at its 'disorderly and unequal assessments'. For the government of Charles I it was a matter of political will as well as financial expediency to secure the full contribution from each county, and the difficulties of collection in Essex were frequently discussed in

London. Complaints against the sheriff of Essex, who was responsible for local assessment and collection, led to the production before the Privy Council of a complete 'account of the money raised in the county of Essex . . . in which the several sums imposed by the sheriff upon the inhabitants and the rates of the whole county are particularly expressed'.[57] This account lists the amount assessed on each parish and gives the assessments on individual payers throughout the county.

Since ship money was not parliamentary taxation there was some ambiguity in the manner of assessment. Contributions were required from landowners, both resident and non-resident, and the latter were distinguished in the sheriff's book as 'outlanders'. Although the assessment was based primarily on land there was some flexibility, as eleven inhabitants of Prittlewell found when they were 'rated in respect of their estates and trades they drive or use, holding little or no quantities of land'. Asked to explain his rating system the sheriff described 'the care he took to ease the poorer sort of people, wherewith the county abounded, whereby the assessment lay something the more upon the abler sort'.[58] The tax burden was progressive according to one's wealth, personal estate was calculated as well as real estate, and poor people were completely exempt.

The sum demanded of each parish, the number of payers both resident and non-resident, and the mean assessment per payer serve as first indicators of community wealth. If the ship-money assessors were consistent in excusing people on grounds of poverty, and if the total population can be judged by the number of subscribers to the declarations of the 1640s, the proportion of men who were exempt can easily be calculated and used as another indicator of community prosperity. We can also calculate how much would have been needed from every man in the community if none was exempt and contributions were equal. The figures for our sixteen parishes are displayed in Table 4.4, alongside figures from the hearth-tax records.

The hearth tax of the Restoration period was a more successful attempt at equitable taxation. Householders were assessed according to the number of hearths in their house on the principle that the prosperous would keep larger and better-heated establishments and should make a greater contribution to public revenue. Poor people with two or less hearths, whose property was worth less than one pound a year and whose annual income was no more than ten pounds could claim exemption, and pauper households were automatically excused. The total of taxpaying households in each parish and the number discharged through

Table 4.4 Illiteracy and wealth in Essex, 1637–71

Parish	% mark	No. of subscribers	Ship-money assessment (£/s/d)	No. of payers	Resident payers	Assessment per payer (£)	Assessment per adult male (£)	% exempt	Hearth-tax households	No. exempt	% exempt	No. of hearths	Hearths per household
Little Baddow	45	71	23/9/4	28	28	0.60	0.33	61	46	11	24	144	3.1
Barnston	63	63	9/18/0	25	25	0.40	0.16	60	35	14	40	98	2.8
Boxted	61	131	21/5/0	79	79	0.27	0.16	40	121	44	36	287	2.4
Dengie	71	28	13/16/0	16	16	0.86	0.49	43	13	0	0	36	2.8
Fyfield	69	106	28/0/8	50	39	0.56	0.26	63	89	35	39	165	1.9
Hadleigh	82	50	8/0/0	22	22	0.36	0.16	56	25	9	36	71	2.8
East Hanningfield	67	67	17/17/0	39	39	0.46	0.27	42	50	15	30	116	2.3
Kelveden Hatch	64	59	17/17/7	15	15	1.19	0.30	75	34	11	32	130	3.8
Middleton	57	21	7/0/4	31	13	0.23	0.33	38	21	12	57	39	1.9
Little Oakley	85	34	6/0/0	20	16	0.30	0.18	53	24	8	33	41	1.7
Great Parndon	58	73	26/15/6	71	71	0.38	0.38	3	74	24	32	218	2.9
Prittlewell	69	157	22/11/8	41	41	0.55	0.14	74	77	17	22	101	1.3
Great Stambridge	69	26	12/0/1	33	33	0.36	0.46	0	28	0	0	78	2.8
Marks Tey	56	36	6/0/0	22	16	0.27	0.17	56	30	5	17	67	2.2
Wanstead	36	59	12/9/4	16	16	0.78	0.21	73	40	9	23	206	5.2
Wormingford	62	100	15/0/0	41	29	0.37	0.15	71	45	13	29	125	2.8

poverty, together with the number of hearths in each house and in each village, are clearly shown in the 1671 hearth-tax assessment for Essex.[59] The proportion of exempt households, the total number of hearths, and the ratio of hearths to households indicate the prosperity of each community a generation after the declarations. These figures relating to the sixteen parishes are also shown in Table 4.4.

Study of the figures in Table 4.4 reveals no straightforward association between literacy and wealth. Ship-money assessments ranged from £6 at Little Oakley and Marks Tey to £28/8d at Fyfield. Individual assessments varied between a few pence and several pounds. Sir Henry Mildmay was assessed £10 at Little Baddow but the mean assessment in the sixteen parishes was less than ten shillings and the median close to seven shillings and sevenpence. The mean assessment in particular places ranged from less than five shillings at Middleton to more than a pound at Kelveden Hatch. If the cost of contribution had been equally distributed among all adult males the men of Prittlewell would have paid least and the men of Dengie the most. Mean assessments would have been just over five shillings a head and the median about four shillings and fourpence.[60] Exemption rates varied enormously, from 75% at Kelveden Hatch to 3% at Great Parndon, while at Great Stambridge there were actually more contributors to ship money than subscribers to the Protestation.

None of these measures decodes the enigma of literacy. A statistical analysis employing rank order correlation and linear regression produced Spearman and Pearson correlation coefficients which are shown in Table 4.5.[61] The results are generally disappointing. The ship-money figures, no matter how they are construed or adjusted, show no measurable relationship with community literacy, while the hearth tax figures are only marginally more suggestive.

The proportion of households in each village whose poverty gained them exemption from the hearth tax bore no relation at all to literacy levels. Exemptions ranged from 17% at Marks Tey to 57% at Middleton, while Dengie and Great Stambridge had none. The wealthier communities, with less than a quarter of the households exempt, included Marks Tey, Wanstead and Little Baddow, and these places were also remarkable for their good literacy. But Prittlewell had a similar level of exemption but a decidedly worse level of illiteracy. Barnston and Middleton had the highest proportion of exempt households, but their poverty was not matched by high illiteracy. No pattern emerges and no clear associations can be found. Indeed, the correlation coefficients

Table 4.5   *Illiteracy and wealth in Essex, 1637–71;*
correlation coefficients

Items correlated with illiteracy	Spearman's rho	Pearson's r
Ship money assessment	−0.117	−0.202
Assessment per payer	0.041	−0.217
Assessment per adult male	−0.059	−0.061
Exemption from ship money	−0.071	−0.126
Hearths	−0.445*	−0.479*
Hearths per household	−0.405	−0.599**
Exemption from hearth tax	0.028	−0.006

*p < 0.05
**p < 0.01

for illiteracy and exemption from hearth tax suggest virtually no correlation at all.

The figures for hearths per household are more promising. Little Oakley, Prittlewell and Fyfield were relatively poor places with less than two hearths per household and it may be no coincidence that they were among the most illiterate communities. At the other end of the scale the most literate communities of Wanstead and Little Baddow had more than three hearths per household. Middleton and Kelveden Hatch upset the pattern, but the evidence points to a possible relationship between literacy and wealth. The statistical analysis confirms this impression. A coefficient of −0.599 indicates a moderately strong association between the ratio of hearths per household and the inability of the menfolk in the community to sign (significant at 0.01 level). It should be noted, however, that the ratio of hearths to households provides no more than a rough summary measure of community prosperity and fails to distinguish places with one or two extremely wealthy households from others where prosperity was more evenly distributed. The Wanstead total included the 43 hearths in the former Mildmay mansion, Kelveden Hatch had one house with 27 hearths and another with 16, Little Baddow had a 26-hearth house, while abnormally large establishments were also recorded at Barnston, Great Parndon and Wormingford.

Our attempt to make sense of the distribution of literacy in one English county has been marked by frustration, uncertainty and negative results. The religious and educational history of a community goes some way towards accounting for its literacy but there was enough contradictory evidence to enjoin extreme caution. Similarly the economic environment played a role in conditioning levels of illiteracy but neither a review of agrarian regions nor an examination of particular measures of community wealth reveals a clear pattern of relationships. Within an area of not much more than 1,000 square miles we have sixteen parishes with very varied literacy characteristics. No single phenomenon, experience or set of conditions will adequately explain this distribution, so we must posit a mixture of influences, a complex matrix of cultural, ideological, economic and perhaps even accidental elements which fashioned the literacy of each community at a particular time.

In some places ideological pressures in favour of literacy harmonized with economic circumstances, while other places had no such good fortune. Little Baddow, for example, a wealthy village in the heart of a prosperous region of mixed farming, equidistant from the towns of Maldon and Chelmsford, centre of a vigorous puritan tradition and supplied with its own school, could hardly fail to stand out as one of the most literate villages in England. Elsewhere, as the experience of Little Oakley testifies, poverty, remoteness, pastoral simplicity and a religious climate shading between conservatism and indifference combined, not surprisingly, to produce massive illiteracy. Other places were subject to different, even countervailing, pressures and tensions in varying degrees which could affect their level of literacy, while every place had migrants, recent and long established, who brought their literacy with them from other places which in turn had their own mixture of conditions.

The local geography of literacy is still bewildering, although this attempt at reconnaissance has suggested some guidelines. Our best hope of untangling the connections lies with community and sub-regional studies, and these will have to go deeper into the themes that have been touched on here and perhaps explore associations that have yet to be recognized.

One more occasion which produced documents akin to a census of literacy was the discovery of a plot to assassinate William III in 1696. A catholic conspiracy with violent plans to restore the Stuarts was exposed. The king may not really have been in great danger but the protestant establishment made use of the scare by circulating an oath, modelled on the Instrument of Association of 1594. The Elizabethan Association was fetched from the archives and a copy was attached to the new Association. Subscribers to the oath promised to protect the king, to revenge his murder should such an event come to pass and to defend the protestant succession. The Association oath was embodied in the 'Act for the better security of his majesty's royal person and government' in 1696.[62]

Like the earlier Protestation and covenants the Association was intended to reveal malignants and expose opposition while binding loyalists together and alerting them to danger. Subscribers announced 'the horror and astonishment wherewith we were surprised upon the news of the execrable plot against your majesty's person', while expressions of concern were commonly incorporated in the preface to the oath. For example:

> we your majesty's most dutiful and loyal subjects, the Lord Lieutenant, Deputy Lieutenant, justices of the peace, officers of the militia, both the grand juries, gentlemen, freeholders and others of the county of Suffolk, do most humbly beg leave to congratulate your majesty's most wonderful preservation, and thankfully acknowledge the signal providence of God in your happy deliverance from so villainous and barbarous a design, carried on by papists and other traiterous persons against your majesty's sacred person.

The spring of 1696 saw the country, orchestrated from London, ablaze with indignation and people of all sorts lining up to take the oath.[63]

The Act of Parliament required only officeholders to swear the Association, and their names were dutifully entered on specially prepared rolls. But so great was the outrage at the threat to the king that there was a widespread and patriotic urge to pledge the Association among ordinary subjects. The oath was taken in London on 25 February 1696 and was soon circulating in the country. The privy council ordered the county lieutenants to secure the subscriptions of 'gentlemen and other persons of any consideration', and was especially interested in the names of refusers and neglecters.[64]

At the quarter sessions in Hertfordshire on 20 April 1696 arrangements were made for every man in every parish, whether householder or lodger, officeholder or not, to set his name to the Association. 'Convenient rolls of parchment' were provided with the terms of the Association printed at the top and three ruled columns 'for the more orderly and regular signing the same'. These were to be distributed through the chain of high constables, petty constables, tything men and headboroughs, 'to be carried from house to house through the parish or place' and tendered 'to every housekeeper and lodger within his or their parish to sign'.[65] The local arrangements far exceeded the requirements of the act and many of the returns survive with the marks and signatures of adult male inhabitants.

Manuscript instructions were sent to the constables of every parish in Suffolk. On 30 April 1696 the constables of Ashfield, Suffolk, were given their specific charge.

Whereas the grand jury did present at the quarter sessions [held at Beccles on 9 April] that they being deeply sensible of the danger the nation lieth under from an intended assassination of his majesty king William and an invasion from France carried on by the late king James and others, these are in his majesty's name to require you to tender [the oath] to all housekeepers, lodgers and others within your parish, to be by them signed, and also a true note in writing of all the christian names and surnames, places of abode, additions and callings of all such persons as shall refuse to sign the same; and you are required to deliver to me the printed roll and the names of all such as shall refuse to sign the same at the Pickerel in Ixworth upon Friday the eighth day of May next by one of the clock, and hereof you are not to fail.

Subscriptions were required of men above the age of sixteen.[66]

Since the Association was taken around the parish by local officials who knew the neighbourhood it is likely that the oath was thoroughly subscribed. Fiscal and demographic records can be checked to see whether the returns are complete. Macfarlane's analysis of the Association roll for Earls Colne, Essex, found some shortfall but concluded that the list contained 'a good cross section from the very poor to the wealthy'. Hearth-tax totals are generally found to be compatible with population estimates from the Association returns.[67]

Very few people dared to refuse, and their names together with names of absentees are usually appended to the record. A characteristic report from Suffolk stated that 'there are no persons in the parish of Chelsworth . . . that have refused to subscribe this declaration', while the constables of Ixworth reported, 'we have none that refuse, so God bless king William'. Wiston, Suffolk, had two refusers, 'both considerable farmers', while at Kelsale the Association was refused by 'Mr John Buxton, usher in the free school'.[68] Despite strong pressure to subscribe there was a thin sprinkling of refusals which drew the attention of the authorities. Catholic recusants were naturally reluctant, while quakers consistently refused to take the Association although they felt no hostility to the king or his government. The quakers of Colchester drew up a lengthy explanation 'touching the present Association' which was signed by 125 quakers and seems to have been accepted as an alternative testament of loyalty. Two country quakers refused the Association at Westhorpe, Suffolk, because 'we cannot for conscience sake revenge for ourselves nor any man else'.[69]

The surviving returns can be treated in the same way as the

better-known declarations of the 1640s if they meet the same criteria of completeness and authenticity. Some 500 rolls with subscriptions to the Association are in the Public Record Office while more are lurking in local collections. The evidence exists to make a detailed analysis of literacy in the late seventeenth century, but the documents are relatively obscure and researchers have been intimidated by the sheer bulk of the records. Table 4.6 shows the level of illiteracy calculated from Association oath returns for Essex, Hertfordshire and Suffolk. Doubtful documents with signatures in a common hand have been excluded from the analysis.[70]

The sample of Suffolk parishes was so large that the figures can surely be trusted as a guide to male illiteracy at the end of the seventeenth century. It is striking that the percentage unable to sign in the adjacent county of Essex was almost the same, indicating that just over half the men in that part of East Anglia were illiterate in the 1690s. The Hertfordshire figures may be less characteristic of their region since they include the market towns of Bishops Stortford and Sawbridgeworth and only one rural parish. They do, however, provide some information about literacy in country towns. Urban returns from Suffolk show a similar superiority, with just 39% unable to sign in seven market towns.[71]

The distribution of literacy shown by the Association oath rolls was no less bewildering than the geography of illiteracy in the 1640s. Map 4 shows the percentage of men unable to sign the oath in Essex parishes, for comparison with Map 2 which showed illiteracy in Essex at the time of the civil war. Some of the variations might be explained by reference to the economic geography of late Stuart Essex but it would take a community-by-community analysis to comprehend and explain the differences between, say, Broxted and Lindsell, or Steeple and Asheldham.

The Suffolk figures are just as variable and are so plentiful as to defy mapping. However, some of the irregularities vanish when parochial returns are arranged by hundreds, and the hundredal variations are further smoothed in the calculation of county summaries. The greater the degree of aggregation the more homogeneous the literacy figures appear. Table 4.7 and Map 5 show illiteracy levels in the Suffolk hundreds in 1696. The evidence could be subjected to a multitude of investigations, but these, for the moment, must be left to the Suffolk historians.

To what extent was illiteracy reduced between the reign of Charles I and the reign of William III? The figures for Essex point to an improvement from 63% to 54% unable to sign, suggesting a moderate advance in elementary education. The difference is

Table 4.6   *Illiteracy in eastern England, 1696*

County	Usable parishes	No. of subscribers	No. mark	% mark	Illiteracy range (%)
Essex	36	1,789	967	54	75—33
Hertfordshire	3	655	233	36	51—28
Suffolk	215	10,056	5,302	53	93—28

statistically significant if the over-all number of subscribers is considered, but if the particular parishes for which we have returns are taken as clusters, each with their own literacy characteristics, the statistical significance evaporates. In other words, there may have been a change in the literacy of Essex males in the second half of the seventeenth century, but it is just as likely that the different figures reflect a different mix of parishes. Not one of the parishes investigated in the 1640s appears among the usable returns for the 1690s.[72]

Suffolk in the 1690s appears to have been like its neighbour to the south, rather than the exceptional county which it was shown up to be in the 1640s. Two of the Suffolk parishes with usable returns to the civil war declarations reappear among the Association oath rolls. In Brantham 47% were illiterate compared to 52% in the 1640s, and Brundish had 42% unable to sign compared to 36% in a previous generation. Both places had better than average literacy, although Brundish was unable to sustain the remarkable performance of the 1640s.

The Protestations and similar declarations of the seventeenth century reveal the outlines of illiteracy and some of its spatial dimensions, firmly establishing the fact that some 70% of mid-Stuart Englishmen were unable to sign their names. The variations from place to place are intriguing and call for further investigation but the over-all level of illiteracy is clear. Since reading was taught before writing it is likely that the percentage who were totally illiterate was somewhat lower than 70%, although how much lower is a matter for guessing. If we can assume that the ability to sign was roughly commensurate with fluency in reading then our measurement shows that more than two-thirds of the men lacked the capacity for basic active literacy.

Our sources are so far silent on the questions of social differentiation and change over time, and they tell us little of the literacy of women. A few of the declarations and Associations

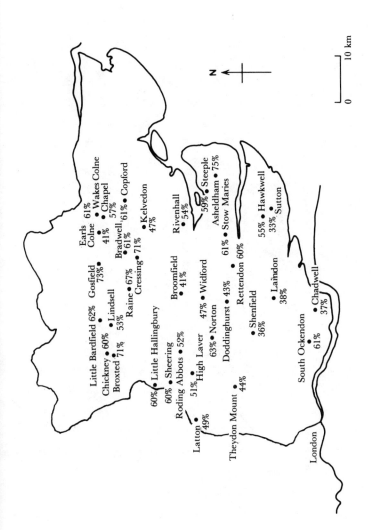

Map 4   Illiteracy in Essex, 1696: percentages of men unable to sign the Association oath

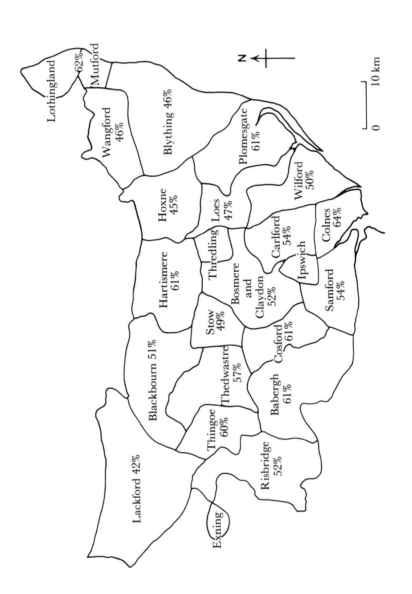

Map 5   Illiteracy in the Suffolk hundreds, 1696: percentages of men unable to sign the Association oath

Table 4.7   *Illiteracy in Suffolk hundreds, 1696*

Hundred	Usable parishes	No. of subscribers	No. mark	% mark
Babergh	7	504	305	61
Blackbourn	20	1,068	546	51
Blything	17	905	420	46
Bosmere & Claydon	24	823	427	52
Carlford	8	344	185	54
Colneis	5	165	106	64
Cosford	12	596	364	61
Hartismere	7	364	221	61
Hoxne	8	385	175	45
Lackford	2	166	70	42
Loes	9	372	173	47
Mutford & Lothingland	11	371	231	62
Plomesgate	7	163	99	61
Risbridge	9	349	181	52
Samford	15	625	338	54
Stow	12	777	383	49
Thedwastre	12	541	307	57
Thingoe	9	393	236	60
Wangford	14	847	386	46
Wilford	7	298	149	50
Total	215	10,056	5,302	53

Note: Returns for Aldeburgh, Bury St Edmunds, Ipswich and Orford boroughs are not usable for the study of literacy.

contained the marks and signatures of women, and occasionally the document gives the occupation or status of male subscribers, but such information is too sporadic to be of much use.[73] Nor do the declarations indicate the development of literacy decade by decade from the sixteenth to the eighteenth century. Their value is limited, and pales beside the sources to be discussed in the next chapter which illuminate literacy in its social, sexual, economic and chronological dimensions.

5

Lay illiteracy in ecclesiastical records

The church courts in post-reformation England enjoyed a vast range of competence touching the affairs of the laity. Matters of life and death, marriage and midwifery, probate and inheritance, sexual offences and defamation of character, as well as questions of tithe, church attendance and religion, were among the dozens of subjects deemed to be 'of ecclesiastical cognizance'. Bishops and commissaries, archdeacons and other churchmen with ordinary jurisdiction regularly sat in judgement on the laity or performed routine administrative tasks which tapped them for fees. Thousands of people appeared before the ecclesiastical judges as parties to a suit, defendants in an action, witnesses, petitioners or bondsmen. In its judicial and administrative capacity as well as in its pastoral role, the church involved itself in the everyday lives of layfolk of all descriptions.[1]

Protestant England was in this respect a much more sacerdotal society than catholic France. By the ordinance of Villers-Cotterets in 1539 the ecclesiastical courts in France lost almost all their powers over the laity.[2] In England the reformation stripped the church courts of their unpopular powers of punishment but left them to serve the state as an adjunct authority for social regulation. A defamation case might be brought, for example,

If any out of an angry, malicious or passionate mind utter these or the like words, "thou art an unhonest liver, or thou art a lier . . . an arrant knave, or thou art a drab or a scold, a jade, a filthy fellow, etc."[3]

The scope for business was enormous. Black-robed ranks of proctors and apparitors, notaries and registrars serviced the machine and maintained the flow of parchment, ink and paper. The appetite of the ecclesiastical bureaucracy under Elizabeth and the Stuarts appears to have been insatiable and a mountain of documentation was created in the process.

Much of this documentation survives and can be used to illuminate the literacy of the laity. Three series of records, reflecting different activities of the ecclesiastical courts, are especially valuable since they record people's signatures or marks along with information about their occupation, social status, age, sex and residence. Probated wills, marriage-licence records and the incomparable ecclesiastical court depositions make possible a much more sensitive study of literacy than is possible with the Protestations and associated declarations.

The evidence from each of these sources clearly establishes the social structure of illiteracy in pre-industrial England and allows us to trace its progress over an extended period of time. The evidence has to be approached with caution. Peculiarities of procedure and unstated principles of selection affect each source in different ways and none of them is free from bias or difficulty. If we wish this documentation to show us the shape of illiteracy in the past we shall need an understanding of ecclesiastical law and practice and of the circumstances in which the records were produced.

The church was responsible for probate and testamentary matters, and churchmen developed strict conventions for handling wills and coping with the myriad disputes which they spawned. Ecclesiastical archives contain vast quantities of probate inventories, cataloguing and valuing the goods of the deceased, and ecclesiastical court records are thick with interrogatories and answers and depositions in testamentary causes. Some of these records can be used in indirect ways to illuminate the problem of literacy, and occasional reference has been made to them in preceding chapters,[4] but here we will focus on wills.

To be valid a will was supposed to be signed or marked by the testator in the presence of witnesses, who also placed their autograph on the document. Nuncupative or oral wills and testaments of irregular format with technical errors could be admitted according to certain rules, since the courts were concerned to interpret and respect the intentions of the deceased as well as to protect the interests of the heirs, but documents of this sort caused problems for everybody.[5]

Thousands of original wills survive from the sixteenth and seventeenth centuries with the autograph signature or mark of their makers. The social status or occupation of the testator is usually recorded in the text of the will or else it can be discovered from the accompanying probate inventory. Additional information, including important details about personal wealth and place of residence, is usually obtainable from the same sources and it should be possible with this evidence to reconstruct the social profile of illiteracy. The most comprehensive survey of literacy in colonial New England is based entirely on the analysis of wills, and similar sources have been used to indicate the level and distribution of illiteracy in English rural communities.[6]

Table 5.1 shows the stratification of illiteracy among a sample of 578 will-makers in seventeenth-century East Anglia. All these wills were proved in the consistory court of the Bishop of Norwich in the 1630s and they include the autographed testaments of people from most parts of Norfolk and Suffolk.[7] This small body of evidence illustrates some of the problems associated with wills as well as the fruitfulness of the source.

Only a tiny fraction of the English population made wills and the people who organized their affairs in such a careful way were mostly drawn from a narrow segment of society. Women were grossly outnumbered by men, and most of the female will-makers were in fact widows. A married woman, as *femme couverte*, could not dispose of property without the consent of her husband, and was in the same general category for testamentary matters as idiots and outlaws.[8]

Wills were chronically afflicted by social bias. Leaving aside the complication that archdeaconry, diocesan and provincial courts had varying competence and claimed jurisdiction over property-owners with different amounts of wealth, the evidence from every collection of probate records points to a social imbalance. Gentlemen, clergymen, yeomen and tradesmen were over-represented, while there was a lack of labourers, husbandmen and the poor. The social distribution of will-makers, indicated in Table 5.1, is not at all surprising, since one would expect such testaments to be made by the more prosperous who had some property to bequeath.

Wealth, however, was not the only criterion for making a will, since a will was an opportunity to dispose of family and other affairs and to settle the care of minor children. The wills clearly demonstrate the social stratification of illiteracy. Even if we are not to place undue reliance on particular figures, the evidence indicates that distinct degrees of writing skill prevailed among the different social groups. Illiteracy was virtually unknown among the gentry and clergy; tradesmen and yeomen shared the middle ground; while husbandmen and labourers, and also women, were massively illiterate at the other end of the spectrum. The structure of illiteracy revealed by the wills is confirmed in the other ecclesiastical records where it can be examined with greater precision. Indeed, this hierarchical ranking turns out to be one of the most striking and constant features of our investigation.

Wills are, unfortunately beset by a serious problem which

Table 5.1   *Will-makers in the diocese of Norwich, 1633–7*

Social group	No. sampled	%	No. mark	% mark
Gentry	43	7	2	5
Clergy	34	6	1	3
Tradesmen and craftsmen	129	22	78	60
Yeomen	165	29	100	61
Husbandmen	64	11	58	91
Labourers	10	2	10	100
Unspecified	49	8	30	61
Women	84	15	74	88
Total	578			
(All men	494	85	279	56)

renders them, as Margaret Spufford says, 'fundamentally un-satisfactory'.[9] Most wills were made close to death when the testator was battling his final illness. Many will-makers were senile or incapacitated, and those amongst them who had once known how to write might now find it impossible to sign their names or even to hold a pen. Instances abound of men who are known to have been fully literate in their prime reduced to making a feeble scrawl when authenticating their deathbed wills. This is a most damaging defect which calls into question all estimates of literacy levels which are based on probate records.

It is sometimes possible to trace the deterioration of writing ability with age, illness and impending death. Old Leonard Woolward of Balsham, Cambridgeshire, was unable to write or sign his will in 1578 and 'his sight was so evil' that he could not even read it. Village opinion recalled that 'the said old Leonard could write in his lifetime' but by the time he made his will, he could no longer 'write well with ease or to his contentation, for that he was then very old and for that his sight failed him much'. Roger Spooner, a gentleman of Fretton, Suffolk, was similarly afflicted by blindness or palsy when he came to sign his will in 1637. After a few sprawling and uncomfortable letters he gave up the attempt and his efforts were recorded as 'the mark of Roger Spooner'. Robert Neve, a minister, signed his will with his usual bold signature, but a codicil added later is remarkable for its shaking and uncertain handwriting. Thomas Oakes, clerk of Norfolk, was completely unable to write when he made his will in

1632, and his apparent illiteracy belies his forty years of incumbency as rector of Brandon Parva.[10]

The figures in Table 5.1 include an unknown proportion of men whose active literacy was masked by the exigencies of a final crisis. When compared with other sources, such as ecclesiastical court depositions and allegations and bonds for marriage licences, it appears that the wills exaggerate illiteracy by as much as 25%. It might be possible to devise a formula or adopt weightings to compensate for this bias, but since there are alternative sources which present fewer problems such a procedure is, fortunately, unnecessary.

Matrimonial matters were, naturally, governed by the church. Only in experimenting societies like Holland and New Plymouth and Cromwellian England was marriage brought under the control of the magistrate. Until Lord Hardwicke's act of 1754 (26 George II c.33) neither bride nor groom was required to sign or mark the marriage register, so we have no seventeenth-century data comparable to that of the late eighteenth and early nineteenth.[11] Bridegrooms who married by licence, however, were required to set their name to allegations and bonds, which were also subscribed by their bondsmen or sureties. The records of this activity are much more tractable than wills, and figures for illiteracy derived from them are more likely to be reliable. The signatures and marks of bondsmen can be set aside, like those of witnesses to wills, allowing us to focus on the literacy of young men at the point of marriage.

Bridegrooms were rarely troubled by the disabling illnesses or decrepitude which so often afflicted will-makers, so a comparison of their autograph signatures and marks should provide a more accurate indication of the extent of illiteracy. Table 5.2 shows the profile of illiteracy among men marrying by licence in East Anglia and in the south-west midlands in the seventeenth century. The figures for Norfolk and Suffolk are based on the one complete file of marriage bonds surviving in the diocese of Norwich, and the Oxfordshire and Gloucestershire figures are reworked from Stone, who does not give the actual numbers in each social or occupational category.[12] The levels of illiteracy shown here are substantially lower than displayed in the wills, but the structure and ranking is roughly the same. Clerks and gentlemen had more or less complete possession of literacy; yeomen and craftsmen came next at some distance; and a much higher level of illiteracy was found among husbandmen. Marriage-licence records give us no reliable information about labourers and none at all about the literacy of women.

Table 5.2   *Seventeenth-century bridegrooms marrying by licence*

Social group	Norfolk & Suffolk, 1628			Oxfordshire & Gloucestershire, c.1635 c.1662	
	No. sampled	%	No. mark	% mark	% mark	% mark
					c.1635	c.1662
Gentry	23	10	0	0	2	3
Clergy	9	4	0	0	0	0
Tradesmen and craftsmen	76	34	41	54	30	26
Yeomen	65	29	26	40	28	28
Husbandmen	40	18	30	75	57	48
Unknown	13	6	10	77		
Total	226	101	107	47		

Marriage-licence records are socially selective in much the same way as wills. The prosperous and the powerful were disproportionately represented while the poor and humble were conspicuously absent. Nor is this surprising in light of the conventions concerning marriage and the trouble and expense involved in obtaining a licence. Most people married by banns, openly published in the parish church. Marriage by licence was a costly alternative, which secured for the marrying parties privacy, flexibility and speed. It also enabled people to marry in the traditionally prohibited periods like lent and advent when banns were not supposed to be read in church. More than 120 days in the year were taboo times for marriage, according to ecclesiastical convention, but these could be over-ridden by purchasing a licence. This could be of pressing importance if there were urgent reasons to speed the marriage, such as the pregnancy of the bride. As many as one-third of all seventeenth-century brides were already pregnant when they went to the altar, and the proportion may well have been higher among those marrying by licence.[13]

Marriage licences were restricted by canon to 'such persons only as be of good state and quality'. The intent may have been to check character and morality but the effect was to harden the social selection. 'Good caution and security' were demanded, along with the oaths of 'two sufficient witnesses' to safeguard against fraud. Fees were paid to the bishop's chancellor and to the registrar, and the paperwork alone could cost the intending bridegroom as much as eight or ten shillings.[14]

Paying fees, providing bondsmen, dealing with church officials and journeying to the often distant consistory court all compounded the expense and trouble of obtaining a licence. No more than a fifth of all marriages were solemnized with this form of authorization, and it cannot be claimed that the bridegrooms who took out licences were representative of all men getting married. Regional customs probably affected the propensity to marry by licence, and it has been suggested that people of humble means might choose this more private way of marrying to avoid the expense of a public wedding feast.[15]

Literacy too may have biased the selection. Without a control group, or much more information about the social interaction of people who could and could not read and write, we cannot discount the possibility that marriage by licence was literacy specific as well as socially selective. It is possible that the yeomen and craftsmen who married by licence were more literate than men of the same rank who married in the ordinary way by banns, or who never married at all. If there is any truth to this suggestion it may mean that the figures in Table 5.2, and any others derived from marriage-licence records, underestimate the actual extent of illiteracy.

Of all the documents produced by ecclesiastical administration the depositions made by witnesses before the various courts reveal the most about the distribution and development of literacy. They include an unrivalled range of information about the social, demographic and geographical correlates of illiteracy, and they pose fewer problems of handling and interpretation than the other ecclesiastical records. They survive in bulk in different parts of the country and can be used to explore the course of social and cultural change from the sixteenth to the eighteenth centuries.

All the cases which were heard and judged in the ecclesiastical courts originated in incidents or disputes which were 'of ecclesiastical cognizance'. People were summoned to appear because they happened to have overheard defamatory remarks or witnessed a churchyard brawl; because they had tended a man on his deathbed and knew something of the circumstances of a will; because they knew the life and reputation of one of the parties in a cause or could speak with authority on the custom of tithes; or because of any other more-or-less accidental connection with the matter before the court. The witnesses spoke their testimony, answered questions and sealed their deposition with a signature or mark.

The court took care to see that the witnesses, often unlettered countrymen, understood the proceedings in which they had

become involved. They were to be set at ease, rather than over-
awed, in the interest of securing an accurate record:

Seeing all positions and articles are usually writ in Latin, by reason whereof
the witnesses, especially countrymen, rarely understand them, therefore it is
very requisite that the registrar or examiner have a great care in explaining
and declaring distinctly and plainly to witnesses all and singular the heads
and contents of these articles and positions.

Similar care was taken to authenticate and protect the evidence so
painstakingly collected. The court was instructed 'to take care
that the witnesses write their names or usual mark to these their
depositions with their own hand lest the register or any other
should afterwards vitiate this deposition in any particular'.[16]
The procedure was designed to minimize fraud, error and future
contention, and it resulted in meticulous documentation. Evidence
was not to be overlooked on account of the financial circumstances
of the potential deponent or his difficulties in attending the court.
Witnesses could be reimbursed for their trouble and the court was
empowered to take into consideration their quality, 'whether they
be horsemen or footmen', as well as the distance they had to travel
and the lodging they required.[17]

A matrimonial case concerning the private exchange of vows
brought Henry Ives, a Norwich craftsman, to testify before the
consistory court of the diocese of Norwich in 1580. The formula
introducing his deposition is quite characteristic (see note for
original Latin text):

Concerning the deposition given on behalf of Richard Richardson and
Suzanna Ives, Henry Ives of the parish of St Andrew in the City of Norwich,
painter, where he has lived for about a month and previously in the parish
of St Michael at Coslany in the aforesaid City for five years past, born in the
borough of Aylesham in the county of Norfolk and aged about fifty years,
a witness free from restrictions etcetera, has known Richard Richardson the
party citing him for three months or thereabouts, and has known Suzanna
Ives since her birth.

Having told how Susan brought Richard to his house and confessed
'that she was sure to him' Henry authenticated his deposition by
signing.[18]

Although different diocesan administrations developed their
own traditions of record-keeping, it was common practice to write
down the name of each deponent with details of his occupation or
rank, which was part of his legal identity, the marital status of
women, and everyone's age, place or residence, previous residence
and place of birth, along with his relationship, if any, to the parties

in the cause. Some dioceses preserved their depositions together with all other papers in a cause, while others filed them separately in special books or bundles. The resulting documentation contains a formidable store of anecdotes and the verbatim testimony of often illiterate people, as well as our best source for charting the actual extent of illiteracy.[19]

Table 5.3 shows the social composition and levels of illiteracy of a sample of 490 deponents before the consistory court of the diocese of Norwich in the 1630s.[20] The figures can be compared to those from the same place and period but from different sources shown in Tables 5.1 and 5.2. The same pervasive structure of illiteracy emerges from the depositions as from all other ecclesiastical records. Clergymen and professional people could all sign their names and so could almost all of the gentry; a third of the yeomen and half the tradesmen could not write their names; husbandmen, labourers and women were massively illiterate. These figures and rankings will be explored in greater detail in later chapters.

The structure and dimensions of illiteracy can be investigated with greater precision and confidence by sampling a large number of depositions from several ecclesiastical jurisdictions. The following discussion is based on evidence from the diocese of Exeter (1574–1688), the diocese of Durham (1561–1631), the diocese of Norwich (1572–1729) and the diocese of London (1578–1729).[21] The evidence covers eleven counties: Cornwall and Devon, Durham and Northumberland, Norfolk, Suffolk and part of Cambridgeshire, and Essex, Hertfordshire, Middlesex and the City of London. Tens of thousands of depositions survive in these areas in boxes and bundles, volumes and files. They run, in some districts, from the beginning of the Tudor period until well into the eighteenth century, but marks and signatures are usually lacking before the Elizabethan period.[22]

Such an enormous body of evidence requires the use of sampling techniques to make it manageable without jeopardizing the quality of the information. Following Schofield, a programme of systematic sampling has been adopted here with safeguards to ensure that every deposition had, as nearly as possible, an equal chance of being selected. Almost 20,000 depositions were examined, roughly a third of the number available and usable from the selected areas.[23]

Before turning to a quantitative analysis of this evidence we must consider its pitfalls and potential problems. The depositions are not immune from the difficulties which weaken the value of

Table 5.3   *Deponents in the diocese of Norwich, 1630—9*

Social group	No. sampled	%	No. mark	% mark
Gentry	37	10	2	5
Clergy and professions	21	6	0	0
Tradesmen and craftsmen	140	37	69	49
Yeomen	90	24	29	32
Husbandmen	84	22	72	86
Labourers and servants	5	1	5	100
Unknown	5	1	2	40
Women	108	22	101	94
Total	490			
(All men	382	78	179	47)

wills and marriage-licence records, although fortunately the problems are far less serious.

People making depositions were not a representative cross-section of the community. Although members of every social group appeared, their presence before the court was not proportionate to their numbers in society. No set of documents provides us with an exact mirror of society in Tudor or Stuart England, so we must do our best to understand and compensate for the bias.

Table 5.4 shows the social and sexual composition of our large sample of deponents from five districts in four dioceses. It confirms the social imbalance encountered among deponents in the diocese of Norwich in the 1630s. Most of the deponents were drawn from the respectable middling ranks of society, with tradespeople, yeomen and their social superiors dominating the record. Indeed, it is striking that, notwithstanding the apparent absence of economic constraints, the deposition sample had much the same social complexion as the samples from the other ecclesiastical sources. Husbandmen were well represented, especially in rural southern England, but labourers and servants were hardly heard at all although they accounted for a quarter or more of the population.

Poor people were as likely as anyone else to have seen or over-

Table 5.4 Social origins of deponents in the dioceses of Norwich, Exeter, Durham and London, 1560–1700

Social group	Norwich consistory court (N = 6,023)	Exeter consistory court (N = 2,990)	Durham consistory court (N = 3,796)	Essex/Herts. commissary and archdeaconry courts (N = 1,906)	London/Middx commissary and consistory courts (N = 4,141)
% of all deponents					
Women	17	20	19	17	43
Men	83	80	81	83	57
% of male deponents					
Gentry	9	11	8	10	10
Clergy and professions	7	4	7	11	7
Tradesmen and craftsmen	37	37	24	28	60
Yeomen	19	15	43	20	5
Husbandmen	24	25	12	29	6
Labourers and servants	2	1	6	1	8
Unknown	2	6	0	1	5

heard an offence, but the courts tended to exclude them as witnesses because their dependence on their masters or employers was thought to diminish their impartiality. Employees as well as kinsmen and 'intimate friends to the party producing them and enemies to the party against whom they are produced' were barred as witnesses because they were expected to be partisan. Similarly, those 'of all ill fame, vicious, poor, indigent and . . . such to whom no credit is given' were to be discharged because the honesty and independence of their testimony could not be trusted.[24] Labourers and servants were excluded on these grounds and so, to a lesser extent, were women. These people also found it more difficult to travel to attend the court, despite the offers of financial reimbursement. This problem was only partly alleviated by the court's travelling from place to place.

Women were severely under-represented, although they appear more frequently in depositions than in any other source which shows levels of illiteracy. Less than 5% of the women were servants, the majority being described as wives or widows. Their social position can often be inferred from the rank of occupation of their husbands, and it appears that they were not quite so select a group as the men. Table 5.5 shows the social standing of the married or widowed women who made depositions in the diocese of Norwich in the seventeenth century. The bulk of them were married to tradesmen, craftsmen and husbandmen, and relatively few were the wives of gentlemen, clergymen or yeomen.[25]

The large number of women appearing as witnesses before the London courts is something of a surprise. Whereas women were responsible for no more than a fifth of the depositions made in rural areas, in London they appeared almost as frequently as the men. One explanation might be that the traditional constraints on female testimony were weakened in the capital city as women occupied a growing role in economic, political and cultural affairs. London women, as will be shown later, were also remarkable for their precocious advances in literacy.[26]

The imbalanced social composition of our sample of deponents would be a serious matter if we intended this evidence to indicate the over-all level of illiteracy, in the manner of the Protestations and declarations. If, however, we are more interested in the levels and relative positions of people in different social categories, and wish to trace those socially dimensioned performances over time, the social bias in the sources is less of a hindrance.

People can be grouped according to their social status or occupation and the sample can thus be stratified and controlled.

Table 5.5   *Social composition of the wives and widows, diocese of Norwich depositions, 1600–1700*

Social group of husbands (N = 119)	%
Gentry	4
Clergy and professions	2
Tradesmen and craftsmen	61
Yeomen	6
Husbandmen	24
Labourers	2

People can be identified as husbandmen, say, or gentlemen, and a comparison of their characteristics can be made at chosen moments and across time to illuminate both social structure and social change. Not much can be said about the penetration of literacy among the labouring population, but for all other groups, including most people engaged in agriculture, crafts and trade, the data are sufficient.

There is nothing to suggest that appearance as a deponent before the ecclesiastical courts was at all literacy-specific, but one other bias might affect the reliability of this evidence. Because custom, precedent and memory were so important to the resolution of certain disputes before the courts, especially in cases concerning tithe, there may at times have been a preference for the testimony of venerable and aged witnesses. If old age was a common characteristic of the deponents and if their ability to write a signature deteriorated with advancing years, such a preference could have the effect of inflating illiteracy figures, distorting them in the same way as wills. It is therefore important to determine the age structure of the deponent sample, to discover whether they were unduly ancient.

Examining a printed collection of seventeenth-century Sussex depositions, Cornwall found 'few persons under thirty years of age and almost an undue proportion of the over sixties'.[27] The depositions examined here are not so seriously skewed. In fact, the witnesses who testified before the courts were of the same range of ages as the adult population at large. Fewer than 15% of the deponents in the diocese of Norwich were more than sixty years old and they were clearly outnumbered by witnesses who had not reached the age of thirty. The mean age of tradesmen and craftsmen who appeared before the courts in East Anglia was 42.1, with 17% under thirty, 26% in their thirties, 24% in their forties, 20% in their fifties, and only 14% aged over sixty. A

Table 5.6   *Age of deponents in the dioceses of Norwich and Exeter, 1570–1700*

Social group	Diocese of Norwich		Diocese of Exeter	
	Mean age	Standard deviation	Mean age	Standard deviation
Gentry	44.1	13.5	43.6	14.1
Clergy	44.1	12.8	44.5	14.3
Trades	42.1	13.4	39.3	13.4
Yeomen	49.1	13.7	48.7	14.4
Husbandmen	45.1	15.2	43.7	14.5
Labourers	48.7	17.7	61.5	0
Servants	28.2	10.4	25.9	4.7
Women	37.1	15.9	38.4	14.4

similar age distribution was found among the other social groups. Table 5.6 shows the mean age (and standard deviation) of all the deponents sampled in each of the major social categories in the dioceses of Norwich and Exeter. Yeomen were slightly older – which is not at all surprising if years of accumulating wealth and esteem were necessary to earn that status – and servants were considerably younger. On the whole the deposition sample is representative of men in their prime. There may have been some loss of writing skill among the few who were entering old age, but if they were well enough to give evidence before the ecclesiastical court they were probably as capable of writing as ever.[28] The age structure of the sample poses no serious threat to the trust-worthiness of the literacy evidence.

Other sources in addition to those mentioned here may yield useful evidence about the structure and dynamics of illiteracy in the pre-industrial period. The secular court examination books, Chancery and Admiralty depositions and hearth-tax documents all demand close attention and may prove fruitful in the future.[29] For the moment, however, no body of evidence is so promising as the ecclesiastical court depositions, and the discussion of literacy and social structure and shifts in the distribution of illiteracy over time which occupies the following chapters is based almost entirely on the ecclesiastical court records.

6

The structure of illiteracy

The hierarchy of social rank in pre-industrial England is precisely and vividly illuminated by the study of literacy. In every area and every period, from the late sixteenth century to the early eighteenth, from the extreme south-west to the far north-east, a profile of literacy emerges which closely conforms to the best contemporary descriptions of the social order. The evidence from the ecclesiastical court depositions allows us to validate the opinions of social observers from Sir Thomas Smith to Edward Chamberlayne, and go beyond their rather legalistic and traditional accounts of English social structure. Historians who have wrestled with the taxonomy of early modern society and others who are disquieted by a social anatomy based almost entirely on literary sources may find in the numerical analysis of signatures and marks a more satisfactory measure of social stratification. This chapter shows how well the ranking based on literacy agreed with the ordering by status and esteem, and also the degree to which literacy was commensurate with alternative rankings by occupation and wealth.

The social hierarchy of literacy, already evident in the East Anglian wills, marriage licences and depositions of the 1630s, is firmly established when the depositions from several ecclesiastical jurisdictions are considered together. Regional peculiarities, sampling procedures and the uneven chronological spread of the evidence make direct comparison difficult, but the over-all impression is clear. Tables 6.1—6.5 show the social structure of illiteracy in the dioceses of Norwich, Exeter and Durham and in the rural and metropolitan areas of the diocese of London.[1] The evidence is collected from counties and regions hundreds of miles apart and covers different years, yet the rankings are remarkably stable. The figures point to the consistency of social differentiation and its continuing, powerful association with literacy. It is likely, then, that the distribution of writing skills shown here existed throughout early modern England.

Three clusters stand out, each composed of people with comparable attainments in literacy. The gentle and clerical elite were well distanced from the yeomen and tradesmen, who in turn

118

maintained a solid superiority over the husbandmen and labourers. Women were mostly illiterate and were clustered with the most illiterate group of men.

The aggregate figures presented in these tables summarize the state of illiteracy in the various areas and periods, but they do not do justice to the dynamics of its history. At times there was dramatic progress in the reduction of illiteracy, followed or interspersed by periods of stagnation. Nor did all groups in all areas change at the same time or pace. An analysis of these movements, with an attempt to link shifts in illiteracy to other historical changes, will follow in chapter 7. Our immediate concern is to relate this structure of illiteracy to the social order of Elizabethan and Stuart England, made familiar to us by contemporary commentators and subsequent historians.

Early social anatomists could describe with ease the gradations of rank among the gentry and aristocracy but they were much less sure of the social distinctions among the other 95% or more of the population. They were not at all certain whether yeomen or tradesmen came next in rank after the gentry, had trouble disentangling the yeomen and husbandmen, had doubts about the position of the clergy and professions, and held vague and confused impressions about the status of artisans and labourers. Nor is this surprising since most of the commentators, gentlemen themselves, cared more about the polity and its governance than the

Table 6.1 *Social structure of illiteracy in the diocese of Norwich, 1580–1700*

Social group	No. sampled	No. mark	% mark	95% confidence interval[1]
Clergy and professions	332	0	0	—
Gentry	450	9	2	± 1
Yeomen	944	330	35	± 3
Tradesmen and craftsmen	1,838	809	44	± 2
Husbandmen	1,198	946	79	± 2
Servants	28	23	82	±14
Labourers	88	75	85	± 7
Women	1,024	911	89	± 2

1. Figures given with 95% confidence that percentage in the general population lie within the range given for the sample. A dash in this column in this and the following tables means 'not applicable'.

Table 6.2   *Social structure of illiteracy in the diocese of Exeter, 1574–1688*

Social group	No. sampled	No. mark	% mark	95% confidence interval
Clergy and professions	101	0	0	—
Gentry	263	7	3	± 2
Yeomen	367	98	27	± 5
Tradesmen and craftsmen	889	419	47	± 3
Servants	8	4	50	±35
Husbandmen	598	471	79	± 3
Labourers	1	1	100	—
Women	609	512	84	± 3

Table 6.3   *Social structure of illiteracy in the diocese of Durham, 1561–1631*

Social group	No. sampled	No. mark	% mark	95% confidence interval
Clergy and professions	208	5	2	± 2
Gentry	252	53	21	± 5
Tradesmen and craftsmen	727	470	65	± 3
Yeomen	1,326	971	73	± 2
Servants	18	14	78	±19
Husbandmen	379	345	91	± 3
Labourers	176	172	98	± 2
Women	706	690	98	± 1

Table 6.4   *Social structure of illiteracy in the diocese of London, Essex and Hertfordshire, 1580—1640*

Social group	No. sampled	No. mark	% mark	95% confidence interval
Clergy and professions	177	0	0	—
Gentry	161	5	3	±3
Yeomen	319	105	33	±5
Tradesmen and craftsmen	448	188	42	±5
Husbandmen	461	337	73	±4
Labourers	7	7	100	—
Women	324	308	95	±3

Table 6.5   *Social structure of illiteracy in the diocese of London, City and Middlesex, 1580—1700*

Social group	No. sampled	No. mark	% mark	95% confidence interval
Clergy and professions	168	0	0	—
Gentry	240	5	2	± 2
Apprentices	33	6	18	±13
Tradesmen and craftsmen	1,398	391	28	± 2
Yeomen	121	36	30	± 8
Servants	134	42	31	± 8
Labourers	27	21	78	±16
Husbandmen	132	104	79	± 7
Women	1,794	1,368	76	± 2

commonwealth and its economy.[2] None the less there was a common ground. According to Sir Thomas Smith, 'we in England divide our men commonly into four sorts, gentlemen, citizens and yeomen, artificers and labourers'. This was a broad enough classification which could accommodate with minor adjustment the views of William Harrison, William Camden, Thomas Wilson and a host of lesser-known commentators. It also corresponds quite well, at least in outline, with the order of literacy.[3]

The clergy and members of the professions were, not surprisingly, the most literate group of people in pre-industrial England. Most of the deponents in this classification were in holy orders, as rectors, vicars or curates, and they have been grouped with a scatter of lawyers, medical doctors and schoolmasters who shared their mastery of the medium. Reading and writing was an essential part of their professional activity and only encroaching senility would rob them of their skill. That, surely, is the explanation of the rare case in which a clergyman could not sign his name. Christopher Thorobye, vicar of Stannington in Northumberland, appeared before the consistory court of the diocese of Durham in 1625 and autographed his deposition with a crude and faltering initial which counts as a mark. His age was said to be 'about 100' and his advanced years rather than the alleged backwardness of the northern clergy are sufficient to explain this instance.[4] It could have happened anywhere.

The social standing of priests and professionals depended on their training and function as well as on their connections and wealth. They were essentially skilled literate specialists, agents and associates of the ruling class. By virtue of their profession alone they were accorded a kind of honorary gentle status and were grouped with the gentry in most contemporary social classifications. 'Lawyers, professors and ministers, archdeacons, prebends and vicars' were included with gentlemen in Thomas Wilson's review of the state of England. William Harrison explained that gentle status was accorded to 'whosoever studieth the laws of the realm, whoso abideth in the university giving his mind to his book, or professeth physic and the liberal sciences'. Thomas Milles in his definitive *Catalogue of honor* recognized a type of gentleman 'which is of reputation only for his learning, or for some office or function which he beareth . . . although he had a common person to his father and leave his sons common persons also'.[5] A gentility based on learning could be a fragile commodity and the same applied to gentle status that was a concession to the cloth. Many of the men in this category, however, and the lawyers in particular, could claim real gentle antecedents, intermarried with the gentry, or were able to set their sons up as gentlemen.

The gentlemen of England included the titled aristocrats of the *nobilitas major* as well as the more plentiful knights, esquires and plain gentry of the *nobilitas minor*. Hardly a single magnate swept into view in the ecclesiastical court records which form the basis for this study, despite their prominence in political history and in the writings of the social commentators. Very few deponents, in fact, had a rank higher than esquire and most were parish gentlemen testifying about local affairs. Gentlemen were expected to be literate. Their education normally prepared them for the business of local administration, estate management, political dealing and civilized exchange which went with their rank, and reading and writing were usually involved in bearing 'the port, charge and countenance of a gentleman'.[6] As a class the gentry were close in literacy to the clergy and professionals and it might be more fitting to enquire what these people did with their literacy than whether they could sign their names. Nevertheless, there were illiterate gentlemen, and not all of them could claim the excuse of advancing age.

Even in London and the prosperous region of East Anglia there were men who were acknowledged as gentle but who could not write their names. James Hanchett, gentleman of Bursted Magna in Essex, and John More, gentleman of Woodford, both made marks instead of signatures on their depositions in 1590. So did William Mowlinge of Holt, Norfolk, in 1635, George White of Silverton, Devon, in 1665, and John Drinkwater of St Dunstan's in the West, London, in 1675.[7] Of the gentlemen sampled 2 or 3% were unable to write their names. Some of these men may have been old or handicapped, palsied, blind or dyslexic, but others were apparently hale and simply could not write. They signal the information that even among the social elite it was not absolutely necessary to have full possession of literacy.

In the Durham region a third or more of the Elizabethan gentry made marks instead of signatures. This high illiteracy was reduced in the early seventeenth century, but even in James' reign the gentry of the north-east were many times more likely to be unable to sign than their southern contemporaries. The diocese of Durham was remote from the cultural impulses of London and was reputedly poor and underdeveloped. The Durham and Northumberland gentry led lives which were rough and simple compared with the gentry of Devon or Suffolk, and were little more literate than southern yeomen, yet their status as gentlemen was not thereby impugned.[8] Gentility was not revoked by illiteracy, although it may well have been inconvenienced. Illiteracy among all social groups was higher in the north-east, but the same hierarchical pattern prevailed.

The gentry, clergy and members of the professions were so similar in their literacy that they can be regarded as inhabiting a single cluster at the accomplished end of the literacy scale. Thirty percentage points or more usually separated them from the next most literate cluster, the yeomen and tradesmen.

Elizabethan and Stuart social anatomists were awkward and inconsistent in ranking the yeomen relative to the tradesmen. Nor is this surprising in light of the ambiguities of yeoman status and the artificial and all-embracing category of trades. In esteem, wealth and literacy they occupied the same general area but the yeoman was sometimes granted a superior social standing by virtue of his traditional position as a landed freeholder entitled to vote in parliamentary elections. Sir Thomas Smith could report that 'next to gentleman be appointed citizens and burgesses', usually urban tradesmen, while announcing with another breath that yeomen are 'in the degree next unto gentlemen'. William Harrison put merchants and citizens and burgesses above yeomen and ordinary artificers and craftsmen below them, while Thomas Wilson reinstated the yeomen's position next to the gentlemen. Almost a century later Edward Chamberlayne insisted on the superiority of yeomen over tradesmen and Gregory King endorsed this view, with reservations about the status of the unquestionably more prosperous 'merchants and traders by the sea'.[9]

So many different occupations made up the grouping of tradesmen and craftsmen that one hesitates to make generalizations about their literacy. They occupied the middle of the range, as likely to be able to sign as not, with enormous variation from trade to trade. The spread, ranking and clustering of illiteracy within this group will be examined in detail in a later section of this chapter. Tradesmen in London and Middlesex, it will be noted, were sharply differentiated from their competitors and contemporaries elsewhere. The depositions in the commissary and consistory courts of the diocese of London are sufficiently plentiful and detailed to permit us to differentiate the tradesmen and craftsmen of the City proper from those who lived in the outparishes, suburbs and villages of Middlesex. True Londoners were decidedly more literate, although this may have had as much to do with the concentration of high-grade trades in the City as with differences in educational background. Whereas 28% of the tradesmen and craftsmen sampled in the entire metropolitan area between 1580 and 1700 could not sign, the proportion in London was 22% and in Middlesex 37%. Their aggregate illiteracy in other parts of England ranged from 42% to 65%.

The literacy of yeomen was substantially inferior to that of the gentry and clergy, comparable to that of the tradesmen, and much better than that of the husbandmen and poorer countryfolk. Only a third of the yeomen in southern England were unable to sign their names. In the diocese of Exeter, using evidence from later in the seventeenth century, the figure for yeoman illiteracy was 27%. In the diocese of Norwich 35% of the yeomen sampled could not sign their depositions, and a similar figure of 33% was recorded in the adjacent rural parts of the diocese of London. Only in the diocese of Durham, where a problem of social terminology as much as cultural backwardness seems to be at issue, was the illiteracy of yeomen out of this comfortable range. Almost three-quarters of the men labelled yeomen in Northumberland and Durham made marks instead of signatures.

The classic Elizabethan descriptions of the yeomen seem not to have applied in the north-east. In the diocese of Durham the term was used more carelessly, or more generously, embracing all sorts of men who would not have been regarded as yeomen in southern England. It seems to have been used as a vague term of respect that could be attached to any decent working person, regardless of his wealth or tenure or whether he was engaged in agriculture. Among the Elizabethan deponents before the consistory court at Durham were Miles Baith of Ebchester, 'yeoman alias blacksmith', William Stoyr of Newcastle, 'yeoman alias porter of the water', and even Christopher Lawson of Walsingham, 'yeoman alias schoolmaster', The word yeoman was linked with occupations which seem incompatible with yeoman status, conventionally considered. Thomas Wawton, 'yeoman alias husbandman', features a common confusion of agrarian status, but what is one to make of James Wally, 'yeoman alias labourer' or Mathew Skorfeld, 'yeoman alias servingman'?[10] These were not isolated instances and collectively they argue that the socially stratified figures for illiteracy in the north should not be compared directly with those from anywhere else. Thomas Leyland, a Lancashire esquire of the early Elizabethan period, made references in his will to 'my servant yeomen' and 'my household yeomen servants' which indicates a form of usage rarely found in southern England except in 'yeomen of the guard'.[11]

By all accounts the yeomen of Elizabethan and Stuart England were a thrusting, dynamic group, working hard as commercial agriculturalists, amassing land and profits, aping their betters and setting their sons up as gentlemen. There may be an element of caricature in the descriptions of the yeomen, but it is apparent that this group made good practical use of its literacy. According to Sir Thomas Smith, the yeomen 'are able and daily do buy the lands of unthrifty gentlemen'. Thomas Fuller described them as 'gentlemen in ore, whom the next age may see refined'. The Middlesex yeomen were said to 'wade in the weeds of gentlemen . . . seldom or not at all setting their hand unto the plough', while the yeomen of Devon could be found 'climbing up daily to the degrees of a gentleman' and bringing their children up accordingly. The Elizabethan yeoman

giveth himself for the most part to such virtues, conditions and qualities as doth the gentleman and delighteth in good housekeeping, fareth well, seemly in his apparel, courteous in his behavior and friendly to his neighbours . . . his chief travails be most in matters of his husbandry wherein he leaveth no pains to make his best profit . . . and now of late they have entered into the trade of usury, buying of clothes and purchasing and merchandises.

Most yeomen were freeholders, but they could just as well rent their land and diversify into other forms of activity.[12]

Contemporary commentators sometimes had difficulty in separating the husbandmen from the yeomen in their classifications of the social order. The problem continues for modern historians, not least because the activity of husbandry was the source of yeoman profits. The difficulty is succinctly put by Peter Laslett: 'all yeomen were husbandmen, because they worked the land, but not all husbandmen were yeomen'.[13] The confusion is similar to that among the social elite where all aristocrats were gentlemen but not all gentlemen were aristocrats. In practice the distinction between yeomen and husbandmen was one of esteem, as estimated by self, family and associates, and status sensitivity could prompt the record-keepers of the ecclesiastical courts to alter a man's addition or description from yeoman to husbandman or the other way around. Gervase Markham, who wrote several books on husbandry at the beginning of the seventeenth century, noted that

we even to this day do seriously observe to call every husbandman, both in our ordinary conference and every particular salutation, goodman such a one, a title if we rightly observe it of more honour and virtuous note than many which precede it at feasts and in gaudy places.[14]

Opportunities for confusion were plentiful, especially since many husbandmen were related to yeomen, farmed like yeomen and grew to be yeomen in the process. Nonetheless, despite overlap and ambiguity, the two terms had separate connotations and identified groups of men at different levels of society.

The difference is clearly shown in their aggregate level of illiteracy. Yeomen had much more engagement with the world of print and script than husbandmen and this is reflected in their considerably superior ability to sign. The percentage of illiteracy in the four rural areas for which we have evidence was 35%, 27%, 73% and 33% for yeomen, compared to 79%, 79%, 91% and 73% among deponents labelled husbandmen. Yeomen had more leisure and more wealth than husbandmen, and were more likely to be able to enjoy the escapist delights of literacy as well as its practical benefits. Husbandmen, on the other hand, might have been more constantly preoccupied with subsistence. Yeomen could manage without literacy — indeed, a third of them could not even write their names; yet their status and prosperity, the very attributes which earned them their yeoman standing, could be enhanced by the ability to read and write. For husbandmen literacy was an uncommon luxury, not a skill that was generally useful in their seasonal routine.

While the yeoman was regarded as energetic and thrifty, the husbandman could be dismissed as clownish and rude. The Suffolk husbandman, 'though he thriveth ordinarily well, yet he laboureth much'. Richard Steele characterized him as 'rather ignorant than knowing, in wisdom rather simple than judicious, in his will rather surly than malleable, in his behaviour rather rude and homely than smoothe and polite'.[15] This may have been patronizing, if not downright insulting, but it can stand as an appropriate comment on one of the least literate groups in pre-industrial England.

Only labourers and women were more illiterate than husbandmen. Labourers were thinly represented in the depositions sample but hardly any who appeared were able to sign their names. Most labourers were non-specialized farm workers, employed by the day or the year to work with their muscles on other men's land. They were often pitifully poor and had neither use for literacy nor opportunities to acquire it. In addition to the 'daily labourer at husbandry' there was an even more depressed labouring countryman. John Hooker of Devon describes

the spader, the daily worker or labourer in the tin works, and there is no labourer to be compared unto him; for his apparel is coarse, his diet slender, his lodging hard, his feeding commonly coarse bread and hard cheese, and his drink is water and for lack of a cup he drinketh it out of his spade or shovel; and he goeth so near the weather as no man can live more frugally and nearer than he doth.

Labourers, according to Edward Chamberlayne, were 'the lowest member, the feet of the body politic'. There were many of them.

Alan Everitt has estimated that in 'the Tudor and early Stuart period the labouring population probably formed about one quarter or one third of the entire population of the countryside', a proportion which would be 'a good deal higher in fertile corn-growing districts'. This estimate is supported by local evidence and the late-seventeenth-century calculations of Gregory King.[16]

Only the women, socially undifferentiated in our sources, displayed a level of illiteracy in the same high range as the labourers and husbandmen. More than four-fifths of the women sampled in the relatively advanced dioceses of Norwich and Exeter were unable to sign their names, while almost all the women in the (admittedly earlier) sample from Durham were illiterate. In all sources and in all areas and periods, the literacy of women lagged behind that of men.

Most women did not need to be able to write. The domestic routine of cooking and sewing and child-rearing had little need for reading, and it scarcely afforded the time. There were, of course, exceptions, and several popular books were aimed specifically at a female audience. There were privileged women whose literacy was a social ornament, daughters who learned to read and write to please their fathers, and wives whose literacy matched that of their husbands. But we must not be misled by examples of gentlemen's ladies and merchant's widows keeping accounts and conducting correspondence into thinking that such abilities were widespread. Even among those social and economic groups where the men had regular dealings with paper and ink, the women were usually illiterate.

Even in matters of religion there was less reason for women to pursue literacy. Men as masters of households had religious responsibilities not normally shared with women, in catechism and in leading of prayers, and wives were supposed to defer to the spiritual guidance of their husbands. Women had souls as precious as men and were just as much Christ's people, but the religious propaganda about reading and writing was pitched less enthusiastically in their direction. The extreme behaviour of some Bible-thumping women in the mid seventeenth century stiffened the element of distrust for female literacy which can be detected in certain puritan sermons. It was as if the male preachers sensed some flaw or incapacity in their female hearers and hesitated to launch them on a path too difficult for their alleged emotional weakness and inappropriate for their social role.[17]

Only in London did women break away from their massive illiteracy. Elizabethan and early Stuart women in the capital city were no more able to sign their names than women anywhere else, but their condition was transformed in the last quarter of the seventeenth century. By the 1690s the level of illiteracy among London women was reduced to 52%, with further improvement into the eighteenth century. London became unusually demanding of literacy among its residents and was uniquely hospitable to developing female accomplishments. The cause and consequences of this geographically limited flowering is a subject for future research, which might focus on the social and cultural networks of the City and the attraction to London of migrants with better-than-average literacy.[18]

Servants and apprentices in London were also extraordinarily literate. Perhaps they took on the literacy colouration of their masters in preparation for careers of their own as London tradesmen. In an admittedly small sample only 18% of the apprentices and 31% of the servants who made depositions in the City and Middlesex were unable to sign. No comparable information could be collected about apprentices elsewhere, but the combined evidence from the dioceses of Norwich, Exeter and Durham shows 76% of the servants sampled in rural England to have been illiterate. While London servants were clustered close to their masters the literacy of servants in the rest of the country was not much better than husbandmen and labourers. Since the ecclesiastical courts were reluctant to admit the testimony of dependent persons, we cannot approach the question of servant literacy with any precision.

The largest group of deponents to appear before the ecclesiastical courts was the composite collection of tradesmen and craftsmen. Closer study of this group throws more light on the structure of illiteracy, revealing another hierarchy inhabited by a further set of clusters. Illiteracy was stratified by occupation and trade as well as by general social categories.

Sir Thomas Smith, viewing the commonwealth from the viewpoint of constitutional arrangements rather than social structure, grouped 'day labourers, poor husbandmen, yea, merchants or retailers which have no free land, copyholders, and all artificers, as tailors, shoemakers, carpenters, brickmakers, bricklayers, masons, etc.' as 'the fourth sort of class amongst us' with 'no voice nor authority in our commonwealth'. Other Elizabethan commentators with more economic sophistication could differentiate the merchants from the rest of the tradesmen and artisans. Richard Mulcaster neatly distinguished 'marchandize' from 'manuarie': 'Marchandize containeth under it all those which live any way by buying or selling: manuarie those whose handiwork is their ware and labour their living. Their distinction is by wealth.'

Edward Chamberlayne more or less repeated this classification, drawing a distinction between merchants and 'mechanicks', while Gregory King separated 'merchants and traders by sea' from 'shopkeepers and tradesmen' and 'artisans and handicrafts'.[19]

None of these classifications takes full account of the broad cultural and social range spanned by the tradesmen and craftsmen, or the aspects of reputation, wealth and skill which connected them or distanced them. Tailors and bricklayers, for example, may have occupied different social realms although both were artisans engaged in 'manuarie'. The evidence of literacy certainly shows the superiority of the one over the other. A ranking of men in different occupations by their ability or inability to sign the depositions reveals a gradation from minimal to total illiteracy. Some tradesmen were as accomplished as the gentry, while others were no more able to write than the labourers.

Representatives of more than 300 distinctly designated occupations appeared before the ecclesiastical courts in the four dioceses under review. Many were commonplace, like smiths and weavers, but the sample encountered men employed as fanwrights and charcoal-burners, cheesemongers and perukemakers. Table 6.6 shows the percentage unable to sign among the most common occupations encountered in the country dioceses, and Table 6.7 shows the ranking of trades by illiteracy in the metropolitan parts of the diocese of London. The evidence in Table 6.6 is collected from all four dioceses, from the reign of Elizabeth to the end of the Stuart era, but is not unduly weighted to any period or district. Some of the samples are small with consequently high standard errors. We can, however, be 95% confident that the true illiteracy level among country merchants was in the range 5—15%, weavers 45—53%, carpenters 55—69% and thatchers 82—100%. A more comprehensive study might revise the figures and alter some of the rankings, but the over-all distribution here has a consistency which makes it convincing.

In rural and metropolitan areas alike, the ability or inability to sign roughly followed the gradient from clean, respectable, commercial pursuits, through various types of specialist craft activities, to rough, manual, outdoor occupations. At the one end were shopkeeper types, like apothecaries and drapers, whose world necessarily included paperwork and might involve literature, while at the other end were fishermen and shepherds and manual workers, such as thatchers and miners, who rarely had to handle a pen or open a page. Five occupational clusters composed of men with roughly similar levels of literacy can be discerned, in rural or provincial England, each associated with a distinctive occupational activity. The relative position of each of these clusters is shown in Table 6.8 with the positions of clergy and gentry, yeomen, husbandmen and labourers for comparison. The ranking and clustering provides compelling evidence that the distribution of literacy in pre-industrial England was powerfully influenced by its economic and social utility.

The commercial elite of the country towns — the apothecaries, drapers, grocers, haberdashers, ironmongers, mercers and vintners — were close to the level of the clergy and gentry: almost completely in possession of literacy. They were joined by scriveners, whose literacy provided them directly with an income, and merchants, for whom the ability to write was a valuable though not indispensable asset. The routine business of these retailers and dealers included correspondence with suppliers and customers, taking notice of regulations and announcements, recording ledger entries and memoranda, and a host of activities facilitated by mastery of the written word. No more than 10% were unable to sign their names, but the few exceptions remind us that even in commercial circles it was possible to get by without full literacy.

The next cluster included a variety of skilled craftsmen and businessmen like goldsmiths and clothiers, innkeepers and saddlers, ranging in illiteracy from 14% to 33%. These men were among the cream of the working population, providing specialist services and supplying expensively wrought products. Their general ability to write their names distinguished them from the middle-ranking artisans in the third cluster.

The third cluster was comprised of 'the industrious sort of people', between 37% and 52% illiterate. Many of them were involved in the textile industry, like woolcombers, weavers and fullers, while others were engaged in the processing of agricultural produce, as brewers and malsters, or in manufacturing articles of dress, as tailors or cordwainers. They were more likely to be literate than not. Apart from the mariner, who might require literacy if he undertook sophisticated modern navigation, or made out cargo manifests, the workmen in this cluster had little need for reading and writing in their actual crafts, but considerable use for those skills if their trade expanded to a business. Literacy was valuable for interaction with customers and creditors, and with the middlemen and dealers who were often in contact with the men of this group.

The next cluster of tradesmen, with illiteracy in the range of 56—68%, had simpler skills and lower esteem, and it is not surprising that fewer of them could write. The cluster included blacksmiths and carpenters, millers and butchers, who were typical

Table 6.6   *Ranking of trades by illiteracy in rural England,*
1580–1700

Trade	No. sampled	No. mark	% mark
Scrivener	21	0	0
Apothecary	15	0	0
Vintner	13	0	0
Ironmonger	10	0	0
Mercer	32	1	3
Draper	46	2	4
Grocer	60	3	5
Haberdasher	14	1	7
Merchant	122	12	10
Dyer	14	2	14
Clothier	86	18	21
Goldsmith	12	3	25
Baker	48	13	27
Innkeeper	36	10	28
Glazier	29	8	28
Saddler	17	5	29
Chandler	16	5	31
Barber	30	10	33
Tanner	101	37	37
Brewer	42	16	38
Maltster	34	13	38
Woolcomber	40	18	45
Mariner	28	13	46
Weaver	524	257	49
Wheelwright	34	17	50
Fuller	30	15	50
Victualler	14	7	50

Table 6.6 cont.

Trade	No. sampled	No. mark	% mark
Tailor	286	145	51
Cordwainer	135	70	52
Turner	11	6	55
Blacksmith	137	77	56
Sailor	40	23	58
Worsted-dresser	33	19	58
Joiner	26	15	58
Wright	27	16	59
Butcher	157	94	60
Miller	44	27	61
Carpenter	201	124	62
Sherman	13	8	62
Glover	72	45	63
Gardener	22	14	66
Shoemaker	57	37	65
Cooper	44	30	68
Bricklayer	45	33	73
Collier	15	11	73
Currier	11	8	73
Mason	57	44	77
Cutler	10	8	80
Ropemaker	10	8	80
Hellier	21	17	81
Fisherman	16	13	81
Shepherd	11	9	82
Thatcher	43	39	91
Miner	25	24	96
Slater	11	11	100

Table 6.7   *Ranking of London and Middlesex trades by illiteracy,
1580—1700*

Trade	No. sampled	No. mark	% mark
Scrivener	46	0	0
Merchant	27	0	0
Vintner	23	0	0
Grocer	21	0	0
Saddler	10	0	0
Apothecary	9	0	0
Goldsmith	29	1	3
Stationer	18	1	6
Chandler	28	2	7
Barber	13	1	8
Ironmonger	13	1	8
Draper	34	4	12
Haberdasher	49	7	14
Dyer	13	2	15
Glazier	13	2	15
Leatherseller	12	2	17
Skinner	12	2	17
Cutler	16	3	19
Cooper	13	3	23
Mariner	13	3	23

of the independent craftsmen found in nearly every village. Their professional skills were mostly manual and the horizons of their business were mostly local.

Finally, the most illiterate cluster of trades included building workers like bricklayers, masons and thatchers, men engaged in mineral extraction like helliers and miners, and all-weather workmen like fishermen and shepherds. Most of this work was heavy and dirty, required more brawn than brain, and often isolated its practioners from regular contact with the rest of society. We cannot judge whether working in a pit, plying a fishing boat or having little company but sheep and the sky was a cause or consequence of illiteracy, but there was certainly a powerful association between work of this sort and the inability to write one's name.

A comparable clustering was found among tradesmen in London and Middlesex. At one end the civic elite of merchants, joined by the pen-wielding scriveners, wholesale dealers and polite shop-keepers, had complete possession of literacy. Specialist distributors and craftsmen came next, followed by a miscellany of people in servicing and processing trades. Industrial workers and

Table 6.7 cont.

Trade	No. sampled	No. mark	% mark
Baker	19	5	26
Cook	11	3	27
Victualler	40	11	28
Sailor	17	5	29
Clothworker	30	9	30
Merchant-Taylor	62	19	31
Cordwainer	42	13	31
Weaver	29	10	34
Butcher	26	9	35
Blacksmith	37	14	38
Joiner	32	12	38
Bricklayer	21	8	38
Carpenter	40	16	40
Feltmaker	10	4	40
Innkeeper	10	4	40
Tailor	97	43	44
Brewer	13	6	46
Shoemaker	19	10	53
Gardener	17	10	59
Waterman	15	10	67

craftsmen occupied the fourth metropolitan cluster, with less-skilled craftsmen and outdoor workers at the bottom. Most of these people were more literate than their provincial and rural counterparts. Mariners and sailors, victuallers and butchers, weavers and bricklayers and more, were more likely to be able to write their names if they dwelt in suburban Middlesex or the City. A few, like haberdashers and inn-keepers, appeared to be less literate in London than in the country dioceses, but this may be a product of the sampling, with neither statistical nor sociological significance. More work needs to be done on the social and occupational structure of the metropolis to determine whether people identified themselves by a livery company affiliation, and what relationship this had to their actual occupation and daily trade.

The evidence of literacy brings into focus some details of social stratification which were hitherto blurred or unseen. Occupations which were outwardly similar can be differentiated by the attainments in literacy of their members. The more specialized, complex, refined or expensive the business the more likely was its practitioner

Table 6.8   *Clusters of illiteracy in rural England, 1580–1700*

% illiterate	Economic activity	Social status
		Clergy and gentry
0–10	Retailers	
	Distributors	
14–33	Specialist crafts	
		Yeomen
37–52	Manufacturers	
	Processors	
56–68	Village crafts	
73–100	Heavy manual trades	Husbandmen
		Labourers

to be able to sign his name. Cordwainers were superior to simple shoemakers, mariners were more literate than mere sailors, and joiners were more commonly able to write than carpenters. Among the many kinds of metal workers, anchorsmiths and white-smiths were more likely to be literate than ordinary blacksmiths, and there was a similar minor hierarchy among the different kinds of weavers. In the diocese of Norwich, for example, dornix weavers and worsted weavers were generally more literate than linen weavers and weavers unidentified by their thread. The Merchant Taylors of London were more literate than ordinary tailors although the finding that almost a third of them could not sign is something of a surprise, considering their association with one of the premier schools of England.[20]

The clusterings and rankings point to the diversity among the working population, where career prospects, social esteem, social interaction and capacity for participation in wider affairs was affected by one's level of literacy. The evidence of literacy shows the weakness of traditional attempts to classify the working popu-lation by their relationship to a particular industry or material, such as textile workers or people who worked with wood.[21] Saddlers were evidently more literate than shoemakers, although they both worked with leather, clothiers were better than worsted dressers although they both dealt with textiles, bakers were better than millers although both were engaged in producing food, and turners were apparently more literate than common carpenters, although both of their trades were in wood. It was the degree of skill and the extent of commercial opportunities involved in the activity, rather than the particular material on the bench or in the shop, which distinguished these people in their community.

Literacy was an important component in local social status and may provide clues to a variety of relationships. It is something of a mystery why the literacy of ironmongers should apparently outstrip that of chandlers, and why bakers were so much better than butchers, but their place in the ranking, assuming the sample has not led us astray, invites us to investigate their roles.

Explanation, of course, is more difficult than observation, and it is easier to delineate this hierarchy of illiteracy than to account for it. The information assembled here points to an overwhelming correspondence between social and occupational status and the ability to sign one's name. The evidence before us permits no more than an outline sketch of the distribution of literacy among men in different occupations. More data will need to be collected and there will have to be a careful examination of the activities and requirements of particular trades before the structure presented here can be accepted with confidence. For the most part, however, the rankings and clusters are plausible, consistent with other things known about the pre-industrial economy.

To what extent was the distribution of literacy conformable to the distribution of wealth? Such an artless question touches on so many difficulties of evidence and interpretation that the disciplined social historian may be forgiven for running for cover. What follows is an attempt to tease a social ranking of prosperity out of yet another set of ecclesiastical court documents, and to compare that ranking to the profile of illiteracy.

A clear gradient of wealth at death emerges from the study of probate inventories. To protect the deceased, his heirs and associates, the church supervised the valuation of goods and chattels as part of its testamentary business and approved a careful appraisal of moveable property, known as a probate inventory. This did not include the value of land, but it might list and value livestock and crops as well as household goods, cash on hand and debts owing and due.[22] Since the inventory usually recorded the status or occupation of the deceased, as well as his parish of residence and date of probate, it is not too difficult to calculate the average wealth of people in different social or occupational categories. The omission of real estate from these probate valuations leads to a serious underestimate of the wealth of land-owners, like gentlemen and yeomen, but probably has no more than a minor effect on the over-all rankings. Despite the vagaries of valuation, the inconsistent inclusion of debts and the usual difficulties of survival, bias and interpretation, the inventories give an adequate indication of the distribution of wealth.

Table 6.9 shows the ranking by probated wealth of the major

social groups of pre-industrial England, and Table 6.10 shows the hierarchy of wealth among some of the most frequently encountered trades. The tables are based on an analysis of 3,261 probate inventories made in fourteen counties between 1580 and 1700.[23] The evidence has been collected from all parts of England for more than a hundred years and, although there may have been changes which advanced some occupations and depressed others, the figures probably provide an accurate indication of the average wealth and relative position of the various ranks and trades in pre-industrial England. The broad range of wealth in each group is indicated by the very high standard deviations.

Valuations, of course, fluctuated with the price movements of the period, so the estate of a yeoman inventoried at £80 in 1600 was worth more in real terms than that of a yeoman inventoried at the same sum half a century later. To take account of these variations the value of each inventory has been adjusted to a common base year. Using the Phelps Brown and Hopkins index of the prices of consumables the net amounts have been converted to 1640 values.[24] In practice this somewhat laborious process makes little difference to the mean valuation for each category or for their rank order, so well were the inventories distributed through the period, but the adjusted as well as raw summary figures have been included in the tables.

The economic ranking of the principal social groups in Table 6.9 shows a mild degree of variation from the rankings by status and literacy. The three components of the *nobilitas minor* — knights, esquires and gentlemen — were ranked in descending order of wealth, befitting their influence in the affairs of the nation. John Norden, enumerating the aristocracy of Middlesex in 1596, craved 'patience, though I have not given to every man his addition of *esquire* or *gent*, for that I may easily err therein without the especial aid of an expert herald'.[25] The distinction might have been easier if he had access to their account books rather than their pedigrees. Esquires died possessed of moveable wealth worth almost twice that of mere gentlemen, while the probated wealth of knights was almost twice again that of esquires. The gentry together were the wealthiest social group, highest in social status, and in literacy second only to the clergy.

The inferior economic position of the clergy is clearly shown in this analysis of inventories, and helps to explain why their social connection with the gentry was conceded so begrudgingly. Clergymen were worth much less than gentlemen, and the difference would be still more acute if real estate wealth was taken into consideration. The clergy were worth even less than the

Table 6.9   *Ranking of social groups by wealth, 1580—1700*

Social group	No. sampled	Mean value (£)	Adjusted mean value (£)	Standard deviation
Knights	11	1,125.64	1,145.70	961.2
Esquires	69	662.03	657.81	831.3
Gentlemen	298	343.31	329.34	346.9
Yeomen	1,071	206.47	194.97	232.3
Clergy	234	197.15	186.30	171.7
Husbandmen	470	75.53	79.95	77.6
Labourers	103	29.70	27.91	37.5

yeomen, although the closeness of their mean probated wealth suggests that they shared an economic cluster in the middle range. Analysis of the content of the inventories, rather than their bottom line, might show the cultural distinctions between yeoman and priest which are implied by their differences in literacy but masked by their similarities in wealth.[26]

Yeomen were clearly much more prosperous than husbandmen, but were still a long way behind the gentry. They were, as Thomas Fuller said they were, 'in the temperate zone, betwixt greatness and want', with comfortable possessions and literacy and status to match.[27] If a weighting could be added for the ownership of freehold land an even greater economic distance would separate yeomen from husbandmen. The economic evidence from inventories and the literacy evidence from depositions strongly endorses the contemporary image of the thrusting yeoman, and lends more support to our insistence that the cultural and social sphere of the yeoman was very different from that of the husbandman. Husbandmen's estates were worth less than half those of yeomen, while the goods and chattels of the poor labourer were less than half those of husbandmen. At the bottom end of the social scale, as at the very top, the order of wealth was in accord with the order of esteem.

The valuations and rankings for particular trades are much more subject to error because of the small size of some of the samples. For all its imperfections, however, the occupational profile of wealth in Table 6.10 confirms the differentiation among the tradesmen and craftsmen which was apparent in their ranking by illiteracy. Distributive tradesmen were worth more than industrial processors and skilled craftsmen were worth more than simpler

Table 6.10   *Ranking of trades by wealth, 1580–1700*

Trade	No. sampled	Mean value (£)	Adjust mean value (£)	Standard deviation
Merchant	22	1,084.9	1,293.2	1,850.8
Mercer	13	280.2	282.2	450.0
Tanner	31	250.7	235.2	239.0
Maltster	12	218.8	202.6	177.5
Glover	13	182.0	169.0	392.5
Butcher	52	153.8	146.5	213.3
Innkeeper	21	157.9	140.1	154.1
Chandler	10	118.3	111.9	176.9
Baker	33	104.0	104.5	103.1
Weaver	78	107.3	97.9	119.7
Miller	38	95.8	85.7	134.0
Shoemaker	26	75.1	84.2	105.6
Locksmith	10	96.3	77.9	52.7
Blacksmith	44	74.3	68.8	65.0
Cordwainer	11	52.8	56.8	52.3
Shepherd	31	61.0	55.2	63.6
Mason	25	53.6	48.7	42.6
Carpenter	51	51.5	46.6	56.3
Nailer	29	44.0	39.7	28.8
Wheelwright	10	39.2	39.4	22.1
Tailor	52	39.6	36.1	30.5
Bricklayer	11	27.6	29.9	26.5

artisans and outdoor workers. The extraordinary wealth of the merchants, more than four times that of the next-nearest tradesmen, explains the attempts of some social anatomists to detach them from the rest of the commonalty and place them next to the gentlemen. The distinct clusterings which emerged from the ordering by illiteracy are blurred in this arrangement by wealth, and some of the rankings are changed, although the differences are not statistically significant. Tanners and maltsters were among the wealthiest tradesmen in this sample, although stock in trade and industrial equipment may have counted heavily in their inventories. Their mean wealth was close to that of the yeomen, just as they were comparable in their aggregate illiteracy. Butchers were apparently wealthier than bakers, although they occupied the opposite positions in literacy. The superiority in literacy of cordwainers over shoemakers and wheelwrights over carpenters is lost in this analysis of wealth, although the probate value of all these village craftsmen was in the same general range between the worth of husbandmen and labourers. Tailors were among the poorest trades, worth little more than bricklayers and labourers, yet their illiteracy was in the middle of the range. A rank-order correlation and linear regression on the twenty-five social and occupational groups for which there is adequate information about both illiteracy and wealth yields coefficients of −0.729 (Spearman's Rho) and −0.584 (Pearson's r, p<0.01), indicating a moderately strong negative association between probate value and the ability to sign. Literacy was evidently an economic function.

The structure of illiteracy and the hierarchy of wealth were in approximate accord with the traditional order of esteem. It was, however, impossible to place a cash value on literacy or to predict that its possessors would prosper. A man's social standing involved so many other things, like pedigree, kinship and bonding, neighbourly interaction, life-style and display, and the source and disposal of income as well as total wealth, that no simple ranking could elicit all its dimensions. Nor do we yet know the mechanism or process whereby literacy and occupation were linked. Did one develop a certain level of literacy in preparation for a particular choice of trade, or were the two fortuitously associated? Did illiteracy constrain career opportunities, or was one's exposure to formal education linked to the expectations one's parents and friends had about one's future source of livelihood? Not enough is known about employment patterns and their perpetuation or about the realm of choices which confronted people in pre-industrial England to illustrate this problem. Perhaps people had not only an amount of literacy appropriate to their needs, but also no more literacy than they thought they were going to need. And this may have had as much to do with circumstance and perceptions of the immediate cultural ambience as with economic utility and occupational advantage.

Despite all these uncertainties it is clear that literacy was a powerful marker of social and economic position. The basic structure withstood the passage of time, although some social groups made progress while others experienced stagnation, as a close study of the dynamics of literacy in the early modern period will reveal in the following chapter.

7

The dynamics of illiteracy

The social structure of illiteracy is relatively simple to chart and not hard to understand. Limited educational opportunity in a hierarchically organized society, together with the scant need for literacy in many occupations, may explain why the response to the promotion of literacy was so thin and socially selective. More troublesome, however, are variations in illiteracy over time. There appears to have been no steady, cumulative progress in the reduction of illiteracy among men in the early modern period. Nor did the different social groups maintain the same level of illiteracy in relation to each other at all times from the sixteenth to the eighteenth century. Rather, the record reveals an irregular fluctuation, a series of spurts and setbacks, plateaux, arrests and accelerations in the progress of literacy, which sometimes involved large sectors of society but at other times were confined to particular sets or specific social groups.

The movement of illiteracy observed in the depositions is simply shown by grouping the evidence in ten-year periods. The abilities of clerics at one end of the scale and of labourers at the other did not change significantly over the seventeenth century. Nor was there much variation in the abilities of gentlemen and women, except for the gentry of the Durham region, who caught up with their southern contemporaries, and women in London, who outstripped their country sisters. Their progress is shown in tables 7.1 and 7.2 and graphs 7.1 and 7.2. The middling groups in society were much more volatile and the switchback performance of the yeomen, tradesmen and husbandmen is shown in tables 7.3–6 and graphs 7.3–6.

Literacy could be taken for granted among the gentlemen of England, and although their educational experience may have altered along with fluctuations in their taste in books there was no variation from their virtually universal ability to sign. The only exception was in the far north-east, where illiteracy still gripped 36% of the Elizabethan gentlemen who made depositions in the diocese of Durham. The evidence from the late sixteenth century shows little improvement, with gentle deponents of the 1590s

142

Table 7.1   *Gentle illiteracy in the diocese of Durham, 1560–1630*

Decade	No. sampled	No. mark	% mark
1560–9	22	9	41
1570–9	40	12	30
1580–9	12	5	42
1590–9	28	10	36
1600–9	63	11	17
1610–19	40	6	15
1620–9	47	0	0

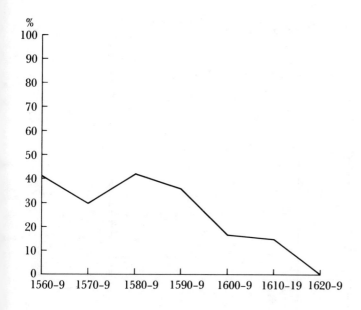

Graph 7.1   Gentle illiteracy in the diocese of Durham, 1560–1630

Table 7.2 Female illiteracy in London and East Anglia, 1580–1730

Decade	Norfolk/Suffolk			London/Middlesex		
	No.	No. mark	% mark	No.	No. mark	% mark
1580–9	37	37	100	68	57	84
1590–9	31	30	97	81	72	89
1600–9	81	76	94	33	30	91
1610–19	57	53	93	175	160	91
1620–9				213	192	90
1630–9	147	137	93	247	222	90
1640–9	22	20	91	21	17	81
1660–9	183	161	88	279	219	78
1670–9	234	203	87	374	241	64
1680–9	204	172	84	303	158	52
1690–9	28	22	79			
1720–9	98	73	74	153	67	44

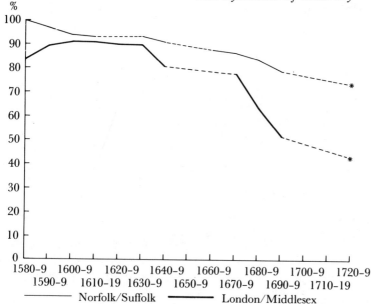

Graph 7.2   Female illiteracy in London and East Anglia, 1580–1730
Note: Solid lines, dots and dashes link consecutive points, broken lines are
estimates of trends, and asterisks represent solid data in the decade indicated,
here and in the following graphs.

barely more literate than those of the 1560s. Successive decades
of the Jacobean period, however, saw the eventual eradication of
illiteracy among this group. Although later evidence is, unfortunately, missing it can be assumed that the gentry of
Northumberland and Durham were as accomplished as gentlemen
anywhere else in the rest of the seventeenth century.
    Women were almost universally unable to write their own
names for most of the sixteenth and seventeenth centuries. The
later Stuart period saw a dramatic divergence between the experience of women in London and women in country districts.
In East Anglia a gradual drift away from complete illiteracy
brought women to the point where no more than four out of five
could not sign at the end of the seventeenth century. The diocese
of Norwich depositions from the 1720s show a further slow
improvement which may have continued for a few more decades
in the eighteenth century. Three out of four women were illiterate
in the early Hanoverian period, a proportion of which was reduced
to about two out of three by the time of the accession of George
III. Evidence from a national sample of marriage registers shows
64% of all brides could not sign in 1750, with a continuing slow

Table 7.3 Illiteracy of tradesmen and craftsmen in the dioceses of Durham, Exeter, Norwich and London, 1560–1730

Decade	Durham/Northumberland			Devon/Cornwall			Norfolk/Suffolk			Essex/Herts.			London/Middlesex		
	No. sampled	No. mark	% mark	No. sampled	No. mark	% mark	No. sampled	No. mark	% mark	No. sampled	No. mark	% mark	No. sampled	No. mark	% mark
1560–9	92	77	84	100	70	70									
1570–9	153	117	76												
1580–9	53	42	79				98	60	61	60	41	68	134	55	41
1590–9	79	45	57				161	89	55				101	43	43
1600–9	132	73	55				151	72	48	68	34	50	65	13	20
1610–19	116	65	56	55	23	42	126	55	44	73	16	22	172	44	26
1620–9	102	51	50							93	34	37	212	63	30
1630–9							140	69	49	113	42	37	154	50	32
1640–9							90	47	52						
1660–9				177	79	45	176	58	33						
1670–9				314	151	48	149	52	35				171	37	22
1680–9				215	89	41	174	77	44				222	58	26
1690–9							125	38	30				167	21	13
1720–9							104	35	34				170	14	8

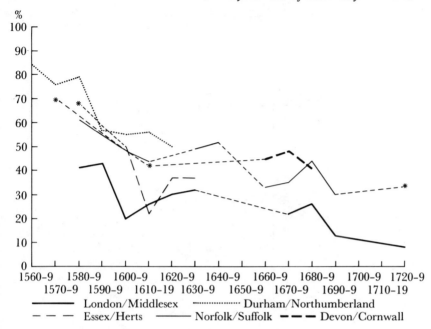

Graph 7.3   Illiteracy of tradesmen and craftsmen in the dioceses of Durham, Exeter, Norwich and London, 1560–1730

erosion of female illiteracy to 50% in the middle of the nineteenth century.[1] The utility of literacy, or its value for spiritual development or frivolous diversion, was steadily if sluggishly impressing itself upon the women of provincial England.

Women in London were not bound by this gradual secular evolution. Under Elizabeth and the early Stuarts they were not much better than women anywhere else, but in the last decades of the seventeenth century their writing ability was transformed. Female deponents from the City and suburbs improved from 78% unable to sign in the 1670s to 64% in the 1680s and 52% in the 1690s. The improvement continued, although its pace may have slackened, to just 44% illiterate in a sample from the 1720s. This was an extraordinary emergence, a halving of illiteracy in the space of two generations. It might, conceivably, reflect a change in the social catchment of female deponents, but there is no evidence to that effect. More likely, this plunging illiteracy points to an educational revolution among late Stuart and early Hanoverian women in the metropolis, a revolution which was geographically specific and to which women in less frenetic parts of the country were not exposed.[2]

Table 7.4   Illiteracy of tailors and weavers in rural England, 1560–1700

Decade	Tailors			Weavers		
	No. sampled	No. mark	% mark	No. sampled	No. mark	% mark
1560–9	8	8	100	11	11	100
1570–9	22	17	73	33	28	85
1580–9	14	9	64	14	10	71
1590–9	25	11	44	25	17	68
1600–9	30	16	53	26	16	62
1610–19	31	17	55	46	27	59
1620–9	9	3	33	15	10	67
1630–9	14	8	57	21	11	52
1640–9	10	4	40	14	5	36
1660–9	29	8	28	58	27	47
1670–9	35	19	54	85	35	41
1680–9	34	15	44	81	25	31
1690–9	10	4	40	56	22	39

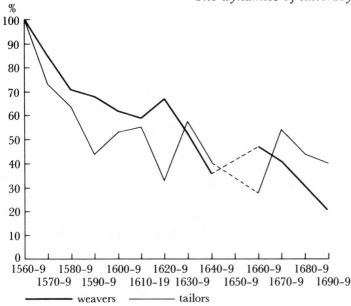

%

Graph 7.4   Illiteracy of tailors and weavers in rural England, 1560–1700

There may be two reasons for this precocity. It is quite likely that the migration of people to London involved a creaming off of talent, education and energy, bringing to the City women as well as men who had learned their literacy elsewhere. Literacy may have been an important factor in internal migration, especially if it was better rewarded in the capital than in provincial England. London may also have developed exceptional facilities of its own for teaching literacy to young ladies. The superiority of schooling in London or the relative ease of access to basic instruction may have been part of the capital's distinction and attraction. Christ's Hospital taught reading and writing to girls as well as boys, and many of the freelance writing-masters of London and Middlesex had female customers. The suburbs north of the City were re-nowned for their academies, although most of them catered more to 'young gentlewomen' than to daughters of ordinary working Londoners.[3] Cash and culture, the wealth of London and the leisure which it purchased, may also have primed this leap into literacy.

Tradesmen and craftsmen, despite the heterogeneity of their composition, can still be considered as a single social group for the purpose of tracing their illiteracy across time. Graph 7.3 shows the progress of tradesmen and craftsmen from 1560 to 1730, and Table 7.3 shows the numbers and proportion unable to sign, decade

Table 7.5 Illiteracy of yeomen in the dioceses of Durham, Exeter, Norwich and London, 1560–1730

Decade	Durham/Northumberland			Devon/Cornwall			Norfolk/Suffolk			Essex/Herts.		
	No. sampled	No. mark	% mark	No. sampled	No. mark	% mark	No. sampled	No. mark	% mark	No. sampled	No. mark	% mark
1560–9	35	22	63									
1570–9	83	45	54									
1580–9	33	17	52	21	9	43						
1590–9	164	116	71				78	43	55	23	8	35
1600–9	394	304	77				112	43	38			
1610–19	389	287	74	14	7	50	89	35	39	73	27	37
1620–9	228	180	79				84	32	38	87	30	34
1630–9							90	29	32	62	14	23
1640–9							36	10	28	56	19	34
1660–9				88	18	20	37	9	24			
1670–9				130	35	27	24	4	17			
1680–9				113	32	28	42	19	45			
1690–9							33	6	18			
1720–9							46	12	26			

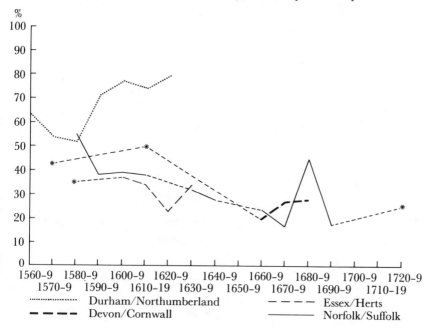

Graph 7.5   Illiteracy of yeomen in the dioceses of Durham, Exeter, Norwich and London, 1560–1730

by decade and district by district. Graph 7.4 and Table 7.4 show the movement of illiteracy among two representative occupations, tailors and weavers, to 1700.

The development of literacy among tradesmen and craftsmen in the four rural areas appears to have been remarkably consistent. Illiteracy was somewhat higher in the Durham region and lower than average in Essex, but neither district diverged excessively from the mainstream represented by the tradesmen of East Anglia and the south-west. The figures for Essex in the 1610s stand out but it is more likely that they reflect the chance of the sample than a sudden and unsustained improvement in local literacy. Essex was adjacent to London and Middlesex and some of its tradesmen had characteristics similar to those in the metropolis, so the general superiority of the group is not surprising. Townsmen and villagers and traders and artisans of all sorts comprised this hybrid category, yet the mix was evidently good enough to smooth out many of the differences.

Most of the early Elizabethan deponents in this group were unable to sign their names. Taking the earliest figures for each region for which we have evidence, a reasonable back-projection

Table 7.6 *Illiteracy of husbandmen in the dioceses of Durham, Exeter, Norwich and London, 1560–1730*

Decade	Durham/Northumberland			Devon/Cornwall			Norfolk/Suffolk			Essex/Herts.		
	No. sampled	No. mark	% mark	No. sampled	No. mark	% mark	No. sampled	No. mark	% mark	No. sampled	No. mark	% mark
1560–9	86	81	94	117	108	92						
1570–9	134	122	91									
1580–9	42	38	90				94	87	93	83	67	81
1590–9	55	50	91				121	105	87			
1600–9	52	45	87				108	85	79	52	42	81
1610–19	7	6		41	34	83	91	70	77	89	64	72
1620–9	3	3								103	68	66
1630–9							84	72	86	101	69	68
1640–9							23	18	78			
1660–9				122	96	79	82	58	71			
1670–9				203	149	73	56	46	82			
1680–9				84	61	73	38	34	89			
1690–9							40	33	82			
1720–9							39	34	87			

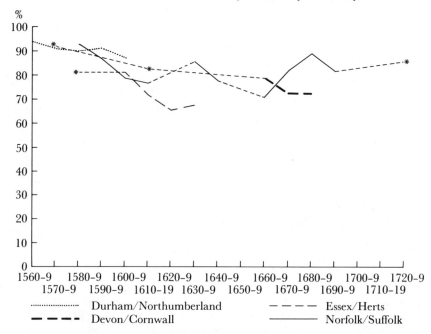

Graph 7.6   Illiteracy of husbandmen in the dioceses of Durham, Exeter, Norwich and London, 1560—1730

suggests that at least three-quarters were illiterate in the 1560s. Progress was rapid, and the evidence from all districts indicates a reduction to just 50% illiterate by the beginning of the seventeenth century. The reign of Elizabeth saw a solid improvement in literacy among tradesmen and craftsmen in all parts of England, reflecting, no doubt, the increased concern for education in that period. Tailors and weavers became increasingly able to sign in the later sixteenth century. A variety of indicators confirms the Elizabethan period as one of educational revolution although, as will be shown later, the greatest advances came before 1580.

The surge towards literacy continued into the Jacobean period before losing its momentum. No further progress was seen until the end of the seventeenth century, and the development of literacy among tradesmen and craftsmen was arrested at a plateau where some 40% to 50% could not sign their names. The general hesitation and fluctuation of the times is reflected in the experience of tailors and weavers, although weavers appeared to consolidate and improve their position later in the seventeenth century. The plateau may represent a point where most of the tradesmen who needed basic literacy had mastered the necessary skills, while the inability to form a signature was not a serious handicap to the others. A more optimistic impression is gained from the East Anglian evidence where tradesmen of the post-war period are shown to have improved upon their predecessors, but in the diocese of Exeter the tradesmen deponents after the Restoration were no more literate than those of the 1610s. In both areas the tradesmen under Charles II and James II showed more signs of drifting back into illiteracy than of its further conquest. The end of the Stuart period saw another phase of improvement, with only one-third of the tradesmen in the diocese of Norwich unable to sign their depositions. The illiteracy of tradesmen and craftsmen in rural England was halved between the reign of Elizabeth and the reign of George II, but relatively little of that long-term improvement took place in the seventeenth century.

Much the same story can be told about tradesmen in London and Middlesex, with the reservation only that their illiteracy was considerably lower. Although tradesmen in the city were generally more literate than their associates in Middlesex, the pattern of change over time was almost identical in both sectors of the metropolis. Just over 40% could not sign in the 1580s and 1590s, and still better performances were recorded in the early seventeenth century when between a fifth and a third could not write their names. Their experience for most of the seventeenth century, however, was not one of continuing progress. Their illiteracy appeared to increase between the beginning of the century and the civil war, and they were no better in the 1670s and 1680s than they had been in the 1610s. The vagaries of sampling may detract from the precision of these comparisons, but a strong impression remains of literacy stagnation in the city in the seventeenth century as well as in the country. Tradesmen and craftsmen in London and Middlesex held to a plateau of around 25% illiterate and did not advance beyond this until the age of William III. The end of the Stuart period saw a renewal of the reduction of illiteracy among metropolitan tradesmen. Only 13% of those sampled in the 1690s could not sign, a figure which was further reduced to 8% in the 1720s. By the early eighteenth century the commercial classes in London had almost complete possession of literacy, the men as well as the women distinguishing themselves from their contemporaries in the provinces.

Reviewing the course of illiteracy sharpens the distinction already made between yeomen and husbandmen. Literacy appealed differently at different social levels in the countryside, for yeomen made progress while husbandmen stagnated. Yeomen halved their rate of illiteracy from around 50% in the late sixteenth century to

roughly 25% in the late seventeenth, but their progress i.
periods of setback and hesitation as well as steady advance.
in the dioceses of Exeter, London and Norwich seem t(
had a comparable experience but the pattern among yeom.
the diocese of Durham was distinctly erratic. In the
Elizabethan period the Durham yeomen improved from ౦౦%
unable to sign in the 1560s to 54% in the 1570s and 52% in the
1580s. Their illiteracy was higher than that of yeomen in the
south but their progress was probably paralleled in other parts of
England. Then the literacy of yeomen in the north-east collapsed
to 71% in the 1590s and deteriorated further to 79% by the 1620s.
No other group of yeomen lost their literacy so suddenly or
slumped so close to the level of the husbandmen. The most likely
explanation for this unique local dislocation involves a shift in the
terminology of status which allowed husbandmen and less literate
workmen to be classed as 'yeomen'. Rather than witnessing the
catastrophe of yeoman illiteracy, the end of the sixteenth century
saw a change in social classification in the Durham region and an
increasingly indiscriminate use of a term which had a much more
specific meaning in the south.[4]

The state of illiteracy among yeomen in the Elizabethan period
is only muddily illuminated by the various diocesan records, and
we cannot say with confidence whether they were improving or
not. The Durham depositions indicate progress in the first few
decades, from 63% to 52% unable to sign, while yeomen in the
diocese of Norwich jumped from 55% to 38% illiterate between
the 1580s and 1590s. These are tokens of advancing education
among the Elizabethan yeomen, but the picture is confused by
evidence from the dioceses of Exeter and London. Yeomen in
Devon and Cornwall in the 1570s and in Essex and Hertfordshire
in the 1580s had already reached a stage where only a third or so
were illiterate and the evidence from subsequent decades points
more to stagnation than advance. The decadal variations reflect
the performance of the sample groups and are not necessarily
invested with statistical significance. The small size of the sample
in each decade makes it difficult to determine the course of educational improvement but it is at least clear that whatever progress
was being made had stopped by the turn of the century. The
Jacobean period was for the yeomen, much more than for the
tradesmen, a time of literacy stagnation or, more charitably, a
period of steadiness and consolidation. The fate of the Durham
'yeomen' should not be allowed to add to the gloom, but every
other set of evidence points to a levelling out or even a retardation
in the early seventeenth century. The scanty evidence from the

south-west suggests that fewer yeomen could sign their names in the 1610s than in the 1570s, and there was surprisingly little progress among the allegedly thrusting yeomen of East Anglia. Yeomen, like tradesmen, seem to have reached a plateau where between a third and a half could not sign.

This hesitation, however, was overcome by the following generations of yeomen deponents. The Essex figures for the 1620s and 1630s can be interpreted as signs of advance or decline, but those from the dioceses of Norwich and Exeter in the 1630s and 1640s and after the civil war indicated a renewed and sustained reduction in illiteracy. No more than a quarter of the yeomen who made depositions in the period of the Restoration were unable to authenticate them with their signatures. Educational standards among yeomen were evidently improving at the very time in the middle decades of the seventeenth century when progress among tradesmen had halted.

The end of the Stuart period saw a further contrast between the experience of yeomen and tradesmen. While there is evidence of shrinking illiteracy which betokens progress among tradesmen and craftsmen our figures point to a late-seventeenth-century setback among the yeomen. There was a drift from 20% to 28% unable to sign in the diocese of Exeter and erratic movement in the diocese of Norwich. Small decadal samples once more frustrate closer analysis, but all the signs suggest that the illiteracy of yeomen had struck another plateau. The yeomen deponents in the Norwich court in the 1720s were barely more literate than their predecessors of the 1640s.

Husbandmen remained deeply illiterate over the entire century and a half for which we have information. Only in early Stuart Essex did husbandmen break through to less than 70% illiterate, and there is no telling whether even there they managed to sustain that abnormal position. The over-all illiteracy of husbandmen in pre-industrial England was close to 80% and they rested near that plateau, relatively unmoved by the educational and political developments of the sixteenth and seventeenth centuries. Our evidence suggests that there was a slow erosion of illiteracy among husbandmen in the Elizabethan and Jacobean periods which may have carried on subtly and gradually for much of the seventeenth century. In the diocese of Exeter there was certainly a long-term but not particularly impressive improvement from 92% unable to sign in the 1570s to 73% in the 1670s, approximately 2% per decade. But in the diocese of Norwich there was no such steady augmentation of skills. After a generation or so of progress between the 1580s and 1610s, there was backsliding in the 1630s and a sequence of repeated advance and retardation which left East

Anglian husbandmen as thoroughly benighted in the reigns of William III and George II as they had been in the reign of Elizabeth. The rhetoric in favour of literacy and the philanthropic provision of education in the heroic years of protestant England seems to have made little impression on husbandmen.

The over-all pattern shows little of the gradual elimination of illiteracy which might have been expected. Most groups improved during the Elizabethan and Jacobean periods, although their movement was neither regular nor in phase. The middle of the seventeenth century saw more irregularities, with at best a slow dwindling of illiteracy and at worst actual recession. Contradictory movements again characterized the end of the Stuart period. The progress of literacy, so promising a hundred years earlier, became sluggish and quagmired and only the commercial classes continued to make strides. Some of these variations may be related to irregularities in the sample, but one's confidence in the developments portrayed here is enhanced by seeing much the same movement in every diocesan collection. Durham yeomen apart, it is remarkable how similar was the performance of representatives of the various social groups and how little they were affected by regional variations. No matter what else may have varied, along with landscape and agriculture, the yeomen of East Anglia and the yeomen of the south-west shared common literacy characteristics, as did husbandmen and many of the tradesmen.

Engaging hypotheses about the links between changes in literacy and educational provision, economic conditions and political and cultural developments might be built around these figures. However, the arrangement of the data by decades and the appearance before the courts of deponents of different generations obscures the chronological connection between literacy and its origins. Greater precision can be achieved in the plotting of illiteracy by attending to the time when people acquired their literacy, as children, rather than when they displayed it, as adult deponents. Accordingly, the depositions have been processed to show the movement of illiteracy by school generations. The age of each deponent was subtracted from the date of his deposition to find his year of birth, and ten years were added to bring him to the age of a schoolboy. The results, shown in graphs 7.7–7.16, have been subjected to an eleven-year moving average in order to overcome some of the problems of a small number of deponents in individual years and to smooth year-to-year fluctuations. Not all the fluctuation has been eliminated, but the general movements which emerge provide the basis for a reexamination of the dynamics of illiteracy.[5]

Additional advantages accrue from resorting the deponents into their school generations. Although we have no direct evidence of the dimensions of illiteracy in the mid Tudor period, they can be reconstructed from data accumulated at a later time. The threshold of knowledge about literacy can be pushed back at least to the 1530s. Witnesses before the various courts in the reign of Elizabeth belonged to every school generation of the sixteenth century. A sixty-year-old yeoman making his deposition in 1583 would have been of school age at the time of the reformation. One who was forty in 1583 could have learned to read under Edward or Mary, while one who was twenty in that year would belong to Shakespeare's generation with exposure to elementary education in the early 1570s.

Survivors from the very earliest school generations have been eliminated from this discussion lest their great age as deponents distort the statistics, but otherwise no attempt has been made to control for age and its possible association with declining skills. The graphs show the eradication of illiteracy among gentlemen in the diocese of Durham and the progress towards literacy of yeomen, husbandmen and tradesmen in the dioceses of Durham, Exeter and Norwich from the reign of Henry VIII to the beginning of the eighteenth century. This resorting also overcomes the problem of gaps in the deposition series, including the revolutionary hiatus of the 1650s. Members of school generations who might have made depositions at those times are found distributed through the records from other decades.

The extent to which the shifts and reversals in the progress of literacy reflect the changing educational climate of Tudor and Stuart England is not immediately clear. The fluctuations in the various graphs are not completely synchronized and there are phases where the directions are ambiguous or contradictory. However, the lines are not so tenuous as to bar discussion. The over-all movement of illiteracy among the different groups of school generations in different parts of the country forms a consistent enough pattern in which a sequence of stages can be discerned. These stages can be related to developments in the history of education, and perhaps to political and economic events which had a bearing on the acquisition of literacy.

Certain aspects of the changing educational climate are susceptible to numerical analysis. Figures showing the number of endowed school foundations each decade, the amount of charitable giving to schools in particular and to education in general, and the flow of students into the University of Cambridge, have been assembled in Table 7.7. These figures are themselves beset with imperfections, and do not in any case purport to represent the

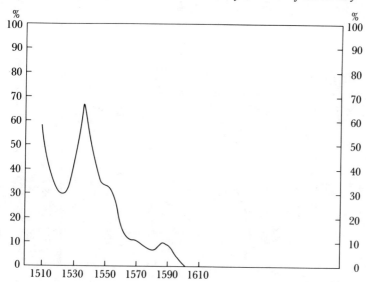

Graph 7.7   Illiteracy of gentlemen, diocese of Durham, by year of education, 1510–1610
Note: This and the following graphs in this chapter are drawn from continuous data, smoothed for every year.

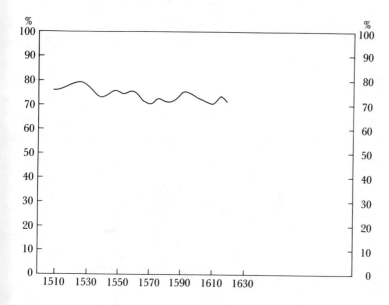

Graph 7.8   Illiteracy of yeomen, diocese of Durham, by year of education, 1510–1620

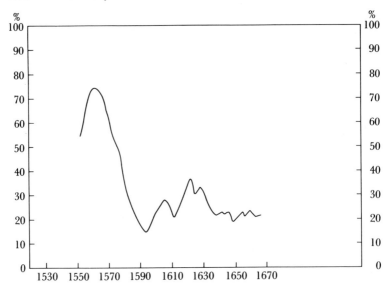

Graph 7.9   Illiteracy of yeomen, diocese of Exeter, by year of education, 1550–1670

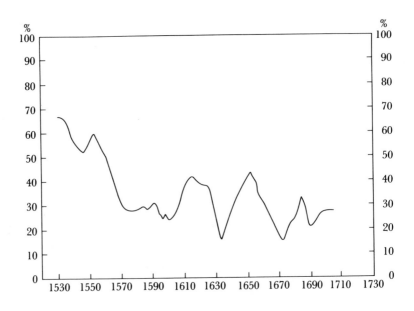

Graph 7.10   Illiteracy of yeomen, diocese of Norwich, by year of education, 1530–1710

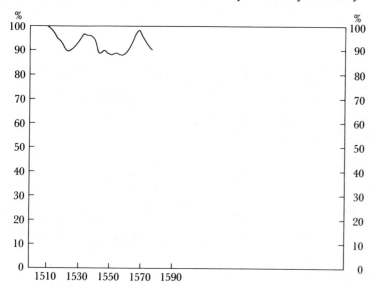

Graph 7.11   Illiteracy of husbandmen, diocese of Durham, by year of education, 1510–90

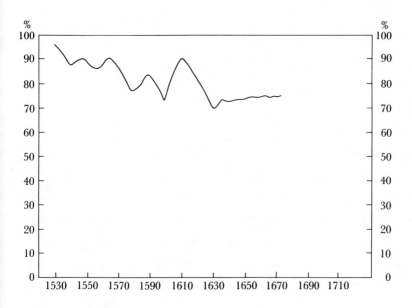

Graph 7.12   Illiteracy of husbandmen, diocese of Exeter, by year of education, 1530–1680

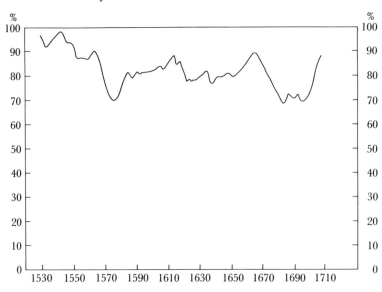

Graph 7.13   Illiteracy of husbandmen, diocese of Norwich, by year of education, 1530—1710

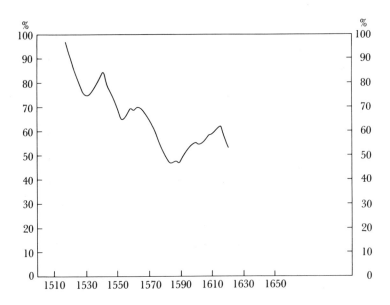

Graph 7.14   Illiteracy of tradesmen, diocese of Durham, by year of education, 1510—1620

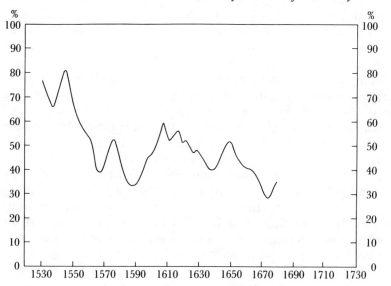

Graph 7.15   Illiteracy of tradesmen, diocese of Exeter, by year of education, 1530—1680

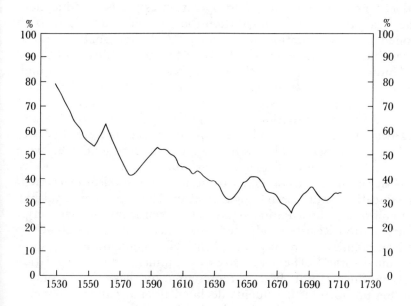

Graph 7.16   Illiteracy of tradesmen, diocese of Norwich, by year of education, 1530—1710

entire educational situation, but they may be taken as a rough index of educational vitality. They allow us to interpret the phases in the movement of illiteracy in terms of developments in the history of education. It could be objected that changes in the level of illiteracy among yeomen, husbandmen and tradesmen in three scattered regions owed little or nothing to changes in the provision of education, mostly of an elite nature, charted for the country as a whole. But even if no direct connection is established we can examine whether conditions favourable to the advance of education were synchronized with periods of diminishing illiteracy.

The totals of school foundations are derived from the work of the Schools Inquiry Commission of 1867–8 which, pursuing historical research in the service of modernization, carefully tabulated the founding of endowed schools from the twelfth to the nineteenth century. No other source so conveniently and accurately documents the creation of schools. Although short-lived private schools are omitted from the list and a few endowments may have been overlooked, a check against other sources proves the Commission's work to be reliable.[6] Nevertheless, caution is enjoined. Some of the foundations listed were in fact refoundations or reorganizations of schools that already existed. Others, though formally established and endowed at a given date, did not immediately come into operation as places of education. The legal creation of an institution did not necessarily lead to an immediate augmentation of learning. A better guide, but less accessible, is the number of practising teachers at different times.

Amounts of educational charity, expressed to the nearest pound, are taken from *Philanthropy in England, 1480–1660*, by W. K. Jordan.[7] The problems with these figures are well known, especially their disregard of inflation, which undercut the real value of later endowments, and the avoidance of probate records from the lesser courts, where many wills of yeomen and modest gentlemen were proved. Nevertheless, Jordan's totals, based on a study of twelve English counties, can be taken to indicate the level of investment in education. Comparable figures after 1660 are not available.

Cambridge matriculation figures are taken from the manuscript Matriculation Registers, adjusted where necessary by reference to college admission books and University graduations to show decennial totals.[8] The actual size of the undergraduate population at Cambridge is not directly represented by these figures since a varying proportion of students declined to matriculate. They may be taken as a guide to the changing intake.

The graphs indicate a quickening of literacy at the time of the Henrician reformation. In every diocese there was improvement

Table 7.7 Indices of educational progress, 1500–1700

Decade	School foundations	Gifts to schools (£)	Gifts to all education (£)	Cambridge matriculations
1500–9	6	4,230	30,174	
1510–19	9	10,062	27,896	
1520–9	13	9,527	46,288	
1530–9	8	7,380	12,235	
1540–9	39	8,227	17,727	1,584
1550–9	47	21,173	30,593	1,624
1560–9	42	10,377	27,296	2,748
1570–9	30	22,647	36,344	3,438
1580–9	20	19,172	44,863	3,443
1590–9	24	20,540	31,444	2,410
1600–9	41	30,315	60,791	2,699
1610–19	41	97,774	133,093	3,879
1620–9	26	63,119	116,239	4,208
1630–9	32	29,392	73,471	3,726
1640–9	15	33,345	53,549	2,623
1650–9	42	55,388	75,750	2,543
1660–9	34			3,035
1670–9	36			2,902
1680–9	28			2,260
1690–9	26			1,905

among tradesmen who were of school age in the late 1520s and 1530s, and there was also growing literacy among the yeomen of this period. Husbandmen showed a flicker of movement, but their participation in educational expansion was no more than marginal. The 1530s also saw great strides in the reduction of illiteracy among the Durham gentry. All the evidence of literacy suggests that elementary education was flourishing in England in the decade after the break with Rome. The revolution of the 1530s, the royal *coup* over the church and the dissolution of the monasteries had no immediate adverse effect on children learning to write. But in the next school generation the growth of literacy was arrested. The reign of Edward VI, famed for its grammar-school foundations, saw setbacks to literacy which continued through the reign of Mary. Progress among tradesmen was halted or slowed, husbandmen stayed much as they were, while among yeomen there was a distinct literacy recession. There was even a hesitation in the progress of the Durham gentry at this time. One cohort of yeomen in the diocese of Norwich, educated about 1548–58, was more illiterate than the previous generation, while there appears to have been a collapse of elementary education for this group in the diocese of Exeter.

Given our limited knowledge of pre-Elizabethan educational conditions, the explanation of these movements must be tentative. Commonweal reformers were agitating on behalf of educational expansion but they are not known to have been particularly successful in creating more schools.[9] The rhetoric of educational reform was not necessarily matched by its performance. Indeed, the record of endowing and founding of schools in the 1530s is not at all distinguished compared to subsequent achievements.

The decade before the reformation saw a peak in the cash value of educational charity, but much of this was composed of gifts to the universities. The 1530s saw a slump both in gifts to schools and in over-all educational philanthropy. A reduced rate of giving continued into the 1540s, but educational charity was again bountiful in the 1550s. Almost three times the amount of money was given to schools in the 1550s as in the 1530s. Yet literacy was improving in the 1530s and deteriorating in the 1550s. Inflation eliminates some of the difference in the worth of the bequests, but an apparent paradox remains. The record of school foundations matches the record of philanthropy: nine schools were founded in the 1510s, thirteen in the 1520s, only eight in the 1530s, and then there was a rush of foundations, 39 in the 1540s and 47 in the 1550s. The charitable and institutional evidence points to an educational expansion in the late Henrician, Edwardian and

Marian periods, when the evidence of illiteracy points to a slump. How is this disparity to be reconciled?

A partial explanation may lie in the elite nature of the schools whose existence is best documented. Most of the foundations recorded by the Schools Inquiry Commission were grammar schools dedicated to the parsing and translating of Latin, while little of the charity that Jordan has documented was intended for elementary instruction. The lack of a clear correlation between endowments and the ability to write is therefore no surprise. Even if educational bequests did contribute to the reduction of illiteracy, a time lag would be expected between the date of an endowment and the time of its impact. It might then be argued that the bountiful educational charity of the 1520s was associated with improving literacy in the 1530s, while the Henrician and Edwardian school foundations of the 1540s and 1550s influenced the growth of literacy under Elizabeth in the 1560s and 1570s.

Unsettling political events rather than reduced support for education may explain the abrupt halt in the reduction of illiteracy at the beginning of Edward's reign. If the chantries really were responsible for a large measure of elementary instruction, as A. F. Leach believed, their dissolution in 1547 would have been temporarily disruptive of teaching to write.[10] Some chantries were made into grammar schools but the legal and organizational problems involved could take a decade or more to resolve. The same problems beset the reorganization of cathedral schools under Henry VIII. The reformation brought confusion. Whatever educational impulse was associated with it in the 1540s and early 1550s was not likely to bear fruit until the next generation. Social and political turmoils frustrated the acquisition of literacy. The troubles of 1549, especially Ket's rebellion in the heart of East Anglia and the rising in the south-west, may have further dislocated an educational system already weakened by the dissolutions and uncertainties. Some of the illiterate deponents of the 1548–58 school generation may not have learned to read and write because educational facilities went untended during their childhood. The setback to literacy, discovered through the depositions, exactly coincides with a decade of local rebellion and revolutions in religious policy, in which schoolmasters were as likely to be as distracted as anyone else.

A period of energetic educational advance, lasting almost to 1580, began with the accession of Elizabeth. Every group in every area, with the possible exception of the boys who were to be tradesmen in the diocese of Exeter, shared in this generation of progress. Even the husbandmen were swept along. The East Anglian husbandmen who were of school age in the first two decades of Elizabeth's reign improved from almost 90% to better than 70% unable to sign their depositions, before drifting back into illiteracy. Similar progress was experienced in the south-west and there are also signs of improving husbandman literacy at this time in the diocese of Durham. Tradesmen improved from more than 60% to less than 40% illiterate in the diocese of Norwich and from more than 70% to less than 50% in the diocese of Durham. Yeomen too made rapid progress in literacy in the early Elizabethan period. The illiteracy among East Anglian yeomen who were of school age in 1560 was close to 55%, but within a generation it was halved to a little over 25%. The experience of the yeomen in south-west England was one of continuing educational improvement at this time and there are faint indications of progress in the north-east, obscured by the problem of nomenclature. The first half of Elizabeth's reign saw substantial steps toward the elimination of illiteracy among the gentlemen of the Durham region.

Every indicator confirms the period from 1560 to 1580 as one of educational revolution. Confidence in education was high, and political, religious and humanist propaganda was running in favour of schooling. Marian exiles were concerned to create a learned protestant community. Ascham and his contemporary pedagogues were perfecting the education of the lay aristocracy and extending their curriculum beyond the most privileged elite. Much was expected of education and such a climate could not but be helpful to the expansion of basic literacy.[11]

Undergraduate admissions at the universities reached unprecedented numbers in the early part of Elizabeth's reign. Matriculations at Cambridge rose from 160 a year in the 1550s to more than 340 a year in the 1570s and 1580s. University graduates (and drop-outs, often met in the records as 'literati'), unable to find immediate employment in the church, became schoolmasters. Thirty-five per cent of the schoolmasters licensed in the diocese of London later in the sixteenth century were graduates and 31% were 'literati'. In the diocese of Norwich in the 1580s 30% of newly licensed teachers were graduates and 47% were 'literati'. The expansion of higher education helped to raise the quality and size of the school teaching force.[12]

There was a proliferation of grammar schools in this period of rising literacy. Edwardian foundations were overcoming their early organizational problems and receiving charters and other forms of endorsement from the Elizabethan regime. New schools were created, but not so many as in the 1550s. The Schools Inquiry

Commission found 42 foundations in the 1560s and 30 in the 1570s, whereas 47 schools dated their origins from the 1550s. Charitable giving to education was at a reduced level in the 1560s, although it reached new peaks in the 1570s. Jordan found bequests of £21,173 to schools in the 1550s, only £10,377 in the 1560s, and £22,647 in the 1570s. If we take inflation into consideration, as Jordan did not, the value of the early Elizabethan endowment is further reduced.

Although the figures for philanthropy and school foundations are out of phase with other indices of educational vitality, the bulk of the evidence, strengthened by the literacy figures, points to the first two decades of Elizabeth's reign as a period of unusual educational excitement and achievement. It may be no coincidence that Shakespeare and his talented literary contemporaries were of school age at this time and that part of his audience was uniquely well educated.

Most accounts of Tudor and Stuart education assume a more or less steady expansion from the accession of Elizabeth to the civil war. The evidence of illiteracy suggests that progress was far from steady. There is substantial evidence to characterize the period 1580–1610 as one of 'educational recession'. Every index of educational progress bears marks of this reversal. The educational boom of the 1560s came to a standstill around 1580 and developed into a serious recession by the end of the century.

Literacy was stagnating or deteriorating in the second half of the reign of Elizabeth. East Anglian husbandmen quickly relinquished the advanced position staked out by the school generation of the 1570s, retiring to the illiteracy doldrums for the next hundred years. Their contemporaries in the south-west suffered setbacks too and were to sink further into illiteracy later in the reign of James. The literacy of tradespeople also went into decline in the 1580s and 1590s after substantial earlier improvements. The recession was experienced in every diocese, with the illiteracy of tradesmen of this school generation worsening by up to thirty percentage points. Yeomen managed to sustain their mid Elizabethan level until the end of the sixteenth century, then they too went into decline at the beginning of James' reign.

All the evidence of literacy points to a shrinkage of elementary education in which the middling groups in society lost ground. It is distressing to find so much damage at a time when schoolmasters and others were enthusiastically publishing works on education. Perhaps their emphasis on pedagogy and the curriculum marks a shift in their clientele, a narrowing of the incidence of education along with a sharpening of its quality.[13] Evidence from educational records also points to a late Elizabethan setback which few historians have noted. Even the observation that admissions to Oxford and Cambridge slumped in the 1580s has not been allowed to overshadow the celebration of the 'educational revolution' of 1560 to 1640. University admissions were falling in the last part of Elizabeth's reign. Although new colleges were founded and building works were undertaken, the undergraduate population was drastically reduced. One-third fewer students matriculated at Cambridge in the 1590s than in the 1580s and matriculations in the 1600s were still below the level of the 1570s.[14] Fewer boys were prepared for university entrance, while the pool of potential schoolmasters with university experience was also diminished. The extent to which religious restrictions or financial problems kept students away is a subject which demands further attention. By the end of the sixteenth century a university education was less desirable, or less possible, than in the previous generation.

Charitable giving to education was also depressed at the end of Elizabeth's reign, while soaring inflation undercut the real value of endowments. The 1590s, a decade of economic crisis, saw the smallest sum philanthropically bestowed on education in thirty years. Fewer new schools came into existence. Only 20 schools were founded in the 1580s and 24 in the 1590s, the smallest decadal totals since the Reformation. In many ways the end of the Elizabethan period was a miserable time to be living in England. Problems of rising prices and unemployment were compounded by bad weather, harvest failures and diseases, and aggravated by the costs of war and the discharge of veterans at its end. The turn of the century saw real wages at their lowest point in the entire Tudor and Stuart period. Perhaps the discretionary income which might formerly have been devoted to education was now being used primarily for survival. All indicators of educational progress point to a serious recession. In so far as it can be glimpsed, the personnel of education also suffered. Country schoolmasters had been highly visible in the ecclesiastical visitation and licensing records of the Diocese of Norwich before 1590, but they had virtually disappeared by 1610. As many as 200 active schoolmasters can be identified in Norfolk and Suffolk in the 1580s, but this dropped to 170 in the 1590s, 92 in the 1600s and even fewer in the 1610s.[15] Although the correspondences are imperfectly synchronized there is substantial evidence to associate the decline in literacy with a national and regional collapse of educational provision.

The recovery began during James' reign. Tradesmen and craftsmen were the first to show progress, improving their literacy throughout the early Stuart period and regaining their mid Elizabethan peak by the eve of the civil war. Yeomen had been stagnating at an uncharacteristically high level of illiteracy for much of the Jacobean period, but in the early part of Charles' reign they improved in both the diocese of Exeter and the diocese of Norwich. The period of the rise of Laud may not have been happy for puritan activists but it saw, more than most times, the successful education in literacy of large numbers of children. East Anglian husbandmen who were of school age in the 1620s were more likely to learn to write than most other husbandman cohorts, while their contemporaries in the diocese of Exeter improved substantially from approximately 90% to 70% illiterate within the space of a generation.

The early Stuart recovery of literacy reflects a second stage in the interrupted educational revolution. All indices confirm this revival. The crisis that had removed country schoolmasters from the diocesan records, whatever its cause, was over by the 1620s. Most of the East Anglian communities which had had schoolmasters at the turn of the century were again being served in the 1620s and 1630s, but freelance teachers were still less widespread than in the 1580s.[16] Students were again populating the universities in large numbers, peaking at Cambridge in the 1620s and Oxford in the 1630s. Between 1610 and 1640 some 400 students a year were matriculating at Cambridge, more than at any other time in the Tudor or Stuart period. Educational philanthropy also reached a peak during James' reign. Record sums were given to schools, £97,774 in the 1610s, £63,119 in the 1620s, trailing off to £29,392 in the 1630s. Much of this money was directed to the endowment of new schools. The Schools Inquiry Commission traced 41 foundations in the 1600s and another 41 in the 1610s. Totals for the 1620s and 1630s, when 26 and 34 schools were founded, reflect the reduced giving of those decades. The greatest investment in education was made in the early part of the seventeenth century, as if to compensate for the weakened educational provision of the 1580s and 1590s. This lavish endowment of educational facilities may be associated with the pronounced improvement in illiteracy levels in the 1630s, especially if there was a spillover from grammar schooling to the teaching of petties.

The revival was abruptly terminated by the onset of civil war. The illiterate deponents who were of school age in the 1640s, even more than their ancestors under Edward and Mary, may be regarded as victims of political events which seriously disrupted educational provision. A sharp reversal set back the literacy of tradesmen and craftsmen by ten percentage points or more before the slide was arrested in the 1650s. East Anglian yeomen suffered a serious dislocation in the 1640s while educational progress was arrested among their counterparts in the south-west. All the evidence from the depositions points to a catastrophic collapse of elementary education in the period of the civil war and its aftermath. Other indices of educational provision support this assessment.

Some schoolmasters left their posts while others were ejected, leaving many of the elementary schools unmanned. At Grimstone in Norfolk, for example, the inhabitants complained that 'through these distracted times . . . the school house is fallen into decay, the master gone, and error and malignancy like to flow in'.[17] University admissions plummeted as Oxford became the royalist headquarters and Cambridge a parliamentary garrison and prison. Only 45 students matriculated at Cambridge in 1643 compared to 315 in 1640 and 450 in 1639. Jordan found more money given to schools in the 1640s than in the previous decade, but educational charity as a whole was depressed. Only 15 schools were founded in the 1640s, compared to 32 in the 1630s. The provision of education was necessarily subordinated to the more pressing military and political concerns, and illiteracy expanded as a result.

However well-intentioned the revolutionaries may have been about extending popular education, they were not able to attend to it until the relative stability of the 1650s. There is no dearth of evidence in the writings of men like Samuel Hartlib and Comenius that great plans were afoot for transforming educational provision, but there is also no evidence that any of them came to fruition.[18] The proponents of mass literacy were never more vocal than in the revolutionary era, and never less effectual.

The restoration of literacy was in hand before the restoration of the king. 1656 brought some relief to the education-starved inhabitants of Grimstone when the Council voted £30 to support a schoolmaster there. Forty-two new schools came into existence in the 1650s, as many as at the height of the 'educational revolution', and there was a moderate expansion of educational charity as the Commonwealth planned to illuminate the 'dark corners of the land'.[19] The graphs show a renewed attack on illiteracy from a little before 1660 to around 1680. Tradesmen and yeomen everywhere made solid progress in the Restoration era and even husbandmen began to emerge from illiteracy in the late 1660s.

University admissions were again buoyant in the 1660s, although matriculations did not reach their pre-war level. Cambridge matriculations in the 1660s were the highest since the 1630s, and higher than in any subsequent decade before the nineteenth century. If there was an educational boom under Charles II it was of modest proportions. Information about the quantity and direction of charity after 1660 is not readily available and there are no figures to compare with those assembled by Jordan. Schools were founded at a substantial if unspectacular rate, 34 in the 1660s and 36 in the 1670s. Country schoolmasters appear infrequently in the ecclesiastical records of the later seventeenth century, but that may reflect evasion of control in the new environment of nonconformity as much as a shortage of teachers. We may conclude that the business of education went on in a routine fashion in the 1660s and 1670s, sufficient to sustain the growth of literacy but without the energy of earlier decades. Leaders of opinion in the second half of the seventeenth century were no longer enthusiastic about education and some, such as Edward Chamberlayne, blamed the schools and universities for 'our late unhappy troubles'.[20]

We have only the evidence from the diocese of Norwich to illuminate the acquisition of literacy in the later seventeenth century, but it looks as if elementary instruction was faltering once again. Tradesmen experienced a setback in the 1690s while the yeomen of school age in the 1680s and 1690s were somewhat more illiterate than their predecessors of the 1670s. Husbandmen performed quite well in the late seventeenth century but slid back into higher illiteracy at the beginning of the eighteenth. This halt to the growth of literacy was associated with a general *malaise* affecting educational provision.

Progressively fewer endowed schools were founded in the late seventeenth and early eighteenth centuries: 36 in the 1670s, 28 in the 1680s, 26 in the 1690s and 24 in the 1700s. University enrolments continued to shrink; fewer students matriculated at Cambridge in the 1690s than at any time since the mid sixteenth century. The rural teaching force in East Anglia, which relied on the universities for much of its manpower, was in steady decline; 195 men had subscribed as schoolmasters in the diocese of Norwich in the 1660s, 94 in the 1670s, 81 in the 1680s and only 37 in the 1690s.[21] Nonconformist reluctance to subscribe may explain part of this shrinkage, but many village schools ceased to function. The educational climate at the end of the seventeenth century was less conducive to the spread of literacy than it had been in some earlier phases.

Faced with a situation of darkening illiteracy, which some commentators associated with idleness and vice, an attempt was made at the turn of the century to reinvigorate popular education.

Charity schools were primarily intended to socialize the poor, to produce 'honest and industrious servants', but they also spread literacy.[22] The slight improvement in the literacy of tradesmen of the 1695–1704 school generation and a similar brief movement among yeomen might be attributable to the efforts of the charity schoolers, but the improvement was not sustained.

The depositions became less informative as the influence of the ecclesiastical courts diminished in the eighteenth century, so we cannot be sure whether elementary education was booming, holding steady or shrinking at the end of the Stuart period. The few deponents of the 1720s who were of school age at the death of queen Anne were generally less literate than their immediate predecessors, indicating another period of decline. We might be able to trace trends of illiteracy among school generations of the early eighteenth century by back-dating from the marriage records of the 1750s, but this is an exercise which has yet to be attempted.

Many of the shifts in educational provision, illuminated by this review of the progress of literacy, have received little attention from other historians. Some of them may prove to be chimerical, statistical apparitions rather than solid social phenomena, but the over-all outline can be accepted. The evidence of the depositions, whether examined by decade of observation or processed to show school generations, shows the movement of illiteracy to have been much more volatile than was formerly suspected. Phases of improvement, stagnation and decline cannot always be explained by reference to indices of educational activity, but their discovery provokes many questions. We particularly need to know how widespread was elementary instruction, how the availability of schooling varied from time to time as well as place to place, and the degree to which education was sensitive to changes in politics or the economy.

It is also worth considering again the relationship between educational needs perceived by working people and their children, the local provision of schooling which was a response to those needs and the pressures from ideological promoters to inculcate literacy for other than utilitarian purposes. The push and pull which affected the transmission of literacy and the ways in which different sectors of society responded to influences which were sometimes contradictory will be discussed in the following chapter. Chapter 8 will also set the English experience with literacy in an international context to show the ways in which it might have been unique.

8

Literacy and society in England and beyond

The development of English literacy from the reign of Elizabeth to early in the eighteenth century may be better appreciated by seeing it in a broader chronological and geographical setting. By sketching the history of literacy back towards the fifteenth century and by tracing it forward almost to the present the movements and conditions discussed in this book can be seen as part of a continuous evolution. Similarly, by collecting information about the state of literacy in other parts of the pre-industrial world the distinctiveness of the English experience can be better evaluated. One purpose of this chapter, then, will be to continue and enlarge the discussion of the dynamics of literacy within a comparative international framework. Since historical work on literacy is relatively new, still getting started or gathering pace, the remarks which follow will be partly speculative and heavily dependent on the recent findings of others.

A second purpose of this chapter will be to resume the discussion of the value and function of literacy, initiated in chapter 1. The period from the fifteenth to the nineteenth century saw, in most parts of the western world, a general transition from restricted to mass literacy. Skills which were once the preserve of a small clerical and specialist elite became laicized, generalized and widely available. But the processes which governed this important change were neither consistent nor universal. Different European societies were subject to different pressures and constraints and emerged into literacy unsynchronized and with varying amounts of enthusiasm. Everywhere there was a multitude of factors assisting and accelerating the growth of literacy or blocking and restricting its expansion. If the utility and significance of literacy varied with social and economic position, as the Elizabethan and Stuart evidence most powerfully demonstrates, the circumstances in which literacy flourished may also have varied with time and place. The English evidence raises a host of questions about the literacy transition, further complicated by the data from abroad. How, why, and under what conditions did literacy expand? Why was that expansion at times so sluggish and so socially selective? Was the literacy attained by the masses the literacy that was wished for them by their superiors? What uses did people make of their literacy, and what did this portend?

By the end of the Stuart period the English had achieved a level of literacy unknown in the past and unmatched elsewhere in early modern Europe. By the time of the accession of George I it is likely that the inability to sign was confined to 55% of the men and 75% of the women. This compared to 70% illiteracy among men and 90% among women at the time of the civil war. Aggregate figures for the sixteenth century are not readily available, but a reasonable guess might place male illiteracy around 80% and female illiteracy close to 95% at the time of the accession of Elizabeth. A projection back to the reign of Henry VII would find perhaps 90% of Englishmen illiterate at the turn of the century, with illiteracy claiming as many as 99% of the women. In the fifteenth century and earlier writing skills were the preserve of a very small minority, although probably a somewhat greater proportion could read.

Most of these figures are estimates, based on a reading of depositions, declarations and such scraps of evidence as can be assembled.[1] They are embodied in Graph 8.1 which shows a schematic outline of illiteracy among men and women in England from 1500 to 1900. The short-term fluctuations which feature in statistical accounts of illiteracy have been removed in order to suggest the most general trend.

A remarkable body of evidence yields information about literacy after 1754. Lord Hardwicke's act of that year required all brides and grooms to sign or mark the marriage register. Only quakers, Jews and members of the royal family were exempt. Employing a carefully controlled sample of 274 parishes Schofield has reconstructed the dimensions of illiteracy in England from 1754 to 1844, with additional figures from the Registrar Generals' reports from 1839 to 1914.[2] A simplified version of Schofield's findings has been incorporated into Graph 8.1.

The evidence from marriage registers shows approximately 40% of the men and just over 60% of the women unable to sign in the middle of the eighteenth century. These figures imply a substantial improvement from the Stuart period but the change was neither sudden nor spectacular. Progress over the seventeenth century had been hesitant and irregular and there is no reason to believe that developments in the first half of the eighteenth century were very different. The general level of literacy in England at the accession of George III would have astonished the proponents of

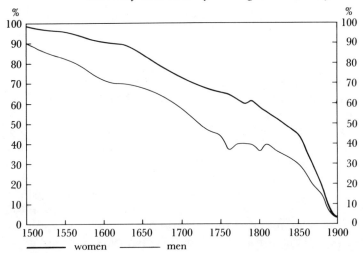

Graph 8.1   Estimated illiteracy of men and women in England, 1500—1900

popular literacy under the Tudors. There was a cumulative augmentation of skills but literacy remained highly stratified.

During the century which followed the civil war the diversifi-
cation of the economy and the growth of towns and trade brought
an increased proportion of the population into occupations or
social settings where literacy was important. Reading and writing
became increasingly useful to an expanding sector of the community. Not only was there the leavening effect of London
literacy, exercised through the cultural, commercial and demographic dominance of the capital, but also a surge of retail activity
and specialist manufacturing in urban centres across the nation
which confronted people with the need to handle letters. With
the expansion of printing in London and the provinces there was
certainly more to read, and with a budding taste for news and
increased political participation and partisanship there was, perhaps, a greater demand for literacy than ever before.

The second half of the eighteenth century, however, saw general
stagnation. Illiteracy among males remained close to 40% until
early in the nineteenth century, while females improved slowly
and almost imperceptibly from year to year. It is possible that this
slowing down in the growth of literacy was associated with social
disruptions of the industrial revolution, to be repaired by massive
public investment in education in the nineteenth century. Male
illiteracy
fell from just over 30% in 1850 to 1% in 1911, and the percentage of women

unable to sign fell from just over 45% in 1850 to 1% in 1913. The fastest rate of improvement was among those marrying after about 1885, or leaving school after about 1870.[3]

What was the geography of European literacy and how did the English compare with their neighbours? We can approach this question with a scatter of data from France, the Low Countries, Sweden and eastern Europe, and additional material about Scotland and England's colonies in North America. Information about other areas is likely to expand as historians engage with this subject. The problem is partly a matter of sources, partly a question of scholarly attack and publication of results.

The sources used here to reconstruct the profile and dimensions of illiteracy in England have no direct continental counterpart. Different legal, religious and bureaucratic traditions have produced different types of record and one cannot always find a source for the measurement of literacy which satisfies our strictest criteria for acceptance. The French and Dutch evidence is based on the ability of brides and bridegrooms to sign the marriage records; some of the evidence from Poland and Hungary comes from signatures on tax and business records; and the findings for North America are based on wills. Each of these sources has information about whether or not people could sign their names. The Swedish evidence is unique since it does not measure whether people could write, but instead records in the church examination books whether they could read.

The peculiar history of literacy in Sweden is exceptionally well documented. The Lutheran church, with full state support, set out to ensure that everyone could read the word of God. A national campaign for literacy which began early in the seventeenth century was energized by the Church Law of 1686 and continued by decree in 1723. Communion and marriage were withheld from those who could not pass a literacy test and there was intense social pressure within the household and community to attain the required standard of reading. Annual examinations were held and the clergy kept meticulous records of parishioners' reading scores. By the end of the seventeenth century 50% or more of the Swedish adult population could read, this figure rising to almost 100% by the middle of the eighteenth century.[4]

Vast numbers of Swedes were coaxed into reading in the all-embracing political and moral world of the Lutheran 'Hustavla'. Very few of them, however, knew how to write. Challenged with a pen and asked to sign their names, it is likely that most of them would have appeared to be illiterate. In southern Sweden at the beginning of the eighteenth century the ability to write was confined to roughly 10% of the population, and little improvement was found before the nineteenth century. The relatively undiversified economy of pre-industrial Sweden made few demands on writing, so the skill was mostly confined to tradesmen and administrators. The national church was able to achieve exactly the kind of literacy it wanted, reading for confessional and liturgical purposes, without much leakage of skills into unregulated areas. This was, perhaps, possibly only in a disciplined rural society with a small population, relatively untroubled by divergent religious opinions. The Swedish accomplishment of widespread reading skills but little knowledge of writing was unique in pre-industrial Europe.

Good information about the extent of signature literacy is available in France. The nineteenth-century educational administrator Maggiolo collected historical data on the abilities of brides and grooms to sign their marriage register in all parts of France, and this trove of material has been analysed and augmented by modern historians. Very little evidence, however, is available before the late seventeenth century. In the period 1686–90 more than 70% of the men and 90% of the women were unable to sign their names, but these figures mask a wide range of regional and social differences. North-east France, marked out by a line from St Malo to Geneva, was considerably more literate than the south and west, and this regional distinction persisted into the nineteenth century. Male illiteracy in the departments to the north and east of Paris was as low as 40%, while 80% or more were unable to sign in some departments of the Midi and the Pyrenees. Maps and graphs showing the progress and distribution of literacy in France are featured in the recent volume by Furet and Ozouf.[5]

Most of the French who were unable to sign were also unable to read. There was no such pressure in France as was applied in Sweden, and although the counter-reformation church was quite keen on education it conducted no persistent campaign to bring about mass literacy. Reading and writing in France, as in England, were closely tied to the demands of the environment. Women did not need full literacy and therefore rarely achieved it, while among the men there was a gradation from town to country and from notables through merchants, independent farmers, artisans and peasants. Some parts of France were as literate as anywhere in England, but over-all the English were more versed in writing. In the period 1786–90, when 40% of English men and 60% of their wives were unable to sign, the corresponding figures for France were 53% and 73%.[6]

Excellent evidence has emerged concerning the extent of

literacy in renaissance Poland. On the basis of a study of fiscal records from the Palatinate of Cracow, 1564–5, it is estimated that 88% of the male population in that area was illiterate. Another study of court records from the Cracow region, 1575–90, points to 83% illiteracy among males and 96% among females. These figures relate to the most developed part of Poland, where levels of illiteracy were not much worse than in Elizabethan England. As might be expected, illiteracy in Poland varied enormously with social class. Table 8.1 shows the structure of illiteracy among men and women in Little Poland in the late sixteenth century, a structure which is remarkably similar to that found in pre-industrial England.[7]

Seventeenth-century Poland was beset by wars and revolts and we are unable to trace the fortunes of literacy. A study of commercial transactions between 1717 and 1724 finds little progress and perhaps even decline from the period of king Stephen (1579–86). Of the urban population 44% was unable to sign, while illiteracy among the multi-ranked Polish aristocracy ranged from 28% to 92%.[8]

The multi-religious society of eastern Europe found Calvinists, Lutherans and other protestants alongside Catholics, Orthodox Christians and Jews. Whether these confessional differences were reflected in different levels of literacy is still a matter for investigation, but in Hungary in the eighteenth century it appears that the protestant communities were best provided with schools. Religion, however, was less important than occupation in setting the conditions for literacy. A study of the ability of village leaders in western Hungary to write their signatures on a government questionnaire in 1768 finds an average of around 15% able to sign (85% illiterate). A complete national survey would almost certainly have found illiteracy much higher. The local variation, however, was enormous, and not surprisingly the greatest ability to sign was found among those peasants farming for the market and engaged in trade.[9]

Much the same was true of Germany, although our knowledge of German literacy is handicapped by the patchwork of imperial, episcopal, civic, princely and electoral jurisdictions into which that country was divided. Protestant parts of Germany may have experienced the same pressures for literacy as Lutheran Sweden, with an evangelical church backed by the arm of the state. The diversity of German society, however, thwarted any concerted literacy campaign, while German catholics were just as likely to be literate if their economic or social environment required it of them. In Baltic Germany in the seventeenth and eighteenth

Table 8.1   *Structure of illiteracy in Little Poland, 1575–90*

Social group	% illiterate	
	Men	Married women
Seigneurs	0	0
Gentry	5	50
Minor aristocracy	25	85
Patricians	30	75
Bourgeoisie	60	88
Plebeians	92	100
Peasants	98	100

centuries it appears that the peasants were mostly illiterate regardless of their faith, while those who were engaged in navigation and trade had a fair knowledge of reading, writing and accounting. Education was well developed with a network of parish schools, but exactly who attended them and what impact they had on literacy remains to be discovered.[10]

Little is known about literacy in Italy and Spain before the nineteenth century. Without the directives of a protestant literacy campaign or the demands of a complex and quickening economy it is likely that most of Mediterranean Europe remained illiterate. Northern Italy was probably more literate than the south, but only in the major cities with cultural and commercial incentives and administrative needs would one expect to find much development of reading and writing. The artisans and tradesmen of Florence and Venice were probably more literate than the peasants of Tuscany and the Venetia, but quantitative evidence is lacking.[11]

Much better evidence is available in Holland. The Amsterdam marriage registers reveal just 43% of the bridegrooms and 68% of the brides unable to write their names in 1630, falling to 15% and 35% by the end of the eighteenth century. Dutch protestantism may be a factor in this achievement but the advanced literacy of the urban Netherlands also reflects its business activity and wealth. Figures for rural Holland are not available but figures for Belgium, not controlled for religion, show 39% of the men and 63% of the women illiterate towards the end of the eighteenth century.[12]

Only Scotland and New England among England's neighbours are believed to have surpassed her in literacy, and in both cases the superior achievement is usually attributed to the activities of protestantism. The evidence and the explanation, however, should be approached with caution.

Most of the evidence for literacy in Scotland is indirect, derived from the history of schooling and policy rather than the ability of people to sign, and some of the writings on Scottish education are tinged with historical nationalism. Calvinist Kirk discipline in post-reformation Scotland was supposed to be 'supplemented by a national scheme for education . . . that none may escape the teachers' net'. Government action in 1616, 1633, 1646 and 1696 promoted a network of parish schools 'considerably in advance of anything known in England or in most other European countries'.[13] Stone has suggested that 'it was perhaps in Presbyterian Scotland that Puritan zeal for a literate, moral, Bible-reading public found its fullest expression', while Lockridge, building on Stone, reports that 'a system of compulsory elementary education appears to have raised adult male literacy from 33% around 1675 to nearly 90% by 1800, a pace surpassing the rate of improvement in male literacy in New England'. These figures, implying illiteracy levels of 67%, then 10%, are purely conjectural but not necessarily wrong.[14]

Firm evidence about the extent of illiteracy in seventeenth- and eighteenth-century Scotland, which can be used to discover whether the Presbyterian educational system had the effect with which it has been credited, is only now being examined. The sources under review include subscriptions to the National Covenant of 1638 and the Solemn League and Covenant of 1643, Kirk Sessions records, port books, and depositions made before the justiciary courts and circuit courts. Quotable figures are not yet forthcoming but the trend of the evidence supports the view that literacy was improving.[15] Calvinism, however, was not the only cause. During its first century the reformed church in Scotland was unable to do much to counter the massive illiteracy of a backward rural society, while the improvements in literacy in the late seventeenth and eighteenth centuries were mostly confined to Edinburgh and the lowland boroughs. The geography of illiteracy in Scotland was strongly associated with Scottish economic development as well as with the incidence of Calvinism. Literacy in Scotland was also socially stratified, another sign that more than religious pressures were at work. Tradesmen and craftsmen, lowlanders and townsmen, were more commonly able to sign their names than people in agriculture and people from the north and west. Nineteenth-century Scotland was, we know, a more literate society than nineteenth-century England, but when and how this superiority came about is still a topic for research.

The most thorough survey of literacy in English North America is based on a study of wills. In England this source yields only a distorted profile of illiteracy, but in colonial America, according to Lockridge, 'the biases affecting signatures on wills were of moderate force and appear to cancel'.[16] This might seem to be more a matter of faith than of scientific judgement, but no alternative evidence is available. The results reveal an astonishing mastery of the written word. Rural Americans were the equals in literacy of the citizens of Amsterdam and of the best-educated sectors of pre-industrial England.

In New England around 1660 just 39% of the men and 69% of the women making wills were unable to write their names, a low proportion which was further reduced in the eighteenth century. Around 1710 31% of the men and 59% of the women could not sign, and around 1760 the figures were 16% and 54%. Low levels of illiteracy were also recorded in Virginia. Roughly half the men making wills in Virginia in the mid seventeenth century could not sign them, while in the eighteenth century illiteracy was confined to one-third.

Lockridge finds the origins of New England's precocious literacy in protestantism. Intense protestantism supplied the drive to found schools and maintain literacy for moral and religious purposes while puritan migration selected the most literate colonists from England. Religious differences above all explain the different history of literacy in Massachusetts and Virginia. More mundane factors, to do with social structure, occupation and wealth, are not discounted but are assigned a secondary role. In New England, as in Sweden and Scotland, mass literacy was achieved at the behest of, and through the agency of, an evangelical church hand in glove with the authority of the state.[17]

This explanation seems not to take full account of the geographic, social, sexual, economic and occupational stratification of illiteracy which is indicated in the New England wills.[18] Reading and writing were used and enjoyed in different ways in different social settings, and the ideological impulses of the puritan leadership could not by themselves achieve near-universal literacy. The ability to read may well have been vital on Sunday, but in a world of litigation and land transfers, with a high degree of involvement in local government and trade, the components of literacy could be valuable every day of the week. It was, perhaps, the combination of religion and utility, rather than protestantism alone, which singled out New England as the most literate society of all in the pre-industrial world.

Migration theorists have made us familiar with the 'push' and 'pull' factors which prompted people into moving long distances. The pressures in the old homeland (the 'push') are weighed against the attractions of the new (the 'pull'), and both sides of the equation are considered when probing people's motives. Some of the vocabulary of this theory has found its way into discussion of literacy.[19] Borrowing the terms, the ideological or external factors promoting literacy can be characterized as 'push', while utilitarian or internal factors might be classified as 'pull'. The distinction is useful if it helps us to understand the range of phenomena involved in the transition to literacy in different parts of the early modern world. Other terms might be preferred. Given adequate data and confident theory we might attempt to anatomize the various elements in the social demand for literacy, spiritual and secular, public and private, material and non-material, imposed from above and drawn from below. We could resort to diagrams and boxes showing arrows and firm and broken lines to suggest the pattern of influences, or we might make analogies with engines pulling trains over difficult terrain. Such aids and images may be dispensed with so long as we are prepared to admit, with the 'push and pull' model, a multitude of economic and ideological factors which bore with varying effect on the progress of literacy. Every combination of pressures is theoretically possible and most can be found in some form in European history.

The 'push' could appear as an official or unofficial campaign for literacy — that is, an ideologically inspired pressure from above which had the capacity to foist on people a skill or pattern of behaviour which they might not otherwise have sought. Its components could include government action by legislation or sponsorship of programmes, specifically aimed at improving literacy, the efforts and exhortations of educators, and the words and deeds of religious activists. It is exemplified by the Swedish state–Lutheran literacy campaign, by the educational policy of the Scottish Kirk, by the puritan educational programme in New England, and by the efforts of divines and philanthropists to improve basic education in England.

The 'pull' factors, on the other side of the equation, locate the origins of expanding literacy in the social and economic environment. Literacy, for some people, had a practical, mundane utility and they sought it for themselves and their children because the particular skills of reading and writing were useful in their everyday lives. They did not need to be inspired or cajoled towards literacy, but, rather, they discovered its value for themselves. Its value in the market place or in private affairs could make literacy attractive regardless of the higher purposes attached to it by the ideologues. We can imagine a grass-roots spreading of functional literacy, with people appropriating whatever skills they found useful to meet their needs, largely independent of the discussion of reading and writing which was taking place among the elite.

In different settings the economic or utilitarian 'pull' into literacy could be strong or weak, mild or irresistible, and it could enhance or undermine the ideological 'push'. Solid and sustained progress towards literacy could be expected where 'push' and 'pull' were equally strong. Where propaganda for literacy was reinforced by educational provision and where this pressure concided with a popular recognition of the day-to-day value of being able to read and write, there was every promise of rapid improvement. New England seems to have experienced this, but such happy conjunctions were unusual in early modern Europe and other combinations of circumstance are easier to imagine.

Where people needed little literacy to manage their affairs it might be difficult to persuade them to embrace a skill which was, for all practical purposes, superfluous. Strong pressure for literacy might make little headway against the indifference of a population not convinced of its immediate utility. The leaders of society, its preachers and teachers, might encourage the expansion of popular literacy for good and godly ends, but their efforts might be wasted if the economic and cultural demand for literacy was slight. Where 'push' was strong and 'pull' was weak the success of any literacy campaign would depend on the muscle behind the rhetoric. The achievement of widespread literacy in a relatively undiversified economy would depend on such factors as the power of the state in support of the idea, the constancy of the leaders in pursuit of their aims and the degree to which their religious or ideological concerns were shared by the people at large.

Very different conditions would prevail where 'push' was weak and 'pull' was strong. Where the ideological message was weak or wavering, ambivalent in its support for literacy or even hostile to popular education, reading and writing could still expand if the demand for those skills was strong. In a society with a complex and developing economy and a rich and variegated culture there might well develop a strong taste for literacy which owed nothing to the opinions of the elite. The ability to read and write might be regarded as an essential skill in some occupations and as a desirable accomplishment in others. The demand for literacy and the use made of it might vary from group to group, leaving pockets of illiteracy among people who did not need reading and writing, and all gradations of literacy and illiteracy among those who did. Such a selective penetration of literacy which was more a product of 'pull' than of 'push' would manifest itself in a hierarchy of attainments closely associated with social rank and occupation.

Finally, we can imagine a situation where both 'push' and 'pull' were weak and underdeveloped. Where ordinary people were content to remain illiterate and where their leaders felt no compulsion to disturb them, where the demands of the economy and society could be satisfied without much use of reading and writing, and where what literacy there was was mostly the preserve of professional specialists, any movement towards mass literacy would wait for radical changes. This seems to have been the case in England during the middle ages and in southern Europe until the nineteenth century.

In England the 'push' towards literacy was sustained by the advocacy of religious and secular writers who urged the importance of reading and writing. Divines like Richard Baxter proclaimed the spiritual benefits of literacy, the gain in knowledge of God's word and the helps to a godly life which could only be obtained through reading. Schoolmasters like David Brown pressed literacy for moral and civic purposes, and hinted that the acquisition of skills might lead to personal profit. There was no shortage of writers to extol the importance of literacy, books and the advantages of education. A selection from these writings was quoted in Chapter 1.

Given such a barrage of rhetoric one might suppose that English men and women were swept on a current of enthusiasm towards widespread literacy. In fact the quantitative evidence, presented in chapters 4 to 7 points to a selective penetration of literacy and suggests that much of the propaganda was ineffective. The evidence strongly suggests that the 'push' towards literacy in Tudor and Stuart England was in fact quite weak, and that the progress which undoubtedly did occur owed more to 'pull' factors than to anything else.

The promotion of literacy was largely ineffective because it failed to secure the firm backing of the state, and found no other means to turn its arguments into practice. The pressure lacked muscle; the clamour lacked force. The stream of rhetoric in favour of reading and writing was swamped in the welter of pluralistic opinions which surged and frothed in renaissance England, and the government, which might have been persuaded to sponsor a programme for mass literacy, was by no means convinced that popular education would serve its interests.

There was, of course, a government interest in popular education from at least as early as the reformation. Thomas Cromwell's injunctions of 1536 required the clergy to oversee the familial education of all children but, like many fine ideas of that time, it came to nothing. The proposal was more a reflection of common-weal idealism than a solid commitment of government resources.[20] Successive regimes lent their names to educational projects provided this cost them nothing. Trained and attended by renaissance humanists, the successors of Henry VIII approved of education in general and were happy to facilitate the attempts of local phil-anthropists to advance public schooling. Most of the grammar schools which bore the name of King Edward or Queen Elizabeth were paid for by someone else or were refoundations of older institutions damaged by the reformation. In so far as there was any Elizabethan policy towards education it was to ensure that those who received it stayed conformable in religion and were taught as far as possible by licensed schoolmasters. There was certainly no thought of extending literacy to the masses, which would surely have been asking for trouble.

The sage Francis Bacon, who was by no means an enemy to the advancement of learning, counselled James I against Thomas Sutton's plans for Charterhouses in 1611, explaining the danger of educational 'excess'. 'Many persons will be bred unfit for other vocations and unprofitable for that in which they are brought up, which fills the realm full of indigent, idle and wanton people which are but *materia rerum novarum*.' People should be allotted only as much education as was appropriate to their social role. That this was not a reactionary view, but part of the educational mainstream, is shown by similar remarks in the writings of such well-credentialled educational reformers as John Brinsley, Comenius, John Dury and Samuel Hartlib. They wished elementary literacy for all, but 'learning' was to be parcelled out in such a way as to protect the social order.[21]

The leadership of society in the sixteenth and seventeenth centuries was far from single-minded in pursuit of popular literacy, and was never prepared to supply the effort, money or legislation which would have been necessary to achieve it. Many might agree with Baxter and the rest about the importance of literacy, but their agreement rarely led to action. Not even during the 1650s, when the promoters of literacy had the ear of the revolutionary regime, was there any substantial progress towards achieving their goals. Indeed, the statistical evidence for the progress of literacy associates a setback with that time, suggesting that elementary education was more disrupted than advanced by the revolution.

No amount of enthusiasm could compensate for the indifference to formal schooling found in many sectors of the community. Piecemeal private philanthropy could not produce enlightenment and only a mass recognition of the advantages of literacy or a concerted, legislated, funded educational effort such as occurred in the nineteenth century could complete the transition. The 'push' towards literacy in early modern England was more strident than effective, and so much of its argument was lost to the wind. This is clearly demonstrated by the occupational ranking and clustering of illiteracy, examined in Chapter 6. The evidence indicates that the penetration of literacy in England was largely a response to need, need felt selectively in different trades and circumstances, rather than a response to ideological pressures which might transcend narrow occupational requirements. The hierarchical structure of illiteracy strongly suggests that in England a weak and indecisive 'push' was powerfully overcome by a 'pull' that was strictly stratified in its incidence and effect. The distribution of literacy varied with activity, status and prosperity, and seemed to follow the functional requirements of different trades. It is doubtful whether so steep a gradient and such regularity of association would have prevailed, over so wide an area and time, if evangelical or ideological promotion was responsible for the spread of basic literacy. Only if the 'push' was socially selective, betraying its own ideological foundations, could a comparable pattern emerge to mask or overlay the effects of the differential economic 'pull'. Labourers and shopkeepers, women and men, were just as much God's people and had as much to gain from reading God's word, but their different social positions conditioned them to different degrees of literacy. Examination of the dynamics of literacy shows how slender and short-lived efforts to promote popular education fared against the long-term tensions of economic 'pull'.

The quantitative evidence, of course, is concerned with gross characteristics, with measures of central tendency. By concentrating on the summary characteristics of social groups and measuring the percentage in each category unable to sign, this account deflects attention from the extraordinary individuals whose literacy was in advance of their peers'. Even among labourers and shepherds there were men who could both read and write, although their literacy was not keyed at all to their trade, while literate women, though a minority, have attracted considerable attention. Religious enthusiasm undoubtedly was a motivating factor, as biographical and autobiographical accounts give testimony, and some people had parents and friends who made literacy available to them as a spiritual and cultural asset. Some people were educated beyond their station, in which case they chafed with frustration, found other employment or channelled their literacy away from their work into religion, politics or popular entertainment. I would not argue that a person's achievement of literacy was rigidly determined by his socio-economic milieu, but rather that the circumstances in which he was reared and found work set the conditions, shaped the influences and supplied the motivations which were, for the most part, stronger than the urgings and encouragements of the educated elite.

Finally, we must ask what good literacy did for the people who possessed it. It is easy to be swayed by the rhetoric of moralists and reformers and agree that literacy was a liberating force which taught man his duty to God and improved his understanding of fellow man. Literacy is associated with independence, political alertness, superior information, rationality, modernity and a host of equally desirable accomplishments. We might pause, however, to consider whether the expansion of literacy brought about all that was promised.

First, it should be stressed that people were capable of rational action, of acquiring and digesting information, and of making well-founded political and religious decisions without being able to read or write. Illiteracy was not necessarily a bar to economic advancement nor did it stand in the way of common sense. Second, we should not assume that people were wiser or more in control of their environment just because they had become literate. The skill could be squandered, used to rot the mind as well as inform it (*pace* Phillip Stubbes), and might find no exercise beyond scanning an almanac or signing a receipt. Popular literacy expanded the audience for politics but it did not inexorably bring about an explosion in political participation. We must distinguish the liberating potential of popular literacy from its more mundane reality. In normal circumstances it is likely that most people were politically quiescent, just as they are today. In moments of crisis, however, when a plot was uncovered or when revolt or change was in the air, controversialists might rush to print and the audience for pamphlets and news sheets might expand. An emergency could have a galvanizing effect and the literate townsman or countryman could come into his own. Literacy unlocked a variety of doors, but it did not necessarily secure admission.

Appendix: Illiteracy in 414 English parishes, 1641–4

Note: This appendix expands the information presented in Table 4.1. It is based on Protestation returns in H.L.R.O. and Protestations, Vows and Covenants surviving in local records, signified by an asterisk (*). Where more than one declaration survives, as in some Essex parishes, that with the greatest number of subscribers has been included. The order of parishes within subdivisions of counties follows the arrangement of the original returns.

County	Parish	No. of subscribers	% mark
Berkshire	Appleton	75	63
	Ashampstead	58	78
	Beenham	56	66
	Besselsleigh	20	65
	Milton	37	65
	Radley	80	93
	Little Shefford	16	81
	Steventon	111	68
	Streatley	84	79
	Sunningwell	59	78
	Little Wittenham	37	57
	Long Wittenham	92	79
	(Total, 12 parishes	725	74)
Buckinghamshire	Foxcott	16	75
	Lillingston Dayrell	58	69
	Thornborough	82	71
	(Total, 3 parishes	156	71)
Cheshire	Chester, Holy Trinity	133	41
	Chester, St Martin	95	82
	Chester, St Mary on the Hill	335	59
	Chester, St Michael	123	30
	Chester, St Olave	50	34
	(Total, 5 parishes	736	52)
Cornwall, East Hundred	Callington	89	72
	Calstock	178	69
	Landrake	226	57
	Linkinhorn	238	63

County	Parish	No. of subscribers	% mark
Cornwall,	St Anthony	215	65
East Hundred	St Dominic	137	67
continued	St Germains	472	72
	St John's	67	78
	Sheviock	157	60
	South-hill	138	66
	Tremayne	37	81
	Tresmeer	33	67
Cornwall,	Budock	294	59
Kerrier Hundred	Constantine	268	81
	Germoe	90	89
	Grade	54	68
	Gunwalloe	64	92
	Helston	241	54
	Landewednack	57	79
	Mabe	46	65
	Manaccan	111	70
	Mawnan	61	72
	Mullion	96	73
	Mylor	132	74
	Penryn	375	59
	Perran Arworthal	55	71
	Ruan Major	31	68
	Ruan Minor	30	90
	St Anthony in Meneage	65	69
	St Martin in Meneage	83	69
	St Stithians	114	84
	Wendron	270	83
Cornwall,	Camborne	175	75
Penwith Hundred	Crowan	178	77
	Gulval	156	79
	Gwithian	69	83
	Illogan	216	83
	Lelant	174	72
	Levan	86	79
	Madron	183	76
	Marazion	150	71
	Morvah	36	81
	Paul	275	87
	Penzance	243	69
	Phillack	73	88
	Redruth	152	86
	St Hilary	101	80
	St Ives	350	65
	St Just	260	90
	Sancreed	121	69
	Towednack	52	86
	Zennor	83	79

County	Parish	No. of subscribers	% mark
Cornwall, Lesnewth Hundred	Advent	34	85
	Altarnun	184	64
	Forrabury	33	85
	Lanteglos	137	69
	Lesnewth	38	47
	Michaelstow	54	63
	Minster	88	58
	Otterham	40	62
	St Clether	30	80
	St Gennys	139	73
	St Juliot	71	66
	Tintagell	161	71
	Trenegloss	52	63
	Trevalga	49	61
	Warbstow	82	77
Cornwall, Powder Hundred	Cornelly	41	63
	Creed	74	85
	Gerrans	168	70
	Gorran	315	78
	Grampound	93	63
	Lamorran	39	77
	Lanlivery	181	76
	Lostwithiel	130	64
	Luxulion	165	79
	Merther	57	91
	Mevagissey	190	69
	Philleigh	84	69
	Ruan Lanihorne	88	67
	St Allen	105	66
	St Anthony	51	63
	St Blazey	115	76
	St Clements	142	71
	St Dennis	67	79
	St Erme	100	71
	St Ewe	199	79
	St Feock	112	78
	St Mewan	98	86
	St Michael Carthayes	46	76
	St Michael Penkevil	45	62
	St Stephens	249	80
	Tywardreth	212	81
	Veryan	233	85
Cornwall, Stratton Hundred	Boyton	94	75
	Bridgerule	31	81
	Launcells	196	61
	Marham Church	112	69
	Moorwinstow	200	76

County	Parish	No. of subscribers	% mark
Cornwall,	North Tamerton	109	68
Stratton Hundred	Poughill	118	60
continued	Stratton	318	64
	Week St Mary	138	62
	Whitstone	98	75
Cornwall,	Blisland	139	81
Trigg Hundred	Breward	143	71
	Helland	72	57
	Minver	260	71
	St Endellion	188	69
	St Teath	162	72
	St Tudy	154	78
Cornwall,	Cardinham	128	77
West Hundred	East Looe	317	65
	Liskeard	516	64
	St Keyne	45	91
	St Pinnock	82	76
	(Total, 116 parishes	15,868	72)
Derbyshire	Kedleston*	36	61
	Pentrich*	181	77
	South Wingfield*	99	75
	(Total, 3 parishes	316	74)
Devon,	Bampton	356	65
Bampton Hundred	Hockworthy	60	87
	Holcombe Regis	202	69
	Morebath	103	71
Devon,	Church Stanton	77	92
Hemyock Hundred			
Devon,	Calverleigh	43	58
Tiverton Hundred	Loxbear	37	62
Devon,	Shobrook	167	68
Budleigh West	Upton Helions	40	68
Hundred			
Devon,	Bishop's Morehard	253	83
Crediton Hundred			
Devon,	Ashprington	141	78
Coleridge Hundred	Blackawton	283	77
	Cornworthy	155	74
	Halwell	102	57
	Harberton	312	67
	Stoke Fleming	201	61

County	Parish	No. of subscribers	% mark
Devon,	Brent, South	268	72
Stanborough Hundred	Diptford	160	66
	Holne	89	74
	Huish, North	106	65
	Morleigh	46	74
Devon,	Ashton	79	59
Exminster Hundred	Shillingford St George	32	66
Devon,	Alverdiscott	78	69
Fremington Hundred	Fremington	291	69
Devon,	Bridford	100	70
Wonford Hundred	Cheriton Bishop	154	83
	Christow	131	73
	Dunsford	148	81
	Hittisleigh	25	84
	Holcombe Burnell	40	73
	South Tawton	233	78
	Spreyton	79	78
	Throwleigh	66	58
	Whitstone	97	84
Devon,	Bickleigh	64	66
Roborough Hundred			
Devon,	Loxhore	48	79
Sherwill Hundred			
Devon,	Brent Tor	37	84
Tavistock Hundred	(Total, 38 parishes	4,903	72)
Dorset	Bryanstone	34	47
	Stratton and Grimston	45	73
	Todbere	12	58
	Upway	97	71
	Warmwell	51	61
	West Knighton	71	66
	Whitcombe	34	74
	Winterbourne Strickland	64	70
	unidentified parish	165	77
	(Total, 9 parishes	573	70)
Durham	Easington*	155	77
	Monk Hesledon*	92	68
	(Total, 2 parishes	247	74)
Essex	Little Baddow*	71	45
	Barnston*	63	63
	Boxted*	131	61
	Dengie*	28	71
	Fyfield*	106	69

County	Parish	No. of subscribers	% mark
Essex	Hadleigh*	50	82
continued	East Hanningfield*	67	67
	Kelvedon Hatch*	59	64
	Middleton	21	57
	Little Oakley*	34	85
	Great Parndon*	73	58
	Prittlewell*	157	69
	Great Stambridge*	26	69
	Marks Tey*	36	56
	Wanstead*	59	36
	Wormingford*	100	62
	(Total, 16 parishes	1,081	63)
Hertfordshire	Walkern*	85	74
	(Total, 1 parish	85	74)
Huntingdonshire,	Bluntisham cum Erith	210	64
Hurstingstone	Colne	92	65
Hundred	Hartford	59	75
	Raveley Parva	29	66
Huntingdonshire,	Barham	45	47
Leightonstone	Buckworth	38	71
Hundred	Gidding Magna	54	57
	Hamerton	38	45
	Kimbolton	223	68
	Swineshead*	51	55
Huntingdonshire,	Alwalton	38	63
Normancross	Caldecote	23	78
Hundred	Chesterton	30	70
	Conington	30	7
	Elton	157	75
	Farcett	47	74
	Folksworth	27	48
	Glatton	77	68
	Haddon	30	63
	Holme	95	80
	Orton Cherry	56	79
	Sawtrey St Andrew and St Judith	56	71
	Standground	92	76
	Water Newton	25	64
	Woodstone	43	77
Huntingdonshire,	Abbotsley	77	62
Toseland Hundred	Fenstanton	147	70
	Toseland	44	77
	(Total, 28 parishes	1,933	67)

County	Parish	No. of subscribers	% mark
Lincolnshire,	Fiskerton	70	80
Lawress Wapentake	Reepham	64	72
	Sudbrook and Holme	30	63
Lincolnshire,	Cammeringham	35	69
Aslacoe Wapentake	Fillingham	92	84
	Hackthorn	50	88
	Ingham	43	70
	Normanby	49	73
	Saxby	17	94
	Spridlington	52	83
Lincolnshire,	Cabourne	29	93
Bradley Haverstoe	East Randall	23	91
Wapentake	Rothwell	44	82
Lincolnshire,	Burwell cum Walmsgate	63	76
Louth Esk	Calcethorpe	20	85
Hundred	Great Carlton	73	77
	North Cockerington	73	84
	Conisholme	32	66
	Farforth cum Maidenwell	25	80
	Grimoldby	69	83
	Louth	81	74
	unidentified parish	395	64
	Muckton	29	69
	Ruckland	16	75
	Saltfleetby St Clement	26	81
	Skidbrook	77	70
	Somercoates South	72	67
Lincolnshire,	Covenham St Bartholomew	56	84
Ludborough	Fotherby	66	82
Wapentake			
Lincolnshire,	Aby	28	61
Calceworth	Calceby	31	68
Hundred	Flaxby	21	71
	Gayton in the Marsh	75	76
	Mablethorpe	35	80
	Maltby	35	71
Lincolnshire,	Oxcombe	12	83
Hill Hundred	Somersby	21	71
Lincolnshire,	Burton super Stather	132	74
Manley	Risby	14	57
Wapentake			
Lincolnshire,	Blyton	107	74
Corringham	Grayingham	58	84
Wapentake			

County	Parish	No. of subscribers	% mark
Lincolnshire,	South Kelsey St Mary	8	50
Walshcroft	East Rasen	202	70
Wapentake	North Willingham	80	74
Lincolnshire,	Croxton	31	87
Yarborough	Saxby	70	81
Wapentake	Wootton	73	84
	unidentified parish	348	60
	(Total, 48 parishes	3,152	73)
London	Holy Trinity the Less*	217	33
	St Clement Eastcheap*	122	17
	St Martin Orgar*	152	21
	St Mary Magdalen, Milk Street*	118	9
	(Total, 4 parishes	609	22)
Middlesex	New Brentford	135	41
	Greenford Magna	79	63
	Hayes	178	77
	(Total, 3 parishes	392	62)
Norfolk	Breccles*	39	72
	Eaton*	25	56
	Hassingham*	19	89
	South Walsham*	63	73
	(Total, 4 parishes	146	72)
Nottinghamshire,	Applesthorp	41	90
Bassetlaw	Askham	53	72
Wapentake	Bole	49	84
	West Burton	42	90
	Clareborough	146	63
	Clayworth	114	82
	East Drayton	65	71
	West Drayton	25	88
	Eakring	109	81
	Edwinston	199	81
	Egmanton	79	75
	Everton	132	81
	Grove	31	45
	Harworth	93	92
	Hayton	68	74
	Laneham	118	74
	Laxton	150	83
	North Leverton	94	81
	South Leverton	127	70
	East Markham	150	77
	West Markham	79	76
	Ollerton	69	75

County	Parish	No. of subscribers	% mark
Nottinghamshire, Bassetlaw Wapentake continued	Ragnall	64	73
	Rampton	114	73
	Stokeham	20	80
	Sturton	145	79
	Treswell	70	63
	Tuxford	170	75
	Walkeringham	131	80
	Warsop	175	71
	North Wheatley	99	78
	South Wheatley	18	67
Nottinghamshire, Bingham Wapentake	Flintham	103	76
	Owthorp	41	68
Nottinghamshire, Broxtow Hundred	Beeston	90	84
	Kirkby in Ashfield	95	66
	unidentified parish	60	70
Nottinghamshire, Newark Hundred	Hawton	34	47
	Staunton	57	84
Nottinghamshire, Rushcliffe Hundred	Costock	30	77
	Kingston	25	80
	Stanford	34	74
Nottinghamshire, Thurgarton Hundred	Bleasby	54	91
	Colwick	26	27
	Edingley	70	93
	Morton	38	66
	Scrooby	49	82
	(Total, 47 parishes	3,845	76)
Oxfordshire	Alvescot	58	62
	Cleydon	62	58
	Mollington	77	69
	Steeple	91	71
	(Total, 4 parishes	288	66)
Shropshire	Wenlock	67	66
	(Total, 1 parish	67	66)
Somerset	Bridgewater	648	67
	Culbone	20	85
	Dodington	30	37
	Winsham*	206	53
	(Total, 4 parishes	904	64)
Staffordshire	Farewell	36	67

County	Parish	No. of subscribers	% mark
Staffordshire	Handsworth	234	63
continued	Hints	42	71
	(Total, 3 parishes	312	64)
Suffolk	Brantham*	56	52
	Brundish*	55	36
	Cretingham*	44	48
	Friston*	27	56
	Ipswich, St Stephen*	88	36
	Linstead Parva*	24	58
	(Total, 6 parishes	294	45)
Surrey,	Buckland	40	70
Reigate Hundred	Burstow	97	71
	Chipstead	68	79
	Gatton	33	61
	Horley	169	70
	Leigh	92	66
	Merstham	97	72
Surrey,	Bletchingley	160	62
Tandridge	Caterham	53	81
Hundred	Crowhurst	25	64
	Farley	26	85
	Horne	63	59
	Limpsfield	64	58
	Oxted	102	65
	Tandridge	74	76
	Tatsfield	21	71
	Titsey	33	49
	Woldingham	11	91
	(Total, 18 parishes	1,228	68)
Sussex,	Billinghurst	225	59
Arundel Rape	Poling	32	75
	Tortington	20	65
	Wiggenholt	56	66
Sussex,	Albourn	86	71
Bramber Rape	Ashington	37	73
	Ashurst	58	64
	Broadwater	128	76
	Buttolphs	15	60
	Clapham	46	78
	Coombs	15	80
	Findon	73	77
	Henfield	164	66
	Kingston	17	71
	Lancing	71	82

County	Parish	No. of subscribers	% mark
Sussex, Bramber Rape continued	Patching	42	69
	Seal	71	73
	Shoreham	39	77
	Southwick	35	80
	Sullington	41	76
	Tarring	156	75
	Wiston	75	71
Sussex, Chichester Rape	Appledram	22	59
	Linchmere	67	69
	Oving	84	73
	Rumbald's Wyke	14	64
	Selham	20	65
	Trotton	88	75
	(Total, 28 parishes	1,797	71)
Westmorland	Appleby St Lawrence	148	78
	Appleby St Michael	142	94
	Clifton	50	78
	Musgrave	40	85
	Orton	346	62
	Patterdale	41	90
	Little Strickland	30	67
	(Total, 7 parishes	797	74)
Yorkshire	Cherry Burton*	55	73
	Pontefract	584	75
	(Total, 2 parishes	639	74)

Abbreviations

B.L.: British Library
C.S.P.D.: *Calendar of State Papers, Domestic*
D.R.O.: Devon Record Office
E.R.O.: Essex Record Office
G.L.: Guildhall Library
G.L.R.O.: Greater London Record Office
H.L.R.O.: House of Lords Record Office
H.R.O.: Hertfordshire Record Office
N.R.O.: Norfolk and Norwich Record Office
P.R.O.: Public Record Office
S.R.O.: Suffolk Record Office, Ipswich branch
R.C.H.M.: Royal Commission on Historical Manuscripts

Note: All places of publication in the notes and bibliography, unless otherwise specified, are London. Spelling and punctuation have been modernized, except in the titles of books.

Notes

Chapter 1. Reading, writing and the margins of literacy

1. Thomas More, *The apologye* (1533), pp. 20—20v. For More's estimate of the extent of literacy see below, p. 44.
2. James Arthur Muller (ed.), *The letters of Stephen Gardiner* (Cambridge, 1933), p. 274. Gardiner's guess of the extent of literacy, very different from More's, is cited below, p. 43.
3. Bishop John Parkhurst's injunctions for Norwich, 1561, in W. H. Frere (ed.), *Visitation articles and injunctions of the period of the reformation*, vol. 3, 1559—1575 (1910), p. 100.
4. The Royal Orders of 1561 required every church to display above the communion table 'the tables of god's precepts imprinted for the said purpose, provided yet that in cathedral churches the tables of the said precepts be more largely and costly painted out, to the better shew of the same' (Frere, *Visitation articles and injunctions*, vol. 3, p. 109). I am grateful to Margaret Spufford for bringing this point to my attention.
5. Frere, *Visitation articles and injunctions*, vol. 3, p. 301 for Bishop Cox's 1571 articles for Ely; vol. 2, 1536—1558, p. 20, for Bishop Lee's 1537 injunctions for Coventry and Lichfield.
6. Nicholas Bownde, *The doctrine of the sabbath* (1595), p. 202. The injunction is from the Swedish church law of 1686, quoted in Egil Johansson, 'The history of literacy in Sweden', *Educational Reports Umea*, 12 (1977), p. 11.
7. James Axtell, *The school upon a hill; education and society in colonial New England* (New Haven, 1974), p. 13.
8. George Swinnock, *The Christian mans calling . . . the second part* (1663), pp. 22—3.
9. Richard Baxter, *A Christian directory* (1673), p. 548.
10. *The office of Christian parents* (Cambridge, 1616), pp. 73, 74; William Gouge, *Of domesticall duties* (1622), pp. 534, 586, 587; Richard Baxter, *The poor husbandman's advocate* (1691), quoted in Richard B. Schlatter, *The social ideas of religious leaders, 1660—1688* (Oxford, 1940), p. 38.
11. *The office of Christian parents*, pp. 64, 73; Richard Steele, *The religious tradesman* (1747), p. 35, formerly published in 1684 as *The tradesman's calling*.
12. Baxter, *Christian directory*, p. 582. See also Richard Baxter, *The poor man's family book* (1674), pp. 287—306.
13. John Ball, *A short treatise contayning all the principall grounds of Christian religion*, 9th impression (1633), p. 165.
14. Richard Baxter, *Reliquiae Baxterianae* (1696), pp. 2, 3. The elder Baxter was converted 'by the bare reading of the scriptures' while Richard was

awakened at the age of fifteen by reading Edmund Bunny's adaptation of *A book of Christian exercise appertaining to resolution.*

15. Baxter, *Christian directory*, p. 60.
16. *Ibid.* p. 580. The courageous Christian could confront false doctrine with confidence, but Baxter was less sure of the reader's reaction to secular literature. See below, p. 8.
17. J. Horsfall Turner (ed.), *The Rev. Oliver Heywood, B.A., 1630–1702; his autobiography, diaries, anecdotes and events books* (1882), vol. 1, pp. 48, 51, 83; A. Monroe Stowe, *English grammar schools in the reign of Queen Elizabeth* (New York, 1908), p. 149; John Brinsley, *Ludus literarius, or the grammar schoole* (1612), p. 255.
18. William Cecil, 'A memorial for Thomas Cecil' (1561), in Louis B. Wright (ed.), *Advice to a son* (Ithaca, New York, 1962), p. 4. Turner, *Oliver Heywood*, vol. 1, p. 83.
19. Roger Ascham, *The scholemaster, or plaine and perfite way of teachyng children to understand, write and speake the Latin tong* (1570), ff. 15v–16; Christopher Wase, *Considerations concerning free schools* (Oxford, 1678), pp. 33–4; David Brown, *The new invention intituled calligraphia* (St Andrews, 1622), p. 59; David Brown, *The introduction to the true understanding of the whole arte of expedition in teaching to write* (1638), sig. B4v.
20. Though dated, the best reviews of this material are in Louis B. Wright, *Middle-class culture in Elizabethan England* (Chapel Hill, 1935) and H. S. Bennett, *English books and readers, 1558 to 1603* (Cambridge, 1965).
21. Thomas Tryon, *Some memoirs of the life* ... (1705), pp. 14ff.
22. A forthcoming study by Mark Goldie of the University of Cambridge should add to our knowledge of politics and the popular press in the seventeenth century. Richard Overton, *An appeale from the degenerate representative body* (1647), p. 37.
23. James Howell, *Epistolae Ho-Elianae*, ed. J. Jacobs (1890), vol. 1, p. 526. For a modern view of the impact of printing see Elizabeth L. Eisenstein, *The printing press as an agent of change: communications and cultural transformations in early modern Europe* (Cambridge and New York, 1978).
24. Phillip Stubbes, *Anatomy of abuses* (1583), ed. Frederick J. Furnivall (1877), pp. 184–5; Steele, *Religious tradesman*, p. 36; Baxter, *Christian directory*, pp. 61, 292.
25. Stubbes, *Anatomy of abuses*, p. 185; Bownde, *Doctrine of the sabbath*, p. 242; Richard Baxter, *Treatise of self-denyall* (1660), ch. 22. Richard Steele referred to the same writings which 'poison the heart, corrupt the fancy, vitiate the affections; and for one useful lesson that can be learned from them are big with a thousand ills' (*Religious tradesman*, p. 36).
26. John Bunyan, *Sighs from hell* (1666?), 2nd edn, p. 148; Baxter, *Reliquiae*, p. 2. Chapmen and book-peddlers distributed 'small godly' as well as 'small merry' pamphlets, and there was a popular appetite for religious as well as worldly stimulation. Their theology tended to be crude and their message sensational, with as much risk of carrying the reader away from 'true religion' as the corrupting 'romances and idle tales'.
27. Martin Billinglsey, *The pens excellencie: or the secretaries delighte* (1618), sigs. B4v, Cv; Brown, *Introduction to the true understanding*, sigs. Bv, B4v. Billingsley, and Brown both remarked on the utility of writing for preserving secrets, implying that a private communication was safe when

relatively few people could read. On the other hand, as Francis Osborne wrote in *Advice to a son* (1656), things committed to paper 'many years after may rise up in judgement against you when things spoken may be forgot', so writing should be treated with caution (Wright (ed.), *Advice to a son*, p. 49).

28. Brown, *New invention*, pp. 58—9; Brown, *Introduction to the true understanding*, sig. B3. A similar argument is made by Billingsley, in *Pens excellencie*, sigs. B4, C, where writing is a defence against 'the manifold deceits of this world', and considered especially useful for the protection of widows.

29. Brown, *New invention*, p. 59. Brown's later book includes details of where potential clients might find him, at the Cat and Fiddle in Fleet Street or at a country house in Kennington, along with further remarks about the private advantages of literacy (*Introduction to the true understanding*, sigs. Bv, F2v, B3).

30. Billingsley, *Pens excellencie*, sig. B4. Christopher Wase noted that literate apprentices were worth more (*Considerations concerning free schools*, p. 33). Modern historians tend to agree with the Stuart penmen, regarding writing as 'one of the essential accomplishments in a practical education' (Herbert C. Schulz, 'The teaching of hand-writing in Tudor and Stuart times', *Huntington Library Quarterly*, 6 (1943), p. 393).

31. Nicholas Breton, *The court and country* (1618), in W. H. Dunham and S. Pargellis (eds.), *Complaint and reform in England 1436—1714* (New York, 1938), p. 468.

32. The Huntington Library, cat. no. 429497, *Almanac for 1652—58*, title page missing.

33. Breton, *Court and country*, p. 469.

34. In a quite extraordinary episode at Willingham, Cambridgeshire, in 1593, the villagers contributed sums equivalent to two years' rent to endow a school by subscription. 'The rector, Dr William Smyth, may well have been the initiator and driving force behind the foundation' (Margaret Spufford, *Contrasting communities, English villagers in the sixteenth and seventeenth centuries* (Cambridge, 1974), pp. 193—4).

35. The story has been told in lectures by Christopher Hill and may be related to the incident involving Richard Shukburgh who 'hunted so merrily' when Charles I was going to 'fight for his crown and dignity' (Sir William Dugdale, *The antiquities of Warwickshire*, 2nd edn (1730), p. 309). It is also referred to in Ian Roy, 'The English civil War and English society', in Brian Bond and Ian Roy (eds.), *War and society* (New York, 1975), p. 31.

36. R. S. Schofield, 'The measurement of literacy in pre-industrial England', in Jack Goody (ed.), *Literacy in traditional societies* (Cambridge, 1968), p. 313; Eisenstein, *Printing press as an agent of change*, p. 130.

37. Frere, *Visitation articles and injunctions*, vol. 3, pp. 98, 277. Some separatists dismissed reading and writing altogether from their religious practice, perhaps in reaction against the bibliocentric features of anglican protestantism. One Brownist pastor in the early seventeenth century argued that 'writing and reading, nay, all letters and characters, are invented by men, while speaking is natural. If consequently writing and reading be artificial devices, so it cannot be spiritual worship.' The Bible, indeed, was acknowledged to be the word of God, but only in the original Greek or Hebrew; the true worshipper should avoid as apocryphal any

translation which was the work of men. Religion came from the heart, not from the text. See J. De Hoop Scheffer, *History of the Free Church-men . . . 1581—1701* (Ithaca, New York, 1922), pp. 103—4, 201—6.

38. More, *Apologye*, p. 20v; Richard Steele, *The husbandmans calling . . . being the substance of XII sermons preached to a country congregation* (2nd edn, 1672), p. 57.

39. Breton, *Court and country*, p. 474.

40. These examples are from ecclesiastical court deposition books, E.R.O., AED/2; G.L. MS. 9585; D.R.O. Chanter 867. Spufford, *Contrasting communities*, pp. 320—3, 332—4.

41. William L. Sachse (ed.), *The diary of Roger Lowe* (1938), pp. 14—46.

42. Thomas Hewke of Wymondham, Norfolk, 'being scrivener by his profession', appeared as a witness before the Norwich consistory court in 1645 (N.R.O., DEP/45). The freelance country writing man should be distinguished from the increasingly professionalized city scrivener, adjunct to the legal profession. Described in Francis W. Steer (ed.), *Scriveners' company common paper . . . to 1678* (1968). Billingsley, *Pens excellencie*, sigs. Bv—B3.

43. Leona C. Gabel, *Benefit of clergy in England in the later middle ages* (Northampton, Mass., 1928), pp. 64—73.

44. William Lambard, *Eirenarcha, or the office of the justices of the peace*, revised edn (1614), pp. 562—7. See also Richard Burn, *Ecclesiastical law* (1763), vol. 1, pp. 131—6. A counter case of the negative value of literacy, a kind of 'cost of clergy', appears in Shakespeare's *Henry VI, Part 2*, IV, ii, where Jack Cade's rebels, hostile to writing in general, convict the clerk of Chatham on account of his literacy.

45. Lawrence Stone, 'The educational revolution in England, 1560—1640', *Past and Present*, 28 (1964), pp. 42—3; John Cordy Jeaffreson (ed.), *Middlesex County Records* (1887), vol. 2, pp. xxxviii—xxxix.

46. Gabel, *Benefit of clergy*, p. 71n.

47. Stone, 'Educational revolution', p. 42.

Chapter 2. The acquisition of literacy

1. T. W. Baldwin, *William Shakespere's small Latine and lesse Greeke* (Urbana, 1941); Kenneth Charlton, *Education in Renaissance England* (1965); Joan Simon, *Education and society in Tudor England* (Cambridge, 1967); W. A. L. Vincent, *The grammar schools: their continuing tradition, 1660—1714* (1969); Foster Watson, *The English grammar schools to 1660* (1908).

2. See, for example, Thomas Laqueur, 'The cultural origins of popular literacy in England, 1500—1850', *Oxford Review of Education*, 2 (1976), p. 257. Perhaps this explains why so few people actually were able to read and write. The best account of elementary education is T. W. Baldwin, *William Shakespere's petty school* (Urbana, 1943).

3. A compelling argument for the vitality of this period is made by Lawrence Stone, in 'Educational revolution', pp. 41—80. A less optimistic assessment is made in David Cressy, 'Educational opportunity in Tudor and Stuart England', *History of Education Quarterly*, 16 (1976), pp. 301—20.

4. William Kempe, *The education of children in learning* (1588), sig. F2.

5. John Hart, *A methode or comfortable beginning for all unlearned to read English* (1570), sig. A4v.

6. Kempe, *Education of children*, sig. F2; Edmund Coote, *The English schoole-master* (1624 edn), p. 1; F[rancis] Clement, *The petie schole* (1587), pp. 12—13. Similar advice appears in John Brinsley, *Ludus literarius* (1612), p. 15, 'first the child is to be taught how to call every letter pronouncing each of them plainly, fully and distinctly, I mean in a distinct and differing sound, each from others'.

7. Charles Hoole, *A new discovery of the old art of teaching schoole* (1660), pp. 4, 20. This was written in 1637, according to Schulz, 'Teaching of handwriting', p. 392.

8. Coote, *English schoole-master*, pp. 3, 26, 28.

9. Alexander Nowell, *A catechism, or first instruction and learning of Christian religion* (1571), required by the church canons of 1571.

10. Hoole, *New discovery*, pp. 22—3. Similar provisions appear in Brinsley, *Ludus literarius*, pp. 17—18 and Kempe, *Education of children*, sig. F3.

11. Clement, *Petie schole*, pp. 36, 40—41. 'Common plays, which do no less, yea rather more, metamorphose, transfigure, deform, pervert and alter the hearts of the haunters', were more still corrupting, according to Clement, and the auditors did not even have to be literate. See also Stubbes, *Anatomy of abuses*, and the other religious critics discussed in ch. 1, pp. 8—9.

12. Richard Mulcaster, *The first part of the elementarie* (1582), 'epistle dedicatory', pp. 53—5.

13. Clement, *Petie schole*, p. 18. The study of punctuation would also be useful for both reading and writing. The child should learn 'the distinction and pointing of sentences, by the observation whereof the breath is relieved, the meaning conceived, the eye directed, the ear delighted, and all the senses satisfied'.

14. Kempe, *Education of children*, sig. F3v.

15. William Bullokar, *A short introduction or guiding to print, write and read Inglish speech* (1580; not paginated).

16. Brown, *New invention*, p. 60.

17. Kempe, *Education of children*, sig. F3v; Brinsley, *Ludus literarius*, p. 29; Clement, *Petie schole*, p. 57. At Peterborough grammar school Saturday afternoon was set aside for writing exercises. 'So many as can write' were to practise their exercises, and 'all such as cannot write' were to 'learn to write two hours that afternoon' (Ordinances of 1561, quoted in Schulz, 'Teaching of handwriting', p. 398).

18. Kempe, *Education of children*, sig. F3v.

19. Brinsley, *Ludus literarius*, p. 32. See also Clement, *Petie schole*, p. 52, for a similar list adding desk and dust-box.

20. Peter Bales, *The writing schoolemaster* (1590), sigs. Q3, Q3v.

21. Clement, *Petie schole*, p. 57. See also W. Pank, *A most breefe, easie and plain receite for faire writing* (1591).

22. Brinsley, *Ludus literarius*, p. 36, actually recommends the beginning writer to practise scribbling.

23. Kempe, *Education of children*, sig. F3v.

24. Coote, *English schoole-master*, p. 23; John Hart, *An orthographie* (1569), pp. 4v—5. A candidate for admission to Shrewsbury grammar school, according to the ordinances of 1577, had to 'read English perfectly, have his accidence without book, and give any case of any number of a noun substantive or adjective, any person of any number of a verb active or passive, and make a Latin by any of the concords, the Latin words

being first given him', and as if this was not enough the entrant 'must be able to write his own name with his own hand' (Stowe, *English grammar schools*, p. 105). Such a requirement was rarely made explicit.

25. Richard Mulcaster, *Positions . . . for the training up of children* (1581), p. 19.
26. Kempe, *Education of children*, sig. F3v; Hoole, *New discovery*, p. 23; Hart, *Orthographie*, p. 4; Bullokar, *Short introduction* (n.p.).
27. Pank, *Receite for faire writing*, 'to the reader'.
28. Brown, *Introduction to the true understanding*, sig. Bv.
29. *Ibid.* sigs. B2, B2v.
30. White Kennett, *The charity of schools for poor children* (1706), p. 18. There was probably an element of wishful thinking in this description.
31. Kempe, *Education of children*, sig. E4v; Clement, *Petie schole*, p. 7; Brinsley, *Ludus literarius*, p. 9; Hoole, *New discovery*, pp. 1—2.
32. *Office of Christian parents*, pp. 73—5, 64—5.
33. Brinsley, *Ludus literarius*, p. 14; Hoole, *New discovery*, pp. 4—5.
34. Thomas Nashe, *A pleasant comedie called Summers last will and testament* (1600), sig. G3v.
35. I owe this information to Margaret Spufford, who kindly allowed me to see the typescript of her paper on humble autobiographers, 'First steps in literacy: the reading and writing experiences of the humblest seventeenth-century spiritual autobiographers', *Social History*, 4, no. 3 (Oct. 1979), pp. 407—35.
36. E.R.O., D/P/30/1/2. The search for early school admission registers and attendance books is an urgent matter since much of the social history of education will remain unwritten without them. See David Cressy, 'School and college admission ages in seventeenth-century England', *History of Education*, 8 (1979).
37. D.R.O., Chanter 872; Consistory court testamentary causes, bundle 192. The original will was destroyed in the bombing of 1942 so we cannot be certain that Henry Facy signed his name. Margaret Spufford has drawn my attention to the eight-year-old son of Alderman Newton of Cambridge, who proudly signed his name in 1667, in the MS. *Diary of Samuel Newton*, Downing College, Cambridge, Library, p. 74.
38. N.R.O., Yarmouth records, L3/13, register of the children's hospital 1682—1745.
39. N.R.O. Yarmouth records, C19/21, f. 196v, Assembly waste book 1683—98.
40. Yarmouth records, L3/13, entry number 241. The other examples cited in this discussion are from entrants 259 to 499.
41. It was common for grammar schools to specify that their entrants should be able to read and write, and as common for this provision to be ignored (Brinsley, *Ludus literarius*, pp. 12—13; Hoole, *New discovery*, pp. 26—8).
42. Cambridgeshire Record Office, P. 177/25/1, discussed in Spufford, *Contrasting communities*, pp. 193—5; Nicholas Carlisle, *A concise description of the endowed grammar schools in England and Wales* (1818), vol. 1, pp. 415—22.
43. Curates were given preference over other freelance teachers, so long as they did not intrude on the masters of established grammar schools (*Constitutions and canons ecclesiastical . . . agreed 1603* (1612), canon 78).
44. N.R.O., SUB/1—4. A similar proportion was found in the diocese of

London, where clergy comprised 11% of the licensed teachers in 1580—1640 and 14% in 1660—1700 (G.L.R.O., DLC/333—45; G.L., MS. 9532/1). *C.S.P.D.*, Charles I, vol. *CCLXX*, 13 (1634).

45. Lichfield Joint Record Office, Bishop Lloyd's survey of Eccleshall, transcribed by Norman W. Tildesley.
46. Clement, *Petie schole*, p. 4.
47. Bagford, Pledger and Roach sought licences to teach from the Bishop of London after the Restoration (G.L., MS. 110116, 2, 9, 7).
48. Dorothy Gardiner, *English girlhood at school* (1929), pp. 204, 205.
49. *Ibid.* pp. 279, 277.
50. E.R.O., D/ACA 15, f. 15; H.R.O., ASA/7/10, f. 200.
51. Hart, *A method or comfortable beginning*, 'epistle dedicatory'.
52. Clement, *Petie schole*, p. 9. This includes one of the rare references to women as teachers.
53. Coote, *English schoole-master*, sig., A2; Brinsley, *Ludus literarius*, p. 16; Hoole, *New discovery*, p. 13.
54. Kempe, *Education of children*, sig. A3. Grammar-school teachers of the seventeenth century were more likely to insist on a pedagogic monopoly, like Richard Reynolds of Great Yarmouth, who accepted a position at Colchester in 1691 only on the 'condition of putting down all other Latin schools' (G.L. MS. 10116, 9).
55. Brinsley, *Ludus literarius*, pp. 13, 15, 20.
56. Illiteracy among tailors in seventeenth-century East Anglia was 44%, and among weavers 42%. See ch. 6.
57. Thomas Tryon, *Some memoirs of the life*, pp. 8, 13—16. More examples are given in Spufford, 'First steps in literacy'
58. Laqueur, 'Cultural origins of popular literacy', p. 257.
59. Brinsley, *Ludus literarius*, pp. 10, 20, 24. See also Kempe, *Education of children*, sig. F.
60. *Office of Christian parents*, pp. 73, 75; Gouge, *Of domesticall duties*, pp. 534, 586; Baxter, *Christian directory*, p. 548.
61. See ch. 6 for estimates of female illiteracy.
62. Baxter, *Christian directory*, p. 582; Swinnock, *Christian mans calling*, p. 22v.

Chapter 3. The measurement of literacy

1. This felicitous phrase is from R. S. Schofield, 'Measurement of literacy', in Goody (ed.), *Literacy in traditional societies*, p. 319. My argument in this chapter is based on Schofield's pioneering work.
2. Bownde, *Doctrine of the sabbath*, p. 241. It is interesting to note the non-literary forms of religious instruction employed by the puritan campaigner.
3. Francis Inman, *A light unto the unlearned* (1622), sig. A2.
4. Schlatter, *Social ideas*, p. 36; Swinnock, *Christian mans calling*, p. 23; Baxter, *Christian directory*, p. 582; Baxter, *Poor husbandman's advocate*, quoted in Schlatter, *Social ideas*, p. 38.
5. Gardiner to Edward Vaughan, 3 May 1547, in Muller (ed.), *Letters of Stephen Gardiner*, p. 274.
6. Overton, *Appeale from the degenerate representative body*, p. 37. Much of the discussion of education in the revolution was predicated on the idea that there was a crisis in elementary schooling as well as an opportunity to transform it.

7. Clement, *Petie schole*, p. 4; Thomas Lye, *A new spelling-book* (1677), 'introduction'.
8. J. W. Adamson, *The illiterate Anglo-Saxon* (Cambridge, 1946), p. 44; H. S. Bennett, *English books and readers, 1475 to 1557* (Cambridge, 1969), p. 27; R. D. Altick, *The English common reader* (Chicago, 1957), pp. 16, 25; Schofield, 'Measurement of literacy', p. 313.
9. Bennett, *Books and readers, 1475 to 1557*, p. 27; Adamson, *Illiterate Anglo-Saxon*, p. 46; Altick, *English common reader*, p. 25.
10. John Rastell, *The grete abregement of the statutys* (1527), preface.
11. Thomas More, *The apologye*, pp. 20—20v.
12. Bennett, *Books and readers, 1475 to 1557*, p. 28. Victor E. Neuburg, *Popular literature, a history and guide* (1977), p. 54, is inclined to accept More's estimate.
13. Spufford, *Contrasting communities*, pp. 208—9, 262—3.
14. For Bible ownership see pp. 50—1.
15. Lawrence Stone, 'Communication', *Past and Present*, 24 (1963), p. 101; J. Jacobs (ed.), *Epistolae Ho-Elianae*, vol. 1 (1890), pp. 523—6. John Amos Comenius, *A reformation of schooles* (1642), p. 3, claimed that 'Books are grown so common in all languages and nations, that even common country people and women themselves, are familiarly acquainted with them'.
16. Adamson, *Illiterate Anglo-Saxon*, p. 43; Bennett, *Books and readers, 1475 to 1557*, p. 24; H. S. Bennett, *English books and readers, 1603 to 1640* (Cambridge, 1970), pp. 78—9; Carl Bridenbaugh, *Vexed and troubled Englishmen, 1590—1642* (Oxford, 1968), p. 339; Lawrence Stone, 'Literacy and education in England, 1640—1900', *Past and Present*, 42 (1969), p. 99.
17. Schofield, 'Measurement of literacy', pp. 314—15. See also Altick, *English common reader*, pp. 19—20.
18. Edward Arber, *A transcript of the registers of the company of stationers of London*, vol. 3 (1876), vol. 4 (1877); W. W. Greg, 'Entrance, licence and publication', *The Library*, 25 (1944), pp. 1—7.
19. *Catalogue of the pamphlets, books, newspapers . . . collected by George Thomason, 1640—1661* (1908); Wilmer G. Mason, 'The annual output of Wing-listed titles 1649—1684', *The Library*, 29 (1974), pp. 219—20; C. John Sommerville, 'On the distribution of religious and occult literature in seventeenth-century England', *The Library*, 29 (1974), pp. 221—5; C. John Sommerville, *Popular religion in Restoration England* (Gainsville, Florida, 1977), p. 9; D. F. McKenzie, *The London book trade in the later seventeenth century* (The Sandars Lectures, Cambridge (mimeograph), 1976), pp. 24—30; Cyprian Blagden, 'The distribution of almanacks in the second half of the seventeenth century', *Studies in Bibliography*, 11 (1958), pp. 107—16; Bernard S. Capp, *Astrology and the popular press, 1500—1800* (1979); Margaret Spufford, 'Samuel Pepys' chapbook collection and the prosperity and stock of some of the chapbook publishers', forthcoming (*The Library*, 1981).
20. Neuberg, *Popular literature*, p. 16. See below ch. 5; the measured illiteracy of husbandmen in East Anglia deteriorated from 77% unable to sign their names in the 1610s to 89% in the 1680s.
21. Spufford, *Contrasting communities*, p. 206.
22. Only 1% of a collection of inventories from sixteenth-century Oxfordshire includes books. In Bedfordshire, Essex, Leicestershire and Devon in the seventeenth century the proportions with books were 14%, 14%,

17% and 22%. In three towns in Kent in the early seventeenth century the proportion of inventories with books rose above 40%, while the figure for the city of Norwich between 1584 and 1638 was 39%. These figures are extracted from Peter Clark, 'The ownership of books in England, 1560–1640', in Lawrence Stone (ed.), *Schooling and society* (Baltimore, 1976), pp. 97–9, 109; Laqueur, 'Cultural origins of popular literacy', p. 264; Peter Laslett, *The world we have lost*, 2nd edn (1971), p. 209 and note; Norwich Survey Unit, report on probate inventories and book ownership, circulated at conference on 'Books and book ownership in early modern England', University of East Anglia, March 1978.

23. Clark, 'Ownership of books', pp. 104–5; Alan D. Dyer, *The city of Worcester in the sixteenth century* (Leicester, 1973), p. 250.

24. Laslett, *World we have lost*, p. 209; Francis W. Steer, 'Probate inventories', *History*, 47 (1962), pp. 287–90; W. B. Stephens, *Sources for English local history* (1973), pp. 36–7; John S. Moore (ed.), *The goods and chattels of our forefathers. Frampton Cotterell and district probate inventories* (Chichester, 1976), pp. 1–4.

25. Roger Lowe the diarist owned books but none is mentioned in his inventory, in William L. Sachse (ed.), *Diary of Roger Lowe*, pp. 133–4; Laslett, *World we have lost*, p. 209; Spufford, *Contrasting communities*, p. 211.

26. Laqueur, 'Cultural origins of popular literacy', p. 264, and Clark, 'Ownership of books', p. 100, have tables showing book ownership and inventorial wealth. The Norwich Survey Unit finds very few book owners with estates worth less than £20 but not much difference between those who did and did not own books among the wealthier citizens.

27. Clark, 'Ownership of books', p. 103; Laqueur, 'Cultural origins of popular literacy', pp. 265, 262. At Houghton-juxta-Harpley in Norfolk a book of homilies cost 6s 6d and a common prayer book cost 8s 6d in 1663, at a time when a labourer might earn a shilling a day. These books, however, might have been finely bound volumes for use in church. In the same parish in 1678 a prayer book was valued at 6d (Churchwardens' Account Books, with incumbent).

28. For Cavendish see note 15 above. Spufford, *Contrasting communities*, pp. 210–11.

29. Spufford, *Contrasting communities*, p. 209; David G. Hey, *An English rural community* (Leicester, 1974), pp. 222, 189, where the bequest of books is taken to suggest 'that some humble people could read tolerably well'; Schlatter, *Social ideas*, pp. 36–8; Baxter, *Reliquiae*, part 1, p. 89.

30. Baxter, *Poor man's family book*, sigs. A3–A3v. Michael Sparke, *Scintilla, or a light broken into darke warehouses* (1641), was 'printed, not for profit but for the commonweal's good; and no where to be sold, but somewhere to be given'.

31. Baxter, *Christian directory*, p. 280, gives characteristic directions for reading the Bible aloud: 'When you read to your family or others let it be seasonably and gravely, when silence and attendance encourage you to expect success, and not when children are crying or talking or servants bustling to disturb you.' Printed ballads as well as Bibles might be owned by illiterates (Bownde, *Doctrine of the sabbath*, pp. 202, 241).

32. Keith Thomas, *Religion and the decline of magic* (1971), pp. 494, 241; John Brand, *Observations on popular antiquities*, ed. Henry Ellis (1813), vol. 2, pp. 597, 641. At least one participant in the divination by book

and key had to be sufficiently literate to write the names of suspects on scraps of paper. Full literacy was also required to enter birth details in a Bible, but this was not necessarily done by a member of the family.

33. Brand, *Observations*, vol. 2, pp. 580, 469; Thomas, *Religion and the decline of magic*, p. 45; Baxter, *Reliquiae*, part 1, p. 46 refers to 'strange providences'.

34. He wrote, 'I rejoice at his mere physical presence; often I clasp him to my bosom and say with a sigh: O great man, how gladly would I hear you speak' (Morris Bishop (ed.), *Letters from Petrarch* (Bloomington, 1966), p. 153).

35. Adamson, *Illiterate Anglo-Saxon*, pp. 47—61; Bennett, *Books and readers, 1603 to 1640*, pp. 79—82; Stone, 'Educational revolution', David Cressy, 'Levels of illiteracy in England, 1530—1730', *Historical Journal*, 20 (1977), pp. 14—16.

36. Some of the difficulties are reviewed in Rosemary O'Day, 'Church records and the history of education in early modern England, 1558—1642', *History of Education*, 2 (1973), pp. 115—132. New endowments for the teaching of reading and writing are noted in Alan Smith, 'Endowed schools in the diocese of Lichfield and Coventry, 1660—99', *History of Education*, 4 (1975), pp. 5—20. Local schoolmasters are traced in David Cressy, 'Education and literacy in London and East Anglia, 1580—1700', Ph.D. thesis, University of Cambridge, 1973, chs. 4 and 5.

37. Laqueur, 'Cultural origins of popular literacy', pp. 257—9, argues for the informal acquisition of literacy. Thomas Tryon learned to read from his work mates, although he had some previous exposure to formal schooling (Thomas Tryon, *Some memoirs of the life*, pp. 13—16, 8). See ch. 2.

38. Cressy, 'Educational opportunity'.

39. Schofield, 'Measurement of literacy', p. 319. See also R. S. Schofield, 'Dimensions of illiteracy, 1750—1850', *Explorations in Economic History*, 10 (1973), which examines the ability to sign marriage registers.

40. Schofield, 'Measurement of literacy', pp. 318, 324—5; Registrar General's report quoted in Stone, 'Literacy and education', p. 98.

41. François Furet and Jacques Ozouf, *Lire et écrire: l'alphabétisation des Français de Calvin à Jules Ferry*, 2 vols. (Paris, 1977), vol. 1, pp. 19—28. An earlier report appeared in François Furet and Wladimir Sachs, 'La croissance de l'alphabétisation en France: XVIIIe—XIXe siècle', *Annales: Economies, Sociétés, Civilisations*, 29, no. 3 (1974), pp. 714—37. (English translation of the quoted passages: [They report] 'a strong correlation between "the ability to sign the marriage contract" and "knowing how to read and write", as strong for men as for women' . . . [Furet and Ozouf are able to conclude that] 'a signature is thus a good measure of literacy'.)

42. Oliver Lawson Dick (ed.), *Aubrey's brief lives* (1950), p. 141. Henry d'Auverquerque, Earl of Grantham, a courtier of the early eighteenth century, could casually be dismissed as illiterate, although not by the strict standards of signing or marking. In 1737 Walpole was instructed to supervize Lord Grantham's copying of a letter to Lord Baltimore,

> to tell him an *o* was to be made like a full moon, a *c* like a half moon, an *m* with three legs and an *n* with two, with other writing master's maxims, or that Grantham's production would never be legible. Lord Hervey said he believed this caution was very necessary, and that as this was the first example, and he believed would be the last, of

Grantham's literary correspondence that would ever appear in history and be transmitted to posterity, it would be pity not to have it perfect.
John, Lord Hervey, *Some materials towards memoirs of the reign of King George II*, ed. Romney Sedgwick, 3 vols. (1931), vol. 3, p. 823.

43. I am grateful to Ms Katherine Wyndham and Professors Dale Hoak and N. P. Sils for drawing my attention to Herbert autographs among the public records, E318/30/1685, PC2/4, p. 391, E101/303/4 and SP46/2, f. 93. Herbert was the only Edwardian councillor not to write in cursive.
44. Peter Clark, *English provincial society* (Hassocks, Sussex, 1977), p. 212.
45. See ch. 2. See also Coote, *English schoole-master*, p. 23: 'Our English proper names are written as it pleaseth the painter, or as men have received them by tradition . . . yea, I have known two natural brethren, both learned, to write their own names differently'.
46. Brown, *New invention*, pp. 58—9.
47. Durham Diocesan Records, D.R.V 2; E.R.O., D/AED 3; N.R.O., DEP/31; D.R.O., Chanter 870; G.L., MS. 9065A/8.
48. Great Yarmouth Manuscripts, C18/6, f. 56v; I am grateful to Mr A. R. Michell for supplying this reference. N.R.O., Case 13/C, Test Oath.
49. Durham Record Office, E/SWG.11; in 1618 Bradley made his mark on a deposition before the episcopal court, where his status was entered as 'gentleman' but then amended to 'yeoman' (Durham Diocesan Records, DR.V 10). William Wheatley, *The history of Edward Latymer and his foundations* (Hammersmith, 1953), pp. 118—9. The boys on Latymer's foundation were to be taught to read English (with no mention of writing) and kept from 'idle and vagrant courses'. The school continues, and I was a pupil there between 1957 and 1964. Facsimiles of John Shakespeare's mark are printed and his literacy discussed in S. Schoenbaum, *William Shakespeare, a documentary life* (New York, 1975), pp. 30—8.
50. Oscar James Campbell and Edward G. Quinn, *The reader's encyclopedia of Shakespeare* (New York, 1966), pp. 752—3. A mark in the shape of a cross, often added to a signature, was indeed a sanctifying symbol in the middle ages but by the sixteenth century its primary indication was illiteracy (Charles Sisson, 'Marks as signatures', *The Library*, 9 (1928), pp. 5—12).
51. Richard Savage and Edgar I. Fripp (eds.), *Minutes and accounts of the corporation of Stratford upon Avon*, vol. 1 (Oxford, 1921), p. xlvii, vol. 2 (London, 1924), p. 1. Schoenbaum repeats these remarks, reserving his own scepticism (*William Shakespeare*, p. 36).
52. Hilary Jenkinson, *The later court hands in England* (Cambridge, 1927), pp. 89—90; Sisson, 'Marks as signatures', p. 22; Spufford, *Contrasting communities*, pp. 182—3, Documents such as wills, which are seriously affected by literacy failing in sickness or old age, give an exaggerated impression of illiteracy, as shown in ch. 5. The most precise measurement of literacy would take the history of epidemics and the age structure of the sample into consideration when compiling annual statistics for the ability to sign.
53. Sisson, 'Marks as signatures', p. 21; Durham Diocesan Records, Probate records 1678, 1689. The will was made in 1687 and proved two years later.
54. William Shakespeare, *Henry VI, Part 2*, IV, ii. The over-all illiteracy of

men is derived from the Protestation Returns, of women from deposition books; see chs. 4, 5 and 6.

55. Andrew Favine, *The theater of honour and knighthood* (1623, translated from the French of 1620), p. 16. See also J. Paul Rylands, 'Merchants' marks and other medieval personal marks', *Transactions of the Historic Society of Lancashire and Cheshire*, 62 (1911), pp. 2, 7, 11 and plates; Sisson, 'Marks as signatures', p. 25 and plates. And see M. G. Guigue, *De l'origine de la signature et de son emploi au moyen age* (Paris, 1863), pp. 79—80 and plates. Sisson reproduced Guigue's plate 30, showing occupational marks in the sixteenth and seventeenth centuries, and translated as labourer the occupation of Le Fay, 'laboureur', whose mark looks like a field harrow. The correct English equivalent of 'laboureur' is yeoman.

Chapter 4. Literacy and loyalty

1. Petitions and receipts of Cromwell's army are used to argue that 'it is probable that a fair proportion of the lower classes, both men and women, could read, and the majority of men, at any rate, could write', in Godfrey Davies, *The early Stuarts*, 2nd edn (Oxford, 1959), p. 359. See also Mildred Campbell, *The English yeoman under Elizabeth and the early Stuarts* (1942), p. 263, for the literacy of yeomen making wills, leases and bonds.

2. Sources and the criteria for their acceptance are discussed in Schofield, 'Measurement of literacy', pp. 319—21. See Table 4.3 below for totals of householders and communicants compared to oath-takers in Essex.

3. 25 Henry VIII c.22, G. R. Elton, *Reform and reformation, England 1509—1558* (1977), pp. 185—6. The oath was not universal but could be applied anywhere at the discretion of the authorities. Thomas More was one of its victims.

4. Muller (ed.), *Letters of Stephen Gardiner*, pp. 56—7; Henry Jenkyns (ed.), *The remains of Thomas Cranmer* (1833), vol. 1, p. 112; James Gairdner (ed.), *Letters and papers . . . of Henry VIII* (1883), vol. 7, nos. 610, 702, vol. 11, no. 29, also nos. 23—6.

5. G. R. Elton, *Policy and police: the enforcement of the Reformation in the age of Thomas Cromwell* (Cambridge, 1972), p. 225. Elton's figures are preferable to those in Gairdner (ed.), *Letters and papers*, vol. 17, no. 689. The number of oath-takers in 1534 can be compared with the number of taxpayers in the 1524 Subsidy, when 54 men were assessed (S. H. A. Hervey (ed.), *Suffolk in 1524, being the return for a subsidy granted in 1523* (Woodbridge, 1910), pp. 17—18).

6. See 28 Henry VIII c.7 for the oath of supremacy.

7. *C.S.P.D., 1581--90*, pp. 207—8, 210—12. P.R.O., S.P. 12/174. The Hertfordshire returns include five marks among the 109 subscriptions to the association.

8. W. B. Stephens: *Sources for English local history*, p. 38; 'Male illiteracy in Devon on the eve of the civil war', *Devon Historian*, 11 (1975), pp. 21—6; 'Male and female adult illiteracy in seventeenth-century Cornwall', *Journal of Educational Administration and History*, 12 (1977), pp. 1—7. Stone, 'Literacy and education', pp. 99—101. A checklist of printed Protestations compiled by L. W. Lawson Edwards appears in *The Genealogists' Magazine*, 19 (1977), pp. 84—5.

9. For the context of the Protestation see S. R. Gardiner, *History of England . . . 1603–1642* (1884), vol. 9, pp. 328–55, and Derek Hirst, *The representative of the people? Voters and voting in England under the early Stuarts* (Cambridge, 1975), pp. 185–7.

10. *Journals of the House of Commons, 1640–42*, vol. 2, p. 132.

11. *Ibid.* vol. 2, pp. 133, 230, 389.

12. *Ibid.* vol. 2, p. 530. Even recusants could be persuaded to take the Protestation, as at Midhurst, Sussex, where thirty-five catholic recusants quickly capitulated (Anthony Fletcher, *A county community in peace and war: Sussex 1600–1660* (1975), p. 99). The Laudian rector of High Ongar, Essex, 'expressed his great dissatisfaction with the Protestation, deferring to read it', but finally took it under the construction that 'the sense of the House was to bind us to maintain the Thirty-Nine articles' (Harold Smith, *The ecclesiastical history of Essex under the Long Parliament and Commonwealth* (Colchester, 1932), p. 138). See T. L. Stoate (ed.), *The Cornwall Protestation returns* (Bristol, 1974), p. vi, for the excuses of absentees and refusers in the hundred of Trigg.

13. G.L., MS. 959/1. The London parishes of Holy Trinity the Less, St Mary Magdalen Milk Street and St Stephen Coleman Street took the Protestation in May (G.L., MS. 4835, 2597, 4458). Thomas M. Blagg and L. Lloyd Simpson (eds.), *Derbyshire parish registers*, vol. 13 (1914), p. 184, vol. 14 (1917), p. 229. E.R.O., Wanstead Register, D/P 292/1, Little Baddow register, D/P 35/1. Hadleigh register, with incumbent. The townsmen of Rye, Sussex, took the Protestation after receiving it from their M.P.s (Fletcher, *County community in peace and war*, p. 252).

14. G. L., MS. 1196/1.

15. H.L.R.O., Protestation returns.

16. S.R.O. Ipswich, Harleston register, FBA 213/D/1. All the names of subscribers are written in a common hand (H.L.R.O., Protestation returns). Women were not required to take the oath, but their names and even their signatures and marks sometimes appear on the returns. The few female autographs have not been included in this study of literacy.

17. *Journals of the House of Commons, 1642–44*, vol. 3, pp. 117, 118, 119, 147. C. H. Firth and R. S. Rait (eds.), *Acts and ordinances of the interregnum, 1642–1660* (1911), vol. 1, pp. 175–6, 493–4.

18. S.R.O., Ipswich, Brantham register, FB 190/D1/1. Ralph Josselin, the Essex clergyman, noted in July 1643: 'another new covenant propounded and begun to be pressed. I took it but the state let it fall' (Alan Macfarlane (ed.), *The diary of Ralph Josselin, 1616–1683* (1976), p. 13).

19. *Journals of the House of Commons, 1642–44*, vol. 3, pp. 223, 241, 254, 344, 382.

20. Firth and Rait (eds.), *Acts and ordinances*, vol. 1, pp. 376–8. Between the Commons discussion in December and the final document in January the youngest age for taking the covenant was changed from sixteen to eighteen. Some men were away in the army and could not take the covenant in their home parishes, but at Marks Tey in Essex it was more heavily subscribed than the Protestation; see Table 4.3.

21. Fletcher, *County community in peace and war*, p. 107. Prittlewell register, with incumbent. At Dengie, Essex, the Restoration rector commented on the covenant, 'rebellion is as the sin of witchcraft'; E.R.O., D/P 301/1. At Ashingdon, Essex, where all three declarations appear in the parish register, somebody added the following verse:

What more? Vow, Covenant and Protestation,
All to maintain the church and English nation.
A threefold cord sure is not easily broken
For so the wise man hath divinely spoken.
But all in vain; men's hearts with guile are fraught,
Great ones break through, small fishes they are caught.
Three nations thus are twisted all in one;
Three nations thus are three times thrice undone.
Smith, *Ecclesiastical history of Essex*, p. 97.

22. G.L., MS. 977/1; Hadleigh register, with incumbent.
23. B. J. Enright, 'Public petitions in the House of Commons', H.L.R.O., typescript (1960), pp. 29—32, describes these petitions and explains that some were presented in a tumultuous manner and some contained fraudulently obtained signatures. Royal Commission on Historical Manuscripts, *Fifth report* (1876), Appendix, pp. 4—14, 18, 21; *Journals of the House of Commons, 1640—42*, vol. 2, p. 387; *Journals of the House of Lords, 1628—42*, vol. 4, pp. 535—6, 539—40, 563—4, 570. On the organization of the Essex petition see Clive Holmes, *The Eastern Association in the English civil war* (Cambridge, 1974), p. 26.
24. B. L. Harleian MS. 2107. This has been wrongly identified as containing the Cheshire Protestation returns in, for example, Maurice F. Bond, *Guide to the records of parliament* (1971), p. 154n. The remonstrance is dated to August 1642 in J. S. Morrill, *Cheshire 1630—1660: county government and society during the English revolution* (Oxford, 1974), pp. 58—9. Protestations of the city of Chester are in H.L.R.O.
25. Thirty-one sets of authentic signatures and marks can be identified from the Essex petition, and only 49% of the subscribers made marks (H.L.R.O., Petitions). Twenty-one sets of original subscriptions to the Cheshire remonstrance yield an illiteracy rate of 53% (B. L. Harl. MS. 2107). Evidence from subscriptions to the parliamentary declarations indicates a much higher illiteracy rate in those areas.
26. R.C.H.M. *Fifth report*, appendix, pp. 3, 120—34. Some of the declarations in local records are mentioned in W. E. Tate, *The parish chest*, 3rd edn (Cambridge, 1969), p. 72. A list of declarations in local records used in this study is given in the bibliography, and figures from all sources are collected in the appendix. Table 4.1 includes figures from the unpublished work of Derek Turner and R. S. Schofield, filed at the SSRC/Cambridge Group. Illiteracy in Kent ranged from 80% at Barfreston through 66% at Walmer to 40% at Eastwell and Ripple, according to Clark, *English provincial society*, p. 448, but the numbers on which these percentages are based are not given and it has not proved possible to inspect the original documents for this study.
27. The evidence of depositions shows that tradesmen in London in the period 1580—1700 had an over-all illiteracy of 22% (a figure identical to that for the declarations), compared to 45% in Norfolk and Suffolk in the same period. The figure includes some tradesmen from Norwich, England's second city, who were often as literate as their London counterparts. Women in London were also uniquely literate (see ch. 6).
28. R. A. P. Finlay, 'The population of London, 1580—1650' (Ph.D. thesis, University of Cambridge, 1976), pp. 79, 208—12, has figures for 1638, when the total population of London within the walls was *c*. 76,000. London illiteracy figures are obtained from civil war declarations in G.L. MSS. 4835, 959/1, 977/1, 2597.

29. S.R.O. Ipswich, FB 107/A1/1; H.L.R.O., Protestation returns.
30. Similar scepticism about urban literacy is expressed in W. B. Stephens, 'Illiteracy and schooling in the provincial towns, 1640–1870: a comparative approach', in D. A. Reeder (ed.), *Urban education in the nineteenth century* (1977), p. 29.
31. Figures are given in the appendix. For the superiority of market towns in 1696 see p. 99.
32. Stone, 'Literacy and education', p. 100. Stone's hypotheses are provocative but he concedes that 'the figures are too fragmentary to justify any conclusions'.
33. E.R.O., Q/RTh/5, Hearth-tax roll, 1671; William Salt Library, Stafford, Salt MS. 33, 'Compton census' of communicants, 1676. A rough estimate of population can be made by multiplying households by 4.5, communicants (males and females over 16) by 1.66 and adult males by 3.2. Multipliers, based on estimates of mean household size and the age structure of the pre-industrial population, are discussed by the editors, correspondents and contributors in *Local Population Studies*, 1 (1968), pp. 30–4, 7 (1971), pp. 22–4, 8 (1972), p. 39. Tables showing household size and age structure appear in Laslett, *World we have lost*, 2nd edn, pp. 72, 108.
34. Clive Holmes, *The Eastern Association in the English civil war* (Cambridge, 1979), pp. 36, 43; Alfred Kingston, *East Anglia and the great civil war* (1897), pp. 63–7.
35. Richard Newcourt, *Repertorium ecclesiasticum parochiale Londinense* (1708–10), vol. 2, pp. 639, 25, 26, 575, 446, 541; Philip Morant, *The history and antiquities of the county of Essex* (1768), pp. 134, 280, 293, 24, 25, 368, 370, 36, 30, 490, 319, 320, 493; T. W. Davids, *Annals of evangelical nonconformity in the county of Essex* (1863), pp. 347, 270, 443, 141, 297; Smith, *Ecclesiastical history of Essex*, pp. 236–320. See also Thomas Wright, *The history and topography of the county of Essex* (1831–5).
36. Davids, *Annals of evangelical nonconformity*, pp. 467–8, 243–4; Smith, *Ecclesiastical history of Essex*, pp. 269, 133, 48, 117; Newcourt, *Repertorium*, vol. 2, p. 262. The conservative rector of Fyfield was evidently mismatched with his puritan patron, the Earl of Warwick.
37. Newcourt, *Repertorium*, vol. 2, pp. 529, 542; Smith, *Ecclesiastical history of Essex*, p. 128.
38. Davids, *Annals of evangelical nonconformity*, p. 439; Smith, *Ecclesiastical history of Essex*, pp. 122, 159; Newcourt, *Repertorium*, vol. 2, p. 307. For Onge as a teacher see G.L.R.O., DLC/343, f. 213v, G.L., MSS. 9537/14, f. 27v, 9537/15, f. 43v, 9539A/2, f. 166.
39. Newcourt, *Repertorium*, vol. 2, p. 352; Davids, *Annals of evangelical nonconformity*, pp. 378, 462, 436; Smith, *Ecclesiastical history of Essex*, pp. 92, 123, 158.
40. Davids, *Annals of evangelical nonconformity*, pp. 156, 296; Smith, *Ecclesiastical history of Essex*, p. 48; Newcourt, *Repertorium*, vol. 2, p. 575. Nehemiah Rogers was rector of Messing, Essex and then of St Botolph Bishopsgate, London. He was also a fellow of Jesus College, Cambridge, and a canon of Ely.
41. Newcourt, *Repertorium*, vol. 2, p. 446; Davids, *Annals of evangelical nonconformity*, p. 297.
42. Davids, *Annals of evangelical nonconformity*, p. 154; Smith, *Ecclesi-*

astical history of Essex, pp. 34, 51, 49, 125; Richard Hooke, the sine-cure rector of Little Baddow who had been presented by the king, was sequestered in 1644.

43. Davids, *Annals of evangelical nonconformity*, p. 162; Smith, *Ecclesiastical history of Essex*, pp. 31—2. Hooker and Eliot both have entries in the *D.N.B.* Despite his battle with the ecclesiastical authorities Hooker's licence as a schoolmaster was quite in order (G.L.R.O., DLC/ 342, f. 44v, Ac.69.88, f. 102)., but I have found no licence for John Eliot. The lay puritan luminaries at Little Baddow included Henry Mildmay, one of the commissioners for the sequestration of scandalous ministers.

44. Davids, *Annals of evangelical nonconformity*, pp. 281, 346—7; Smith, *Ecclesiastical history of Essex*, pp. 4, 47, 103.

45. Newcourt, *Repertorium*, vol. 2, p. 291; Davids, *Annals of evangelical nonconformity*, p. 270; Smith, *Ecclesiastical history of Essex*, pp. 397, 418.

46. Davids, *Annals of evangelical nonconformity*, pp. 116, 569, 443, 444, 268, 318; Smith, *Ecclesiastical history of Essex*, pp. 13, 388, 261.

47. Newcourt, *Repertorium*, vol. 2, p. 639; Smith, *Ecclesiastical history of Essex*, pp. 17, 193, 108, 247, 351; Davids, *Annals of evangelical nonconformity*, p. 255.

48. Episcopal visitations noted 96 schoolmasters in Essex in 1598, distributed through every deanery. In the visitation of 1612 there were 44, in 1628, 30, and in 1637, 55 (Cressy, 'Education and literacy in London and East Anglia', p. 100 and appendix).

49. For the ecclesiastical control of schoolteachers see David Cressy, *Education in Tudor and Stuart England* (1975), pp. 28—42; O'Day, 'Church records and the history of education', pp. 120ff.; Spufford, *Contrasting communities*, pp. 184—90; and the examples given in ch. 2 above.

50. Some of these limitations are discussed in Cressy, 'Educational opportunity', pp. 306—9.

51. Walthamstow schoolmasters included Thomas Colbey from 1598 to 1607, John Wilson in 1609, John Collard in 1612, Robert Seager in 1616, John Daston from 1621 to 1628, Charles Kemp and Robert Yarner in 1624, William Groome and Henry Wheeler in 1637 (G.L., MS. 9537/9, f. 141, MS. 9537/10, f. 77v, MS. 9539A/1, f. 87v, MS. 9537/15, f. 6v; G.L.R.O., DLC/339, f. 75, DLC/340, f. 67, DLC/341ff. 1, 2v, 236, DLC/342, f. 118v, Ac.69.88, f. 239). One Taylor was teaching at Ilford in 1619, followed by William Miller in 1622 (G.L.R.O., Ac.69.88, f. 125, DLC/325, f. 1v). Barking schoolmasters in the early seventeenth century included messrs Amsten, Leeche and Milling in 1605, messrs Greenham, Marsh, Milling, Plumtree and Richardson in 1607, Bett, Cowdrey, Robert and Trench in 1616, and so on (G.L.R.O., Ac.69.88, f. 26v, DLC/338, f. 216, DLC/324, f. 2, DLC/340, f. 210, G.L., MS. 9537/10, f. 75v). The recognized teachers at Colchester are too numerous to mention. Early Stuart schoolmasters at Sudbury included William Jacob, Robert Buxton, Philip Clarke, Mr Parnell and Thomas Haggurth (N.R.O., VSC/1, VIS/2). One Butler was teaching at Ramsey in 1612 and Francis Cooke was there in 1615. Other teachers are recorded at Ramsey back to Elizabethan times. (G.L., MS. 9537/11, ff. 38v, 136). Harwich schoolmasters included Richard Reynolds from 1604 to 1628, James Man from 1629 to 1634, with John Forbes in 1604, Mark Carr in 1621, and John Ashley in 1624

(G.L.R.O., DLC/338, f. 176, DLC/341, f. 212, DLC/342, 98v, DLC/322, f. 6, G.L., MS. 9537/11, ff. 37, 135, MS. 9537/13, f. 25v, MS. 9539A/1, f. 35).

52. G.L., MS. 9537/15, f. 8, G.L.R.O., DLC/343, f. 176v, DLC/341, f. 109. For Francis Onge see note 38 above.

53. Boxted schoolmasters included Richard Pierson in 1612 and Richard Robinson in 1615 (G.L., MS. 9537/11, f. 26, G.L.R.O., DLC/340, f. 165). The schoolmaster at Wormingford in 1615 was Samuel Cock (G.L., MS. 9537/11, f. 129). Richard Bridges taught at Prittlewell in 1611 (G.L.R.O., Ac.69.88, f. 156). Ethan Glascoke, son of a Prittlewell tailor, came up to Cambridge in 1627 after attending five separate schools (Sidney Sussex College, MS. Admission register, vol. 1, p. 196).

54. G.L.R.O., DLC/334, f. 312, G.L., MS. 9537/11, f. 14v, MS. 9537/11, ff. 16v, 110. Other Leigh schoolteachers included Francis Hewitson, who taught reading, writing and arithmetic from 1619 to 1625, John Harrison in 1628 and Gabriel Price in 1637 (G.L.R.O., DLC/341, f. 148v, E.R.O., D/ACV 1, f. 12, G.L., MS. 9537/13, f. 15v, MS. 9539A/1, f. 90).

55. Spufford, *Contrasting communities*, pp. 218, 173.

56. The map and the description of the Essex rural economy are based on Felix Hull, 'Agriculture and rural society in Essex 1560—1640', Ph.D. thesis, University of London, 1950, p. 99 and *passim*; Joan Thirsk (ed.), *The agrarian history of England and Wales*, vol. 4, 1500—1640 (Cambridge 1967), pp. 4, 53—5, and J. E. Pilgrim, 'The rise of the new draperies in Essex', *University of Birmingham Historical Journal*, 7 (1958—9), p. 57.

57. *Calendar of State Papers, Domestic, 1635—6*, p. 6; *C.S.P.D., 1637*, pp. 132, 177; P.R.O., SP 16/358. For the background to this matter see William Chapman Waller, 'Ship-money in Essex, 1634—1640', *Transactions of the Essex Archaeological Society*, n.s., 8 (1903), pp. 8—14.

58. P.R.O., SP 16/358; *C.S.P.D., 1637*, p. 132. Having explained his rating sheriff Lucas received the personal congratulations of the king.

59. John Patten, 'The hearth taxes, 1662—1689', *Local Population Studies*, 7 (1971), p. 18; E.R.O., Q/RTh/5.

60. The assessments were decimalized for the purposes of calculation and then re-converted to pounds, shillings and pence.

61. These non-parametric statistical procedures were carried out using SPSS. See Norman H. Nie *et al.*, *Statistical package for the social sciences*, 2nd edn (New York, 1975), pp. 290—2.

62. *C.S.P.D., 1696*, p. 52. 7 & 8 Wm. III c.27.

63. P.R.O., C 213/108, /264.

64. The circulation of the oath is discussed in Wallace Gandy, *The Association oath rolls of the British plantations* (1922), pp. 16—19. See also his *Lancashire Association oath rolls* (1921). *C.S.P.D., 1696*, p. 177, has some correspondence between the privy council and the Deputy Lieutenants of Worcestershire and Herefordshire indicative of their supervising activity.

65. William LeHardy (ed.), *Hertfordshire county records, calendar to the sessions books*, vol. 4 (Hertford, 1930), pp. 485—6. Some of the returns are in the H.R.O., QS. Misc. 912—917.

66. P.R.O., C 213/264/20. The Suffolk returns are all in the P.R.O., C 213/264—268. The certificate of Coney Weston reported the names of all

'householders and lodgers, young men and servants, above the age of sixteen . . . we had not any did refuse'.

67. Alan Macfarlane, *Reconstructing historical communities* (Cambridge, 1977), pp. 189–90. Hearth-tax figures from E.R.O. Q/RTh/5 and totals of communicants from William Salt Library, Salt MS. 33, are compared with Essex Association oath roll totals in Cressy, 'Education and literacy in London and East Anglia', pp. 298–300.
68. P.R.O., C 213/264/3, 20, 7, 19. In Hertfordshire Mr Pryce the parson of Gilston refused to sign the Association (H.R.O. QS. Misc. 914).
69. P.R.O., C 213/473. Of the 125 subscribers, 24 made marks (C 213/264/17).
70. E.R.O., Q/RRo/2/1 has returns for 58 Essex parishes, of which 36 are usable. H.R.O. QS. Misc. 912–917 has 6 returns, of which 3 are usable. P.R.O., C 213/264–268 has returns for all the parishes in Suffolk, including 215 which are acceptable. Returns for other parts of England are in C 213.
71. A total of 1,146 men subscribed the Association in the market towns of Beccles, Ixworth, Nayland, Newmarket, Southwold, Stowmarket and Woolpit. Other market towns in Suffolk appear in the Association oath rolls but are vitiated for the analysis of literacy by having some names written by proxy. The identification of market towns is from Everitt, 'The marketing of agricultural produce', p. 475.
72. A Kolmogorov-Smirnov test showed that the difference was not statistically significant at the 0.05 level. See H. M. Blalock, *Social Statistics* (New York, 1960), pp. 405–9, 203–6.
73. The Protestation was rarely taken by women, although some of the Middlesex returns include the names of wives and widows. See note 16, above. Women sometimes took the Association as housekeepers (i.e. householders). At Wakes Colne, Essex, 2 women wrote signatures and 7 made marks. At Bulpham, Essex, and at Great Livermore, Suffolk, we are given the occupations of all the subscribers, but neither list has all the original marks and signatures. The list for Theberton, Suffolk, distinguishes lodgers, servants, apprentices and journeymen from housekeepers, while Ilketshall St Andrew divided its subscription between owners, tenants, single persons and lodgers (E.R.O., Q/RRo/2/1, P.R.O., C 213/264/22, 2, 10).

Chapter 5. Lay illiteracy in ecclesiastical records

1. 'Cox's case, Michaelmas 1700', *The English Reports*, 24 (1903), pp. 281–2; Henry Conset, *The practice of the spiritual or ecclesiastical courts* (1685), pp. 15–21; James T. Law, *Forms of ecclesiastical law* (1831), pp. 42–5. Between a third and a half of all ecclesiastical court cases concerned defamation, and almost a third more involved tithes (R. A. Marchant, *The church under the law* (Cambridge, 1969), pp. 20, 62, 194).
2. Gaston Zeller, *Les institutions de la France au XVIe siècle* (Paris, 1948), pp. 357–8; Roger Doucet, *Les institutions de la France au XVIe siècle* (Paris, 1948), vol. 2, pp. 783–9. Although the French ecclesiastical court procedures were similar to those in England, and included the collection of signatures and marks, the volume of business was minute. See Louis de Héricourt, *Les loix ecclésiastiques de France* (Paris, 1756), pp. 141–54.

3. Conset, *Practice of the spiritual courts*, p. 18.
4. See, for example, the discussion of village scribes in ch. 1, and the possession of books in ch. 3. Probate inventories are used in ch. 6 to establish the social distribution of wealth for comparison with the distribution of illiteracy.
5. Richard Burn, *Ecclesiastical law* (1763), vol. 2, pp. 503—774; Conset, *Practice of the spiritual courts*, pp. 371—4; Law, *Forms of ecclesiastical law*, pp. 55—9. In a deposition before the consistory court of the diocese of Norwich in 1633, for example, William Bradford, a schoolmaster of North Walsham, testified about his part in writing the will of Susan Woodroste, 'according to such directions and instructions as she the said Susan then gave unto him this deponent from her own mouth' (N.R.O., DEP/41, f. 465). Most wills were proved without difficulty.
6. Kenneth Lockridge, *Literacy in colonial New England* (New York, 1974). Spufford, *Contrasting communities*, pp. 192—205. Nesta Evans, 'The community of South Elmham, Suffolk', M.Phil. Thesis, University of East Anglia, 1978.
7. The table is based on an analysis of all surviving wills from 1633, 1635 and 1637 (N.R.O., wills).
8. Burn, *Ecclesiastical law*, vol. 2, pp. 505—10.
9. Spufford, *Contrasting communities*, p. 196. Lockridge argues that the bias of selection and the problem of failing literacy are 'roughly equal' and cancel each other, but this seems to be wishful thinking (*Literacy in colonial New England*, p. 11).
10. Spufford, *Contrasting communities*, pp. 182—3; N.R.O., wills, 1637, 1633. Feeble will-makers were vulnerable to unscrupulous executors and heirs and it was not entirely unknown for wills to be altered and 'signatures' to appear after the testator had lost consciousness. In Hudson's case the testator was dying and 'another guided his hand and . . . the testator made his mark but said nothing, nor was he capable' (Burn, *Ecclesiastical law*, vol. 2, p. 523).
11. Schofield, 'Dimensions of illiteracy', pp. 441—54. Further analysis of this data appears in Michael Sanderson, 'Literacy and social mobility in the industrial revolution', *Past and Present*, 56 (1972), pp. 75—104, and the debate between Thomas W. Laqueur and Michael Sanderson in *Past and Present*, 64 (1974), pp. 96—112.
12. The data for Norfolk and Suffolk are mine (N.R.O., MLB/2 and 3; see also MLB/1 and 4, SUN/6); the information for Oxfordshire and Gloucestershire is based on Stone, 'Literacy and education', pp. 103—7. The bond assured the court that there was 'no lawful let or impediment by reason of consanguinity or affinity . . . or of precontract, strife or suit in law', and arranged for the marriage to be performed 'publicly in the face of the church between the hours of eight and twelve of the clock in the forenoon' (N.R.O., MLB/2, 51).
13. Brian Frith (ed.), *Gloucestershire marriage allegations 1637—1680* (Gloucester, 1954), p. xvi, and Patrick McGrath, 'Notes on the history of marriage licences', in *ibid*. pp. xx—xxx; Vivien Brodsky Elliot, 'Marriage and mobility in pre-industrial England', Ph.D. thesis, University of Cambridge, 1978, pp. 12—15. Marriage, except by licence, was inhibited from Septuagesima Sunday to the Sunday after Easter, from Rogation Sunday to Trinity Sunday, and from Advent Sunday to the feast of St Hilary in the following January; most almanacs gave the details for particular years. 'Marriages are prohibited in Lent and on

fasting days, because the mirth attending them is not suitable to the humiliation and devotion of those times; yet persons may marry with licences in Lent, although the banns of marriage may not then be published' (Jacob, *Law dictionary* (1729), quoted in McGrath, 'Notes on the history of marriage licences', p. xxx). For the advantage of the licence to pregnant brides see R. B. Outhwaite, 'Age at marriage in England from the late seventeenth century', *Transactions of the Royal Historical Society*, 5, 23 (1973), p. 67.

14. J. V. Bullard (ed.), *Constitutions and canons ecclesiastical* (1934), p. 108; Burn, *Ecclesiastical law*, vol. 2, p. 21; Frith, *Gloucestershire marriage allegations*, p. xviii; Marchant, *Church under the law*, p. 21.

15. Elliot, 'Mobility and marriage', p. 15.

16. Conset, *Practice of the spiritual courts*, pp. 117, 116.

17. *Ibid*. p. 113.

18. N.R.O., DEP/18, book 19, f. 8v, 25 October 1580. The following is the original Latin text, reproduced here with modern punctuation and extension of abbreviations to improve its legibility:

> Super libello ex parte Richardi Richardson et Suzannam Ives dato, Henricus Ives parochie Sancti Andree civitatis Norvici, Paynter, ubi moram fecit per mensem fere aut circiter et antea in parochia Sancti Michaelis de Coslanie civitatis predicte per V annos elapsos, natus apud Aylesham Burroughe in comitatu Norffolciense, etatis L annorum aut circiter, libere condicionis testis etcetera, novit Richardum Richardson partem producentem per tres menses aut circiter novit, et Suzannam Ives a nativitate sua novit.

The 'etcetera' covers a formula abbreviation for 'libere condicionis ut dicit testis productus, admissus, iuratus et diligenter examinatus super noticia partium litigantium'. Some examples in print are Walter C. Renshaw, 'Witnesses from ecclesiastical deposition books, 1580–1640', *Sussex Archaeological Collections*, 55 (1914) and Arthur J. Willis, *Winchester consistory court depositions, 1561–1602* (Lyming, Kent, 1960).

19. For examples, see F. G. Emmison, *Elizabethan life: morals and the church courts* (Chelmsford, 1973).

20. N.R.O., DEP/38–44.

21. N.R.O., DEP/14–60; D.R.O., Chanter 858–880, 8297–8299, 11035–11038; University of Durham, Department of Palaeography and Diplomatic, D.R. V, 1–12; G.L.R.O., DL/C 222–267, 629–630; G.L., MS. 9065A/2–9, MS. 9189, MS. 9585; E.R.O., D/ABD 1–8, D/ACD 1–7, D/AED 1–10, D/AXD 1. No diocese preserves a complete set of depositions from the sixteenth to the eighteenth century. The Exeter depositions are sparse in the 1590s and 1600s and missing from 1608–13, 1619–34 and 1640–61. Those for Durham are missing after 1631. The Norwich depositions have gaps from 1611–14, 1620–8 and 1646–61. The London depositions come from a variety of courts, consistory, commissary and archdeaconry; while the City and suburban evidence is more or less continuous the depositions for Essex and Hertfordshire are thin in the 1590s and mostly missing for the later seventeenth century. The ecclesiastical courts throughout the country were suppressed during the revolution, although the consistory court of the bishop of Norwich was still conducting business as late as July 1647 (N.R.O., DEP/45, book 49, f. 160).

22. The Norwich depositions survive from 1499 but were rarely signed

before 1572. A small file of London depositions from 1467 to 1476 yields some information about the literacy of City tradesmen (Sylvia L. Thrupp, *The merchant class of medieval London* (Chicago, 1948), pp. 156—7). Another file for 1489—1516 is in G. L., MS. 9065.

23. R. S. Schofield, 'Sampling in historical research', in E. A. Wrigley (ed.), *Nineteenth-century society* (Cambridge, 1972), pp. 146—90. No pattern of social precedence appeared to determine the order in which witnesses came before the judge and no periodicity could be discovered which might undermine the value of a systematic sample. Random number tables were used to select the first deposition in each volume or bundle, and sampling intervals were varied only from bundle to bundle to secure roughly equal numbers in each period. In areas with dense documentation, such as the diocese of Norwich, one in five of all depositions was sampled, but elsewhere it was sometimes necessary to examine every single document.

24. Conset, *Practice of the spiritual courts*, pp. 115, 140—2; Thomas Oughton, *Ordo judiciorum* (1738), pp. 130—56. Henry Ives, whose deposition is cited on p. 111, was a witness in a case involving his sister but his kinship did not bar him since he was produced by the opposing party.

25. Although the names of husbands were normally given, their status or occupation appears in no more than a quarter of the depositions made by wives and widows. The figures in Table 5.5 are drawn from a sample of 119 depositions with this information in seventeenth-century East Anglia (N.R.O., DEP/31—52).

26. The cultural acceleration of London and the unique position of women in the metropolis demands closer attention. Useful leads are given in Keith Thomas, 'Women and the civil war sects', *Past and Present*, 13 (1958) and E. A. Wrigley, 'A simple model of London's importance', *Past and Present*, 37 (1967).

27. Julian Cornwall, 'Evidence of population mobility in the seventeenth century', *Bulletin of the Institute of Historical Research*, 40 (1967), p. 144.

28. To chart the progress of illiteracy with advancing years a sample of these deponents was sorted into birth cohorts (by subtracting their age from the date of their deposition), and their inability to sign was examined at progressively higher ages. Not until the sixties was there any clear evidence of alteration; craftsmen aged sixty and above were some 12% more illiterate than those born at the same time but who made depositions at younger ages. This has no more than a marginal effect on the over-all figures.

29. The Examination Books of Colchester, Essex, for the period 1574—81 reveal a structure of illiteracy similar to the depositions. In a sample of nearly 1,000, gentry and clergy could all sign, but illiteracy was widespread among all other groups, with 50% of yeomen, 55% of tradesmen, 67% of servants, 95% of husbandmen, 97% of women and 100% of labourers unable to sign their names. My analysis of figures supplied by Dr Joel Samaha, University of Minnesota. See also Richard T. Vann, 'Literacy in seventeenth-century England: some hearth tax evidence', *Journal of Interdisciplinary History*, 5 (1974), pp. 287—93.

Chapter 6. The structure of illiteracy

1. Sources are cited in ch. 5, note 21.

2. David Cressy, 'Describing the social order of Elizabethan and Stuart England', *History and Literature*, 3 (1976), pp. 29–32.
3. Sir Thomas Smith, *De republica anglorum* (1583), p. 20. Similar accounts are found in William Harrison, *The description of England*, ed. Georges Edelen (Ithaca, New York, 1968); William Camden, *Britain* (1610); Thomas Wilson, *The state of England, anno dom. 1600* ed. F. J. Fisher, *Camden Miscellany*, 16 (1936), pp. 1–43.
4. B. W. Beckingsale, 'The characteristics of the Tudor north', *Northern History*, 4 (1969), p. 76; Durham depositions, D. R. V 11. An administration bond granted to executors showed that this survivor from the reformation period was dead by 1629.
5. Wilson, *State of England*, p. 23; Harrison, *Description of England*, pp. 113–14; Thomas Milles, *The catalogue of honor, or tresury of true nobility peculiar and proper to the isle of Great Britaine* (1610), p. 79.
6. Harrison, *Description of England*, p. 114.
7. E.R.O., D/AED 3; N.R.O., DEP/42; D.R.O., Chanter 870; G.L., MS. 9065A/8.
8. Mervyn James, *Family, lineage and civil society. A study of society, politics and mentality in the Durham region, 1500–1640* (Oxford, 1974), pp. 31, 106–6; David Cressy, 'Social status and literacy in north-east England, 1560–1630', *Local Population Studies*, 21 (1978), pp. 19–23.
9. Smith, *De republica anglorum*, pp. 29, 31; Harrison, *Description of England*, pp. 115, 117–18; Wilson, *State of England*, p. 19; Edward Chamberlayne, *Angliae notitia*, 3rd edn (1669), p. 441; Gregory King, 'A scheme of the income and expence of the several families of England, calculated for the year 1688', in Charles Davenant, 'An essay upon the probable methods of making a people gainers in the balance of trade', in *Political and commercial works*, ed. Sir C. Whitworth (1771), vol. 2, p. 184, and often reproduced.
10. The peculiarities of yeoman status in the Durham region are discussed in Cressy, 'Social status and literacy in north-east England'. The dual status deponents are found in Durham depositions, D.R. V 2.
11. G. J. Piccope (ed.), *Lancashire and Cheshire wills and inventories* (Chetham Society, 1857), pp. 163, 167.
12. Smith, *De republica anglorum*, pp. 29–31; Thomas Fuller, *The holy state*, 2nd edn (Cambridge, 1648), p. 105; John Norden, *Speculi Britanniae pars: an historical and chorographical description of Essex* ed. Sir Henry Ellis, (Camden Society, 1840), p. xii; William J. Blake, 'Hooker's synopsis chorographical of Devonshire', *Report and Transactions of the Devonshire Association*, 47 (1915), pp. 341–2. Edward Chamberlayne opined that the yeomen, 'at their ease and almost forgetting labour, grow rich and thereby so proud, insolent and careless that they neither give that humble respect and aweful reverence which in other kingdoms is usually given to nobility, gentry and clergy' (*Angliae notitia*, 3rd edn, p. 61).
13. Laslett, *World we have lost*, p. 45. There has been a tendency, perhaps unwise, for historians to group yeomen and husbandmen together as the 'peasantry' of England.
14. Gervase Markham, *The English husbandman* (1613), sig. A3. Sir Thomas Smith notes, 'commonly we do not call any a yeoman till he be married and have children and have as it were some authority among his neighbours' (*De republica anglorum*, p. 32).

15. Robert Reyce, *The breviary of Suffolk, 1618*, ed. Lord Francis Hervey (1902), p. 58; Richard Steele, *The husbandmans calling*, 2nd edn, (1672), pp. 55–6.
16. Blake, 'Hooker's synopsis', p. 342; Chamberlayne, *Angliae notitia*, 3rd edn, p. 445; Alan Everitt, 'Farm labourers', in Joan Thirsk (ed.), *The agrarian history of England and Wales*, vol. 4 (Cambridge, 1967), p. 398. In King's scheme for 1688 labouring people comprised 27% of the families, 51% if cottagers and paupers are added.
17. One thinks of the problems in New England with Anne Hutchinson and the episodes cited in Thomas, 'Women and the civil war sects', pp. 42–62. See also Wallace Notestein, 'The English woman, 1580 to 1650', in J. H. Plumb (ed.), *Studies in social history* (1955), pp. 69–107, and remarks on the 'folly' and 'weakness' of women in J. A. Comenius, *The great didactic* (1657), ed. M. W. Keating, 2nd edn (1910), p. 67, and Billingsley, *Pens excellencie*, sig. B4v.
18. Useful clues might be found in Wrigley, 'A simple model of London's importance', and David Cressy, 'Occupations, migration and literacy in east London 1580–1640', *Local Population Studies*, 5 (1970).
19. Smith, *De republica anglorum*, p. 33; Mulcaster, *Positions*, p. 198; Chamberlayne, *Angliae notitia*, 3rd edn, p. 445; King, 'Scheme . . . for the year 1688'.
20. Sons of Merchant Taylors were the largest group at Merchant Taylors' School, taking 29% of the free scholarships in the period 1570–1600 and accounting for 20% of the entrants in the period 1644–50; figures calculated from C. J. Robinson (ed.), *A register of the scholars admitted into Merchant Taylors' School, from a.d. 1562 to 1874* (Lewes, 1882–3), pp. 2–41, and William Dugard's register, Merchant Taylors' Hall, MS. 'Nomina discipulorum'.
21. The classic exposition of this system of industrial classification is A. J. and R. H. Tawney, 'An occupational census of the seventeenth century', *Economic History Review*, 5 (1934–5), pp. 25–64. An industrial ranking of illiteracy, based on the Tawney occupational classifications, is in Cressy, 'Education and literacy in London and East Anglia', pp. 330–40.
22. Burn, *Ecclesiastical law*, vol. 2, pp. 644–52; Francis W. Steer, 'Probate inventories', *History*, 47 (1962), pp. 287–90; Stephens, *Sources for English local history*, pp. 36–7.
23. Peter C. D. Brears (ed.), 'Yorkshire probate inventories', *Yorkshire Archaeological Society Record Series*, 134 (1972); Margaret Cash (ed.), 'Devon inventories of the sixteenth and seventeenth centuries', *Devon and Cornwall Record Society*, 11 (1966); Lucy Drucker (ed.) 'Administrations in the archdeaconry of Northampton, 1667–1710', *British Record Society* (1947); A. D. Dyer (ed.), 'Probate inventories of Worcester tradesmen, 1545–1614', *Worcester Historical Society Miscellany*, 2 (1967); F. G. Emmison, 'Jacobean household inventories', *Publications of the Bedfordshire Historical Record Society*, 20 (1938); M. A. Havinden (ed.), *Household and farm inventories of Oxfordshire, 1550–1590* (Historical Manuscripts Commission, 1965); P. A. Kennedy (ed.), 'Nottinghamshire household inventories', *Thoroton Society Record Series*, 22 (1963); G. H. Kenyon, 'Kirdford inventories, 1611 to 1776', *Sussex Archaeological Collections*, 93 (1955); G. H. Kenyon, 'Petworth town and trades 1610–1760, part 2', *Sussex Archaeological Collections*,

98 (1960); Moore (ed.), *Goods and chattels of our forefathers*; John S. Roper, *Dudley probate inventories* (Dudley, 1965—6); John S. Roper, *Sedgley probate inventories, 1614—1787* (Dudley, 1960); Francis W. Steer, *Farm and cottage inventories of mid-Essex 1635—1749*, 2nd edn, (Chichester, 1969); D. G. Vaisey, 'Probate inventories of Lichfield and district, 1568—1680', *Collections for a History of Staffordshire*, 5 (1969); James Raine, William Greenwell, J. C. Hodgson and Herbert Maxwell Wood (eds.), 'Wills and inventories from the registry at Durham', *Surtees Society Publications*, 2 (1835), 38 (1860), 112 (1906), 142 (1929). Other printed collections of probate inventories are inadequately edited, or came too late to my attention for inclusion in this analysis. I am indebted to Dr Mark Overton of Emmanuel College, Cambridge, for allowing me to use his transcription of probate inventories from the consistory court of the diocese of Norwich. The computer processing of all these inventories was greatly assisted by use of the Statistical Package for the Social Sciences.

24. E. H. Phelps Brown and Sheila V. Hopkins, 'Seven centuries of the price of consumables, compared with builders' wage rates', *Economica*, 23 (1956), pp. 296—314. The index for 1640 is 546. The adjusted value= inventory value (base year index/inventory year index). I am indebted to Professor Peter Lindhert of the University of California, Davis, for his assistance with this calculation.

25. John Norden, *Speculum Britanniae: an historical and chorographical description of Middlesex and Hartfordshire* (1723), p. 50.

26. John Whitgift claimed that 'every waterman on the Thames earneth more by his labour than the greater part of several ministers in England should do by their benefices', and Richard Hooker judged the 'ordinary pastors of the church' to be comparable in wealth to 'common artisans or tradesmen', quoted in Christopher Hill, *Economic problems of the church, from Archbishop Whitgift to the Long Parliament* (Oxford, 1956), pp. 189, 207. Rachel P. Garrard of Darwin College, Cambridge, is engaged on a study of Suffolk probate inventories which will measure the social significance of the domestic interior.

27. Fuller, *The holy state*, 2nd edn, p. 105.

Chapter 7. The dynamics of illiteracy

1. Schofield, 'Dimensions of illiteracy', pp. 442—6.

2. An additional opportunity to examine the literacy of women in London is provided by the autograph acknowledgements of discharge of children from Christ's Hospital: 88% of the mothers of boys admitted 1637—9 could not sign, reducing to 68% for mothers of 1667—70 entrants and 60% for the mothers of 1687—9. (Sample from G. L. MS. 12818, vols. 3, 5, 6).

3. Gardiner, *English girlhood at school*, pp. 201—2, 209—14, 224.

4. Cressy, 'Social status and literacy in north east England', pp. 20—2.

5. The sorting and averaging was done on the DEC 10 computer at the Seaver Computer Center, Claremont, California. The first fruits of this process and an earlier version of the argument in this chapter appeared in Cressy, 'Levels of illiteracy in England', pp. 11—23.

6. Reports of Schools Inquiry Commission, Appendix 4, *Parliamentary Papers*, 1867—8, vol. 28, pt 1, pp. 700—54. A check was made in

the relevant sections of the *Victoria County History* and in Carlisle, *Concise description of the endowed grammar schools.*

7. (1959), esp. pp. 279—97 and table, p. 373.

8. Cressy, 'Education and literacy in London and East Anglia', pp. 218—37; Lawrence Stone, 'The size and composition of the Oxford student body 1580—1910', in Stone (ed.), *The university in society*, vol. 1 (Princeton, 1974), p. 91.

9. G. R. Elton, *Reform and renewal, Thomas Cromwell and the common weal* (Cambridge, 1973), pp. 29—32; Thomas Starkey, 'A dialogue between Cardinal Pole and Thomas Lupset', in Sidney J. Herrtage (ed.), *England in the reign of Henry VIII* (1927), pp. 205—6.

10. A. F. Leach, *English schools at the reformation*, 2 vols. (1896); Simon, *Education and society in Tudor England* (Cambridge, 1967), pp. 179—96, 215—44, 268.

11. Simon, *Education and society in Tudor England*, pp. 299—332; John Lawson and Harold Silver, *A social history of education in England* (1973), pp. 100—15.

12. G.L.R.O., DL/C 333—4, N.R.O., SUN/2.

13. See ch. 2.

14. My figures in Stone, 'Size and composition of the Oxford student body', pp. 17, 28—9. The total of matriculations in the 1590s is extrapolated from the number of graduations in that decade and the numerical relationship between matriculations and graduations in the previous and following decades. The Cambridge matriculation register was poorly maintained in the 1590s, another symptom of decline.

15. Brown and Hopkins, 'Seven centuries of the price of consumables', pp. 302, 312. N.R.O., VIS/1—6, VSC/1—2, REG/16. The fluctuating numbers of teachers is discussed in Cressy, 'Education and literacy in London and East Anglia', pp. 86—137.

16. N.R.O., VIS/1—6, VSC/1—2, REG/16.

17. *C.S.P.D.*, 1655—6, pp. 387—8. Parliamentary Ordinances were more concerned to remove 'ill affected' personnel than to secure widespread schooling (Firth and Rait, *Acts and ordinances of the interregnum*, vol. 1, p. 431, vol. 2, pp. 958—90).

18. For good intentions and slight achievements during the Revolution see Charles Webster, *Samuel Hartlib and the advancement of learning* (Cambridge, 1970) and W. A. L. Vincent, *The state and school education 1640—1660* (1950).

19. *C.S.P.D.*, 1655—6, p. 388; Vincent, *The state and school education*, *passim*; Christopher Hill, 'Puritans and the "dark corners of the land"', *Transactions of the Royal Historical Society*, 5, no. 13 (1963).

20. Chamberlayne, *Angliae notitia*, 3rd edn, pp. 320—2.

21. N.R.O., SUB/1—4.

22. M. G. Jones, *The charity school movement* (1964), p. 73. See also Joan Simon, 'Was there a charity school movement? in Brian Simon (ed.), *Education in Leicestershire* (Leicester, 1968), pp. 55—100.

Chapter 8. Literacy and society in England and beyond

1. It will be recalled that 89% of the men of Little Waldingfield, Suffolk, failed to sign the oath that was tendered to them in 1534 and this is compatible with our estimate of national illiteracy at that time of

between 80% and 90%. See ch. 4 for the declarations of the 1640s and 1690s and chs. 5, 6 and 7 for the evidence of depositions.

2. Schofield, 'Dimensions of illiteracy', pp. 437—54. For another review of the registrar general's figures see E. G. West, 'Literacy and the industrial revolution', *Economic History Review*, 2nd series, 31 (1978), pp. 369—83.
3. Schofield, 'Dimensions of illiteracy', p. 443.
4. Egil Johansson, 'The history of literacy in Sweden in comparison with some other countries', *Educational Reports Umea*, 12 (1977).
5. Furet and Ozouf, *Lire et écrire*, facing p. 9, pp. 59—68 and *passim*.
6. Roger Chartier, Cominique Julia and Marie-Madeleine Compère, *L'éducation en France du XVIe au XVIIIe siècle* (Paris, 1976) pp. 87—109.
7. Andrzej Wyczanski, 'Alphabétisation et structure sociale en Pologne au XVIe siècle', *Annales, E.S.C.*, 29 (1974), pp. 705—13; Waclaw Urban, 'La connaissance de l'écriture en Petite-Pologne dans la seconde moitié du XVIe siècle', *Przeglad Historyczny*, 68 (1977), p. 257.
8. B. Geremek, communication to the colloquium on 'Alphabétisation, changement social et développement', Werner Reimers Stiftung, Bad-Homburg, 1979.
9. K. Benda, 'L'alphabétisation parmis les paysans de Hongrie a l'époque des Lumières', circulated at the Bad-Homburg colloquium.
10. This paragraph is based on remarks by R. Engelsing, P. Lundgreen and F. Vierhaus at the Bad-Homburg colloquium.
11. Carlo M. Cipolla, *Literacy and development in the west* (1969), pp. 57—9, 83, 93, 114.
12. Simon Hart, 'Enige statistiche gegevens inzake analfabetisme te Amsterdam in de 17e en 18e eeuw', *Amstelodamum*, 55 (1968), p. 4. Belgian figures communicated by François Furet at the Bad-Homburg colloquium.
13. T. C. Smout, *A history of the Scottish people 1560—1830*, 2nd edn (1970), pp. 73, 88, 89, 94, 96. See also Donald J. Withrington, 'Lists of schoolmasters teaching Latin, 1690', *Scottish History Society, Miscellany*, 10 (1965), p. 125, and Daniel Defoe, *A review of the state of the British nation*, 5, no. 80 (1708), p. 318.
14. Stone, 'Literacy and education', pp. 80—1, 126—7. Lockridge, *Literacy in colonial New England*, p. 99.
15. I am grateful to Rab Houston of Peterhouse, Cambridge, for drawing these sources to my attention and sharing with me some of his unpublished findings.
16. Lockridge, *Literacy in colonial New England*, pp. 12 and *passim*.
17. *Ibid.* pp. 5, 45—6, 83.
18. Lockridge discusses these factors but gives them less weight than religion.
19. Johansson, 'History of literacy in Sweden', pp. 7—8.
20. *Injunctions gyven by the auctoritie of the kyngs highnese to the clergie* (1536).
21. J. Spedding (ed.), *The letters and life of Francis Bacon*, vol. 4 (1868), pp. 252—3; John Brinsley, *A consolation for our grammar schooles* (1622), pp. 10—11; Comenius, *The great didactic*, 2nd edn, pp. 66—9; John Dury, *The reformed school* (1649), pp. 18—19; Samuel Hartlib, *Considerations tending to the happy accomplishment of England's reformation* (1647), pp. 21—2.

Bibliography

Manuscript sources

British Library (B. L.)
    Harleian MS. 2107. Cheshire remonstrance 1642
Cambridge University Archives
    Matriculation registers 1544–1702
Cambridgeshire Record Office
    P 177/25/1. Willingham school subscription list
Devon Record Office (D.R.O.)
    Chanter 858–880, 8279–8299, 11035–11038 Depositions 1570–1709
    Consistory court testamentary causes
    1920A/PR37 Uffculme parish register
Durham County Record Office
    Easington parish register
    Monk Hesleden parish register
Durham University, Department of Palaeography and Diplomatic

D.R. V 1–12	Depositions 1565–1631
D.R. VII 2	Act book 1561–1570
Probate records	1678–1689
E/SW/G.11	Bishop Auckland grammar school governors' minute book

Essex Record Office (E.R.O.)

D/ABD 1–8	Depositions 1618–1642
D/ACA 15	Act book
D/ACD 1–7	Depositions 1587–1641
D/ACV 1	Act book
D/AED 1–10	Depositions 1576–1642
D/AXD 1	Depositions 1631
D/P 30/1/2	Witham school attendance book, 1787–1800
D/P 35/1	Little Baddow parish register
D/P 114/1	Fyfield parish register
D/P 153/1	Barnston parish register
D/P 184/1	Great Parndon parish register
D/P 292/1	Wanstead parish register
D/P 301/1	Dengie parish register
D/P 388/1	Little Oakley parish register
Q/RRo/2/1	Association oath roll, 1696
Q/RTh/5	Hearth-tax roll, 1671
T/A42	Transcript of 1636 ship-money account

Greater London Record Office (G.L.R.O.)

DL/C 222–267	Depositions 1613–1731
DL/C 304–329	Correction books 1606–1706
DL/C 333–345	Vicar Generals' books 1580–1686

DL/C 618–626	Correction books 1605–1671
DL/C 629–630	Depositions 1578–1634
Ac.69.88	Depositions and corrections

Guildhall Library (G.L.)

MS. 959/1	St Martin Orgar vestry minutes
MS. 977/1	St Clement Eastcheap vestry minutes
MS. 1196/1	St Katherine Cree vestry minutes
MS. 1303/1	St Benet Fink Churchwardens' accounts
MS. 2597	St Mary Magdalen Milk Street vestry minutes
MS. 4384/2	St Bartholomew Exchange vestry minutes
MS. 4415	St Olave Jewry vestry minutes
MS. 4458	St Stephen Coleman Street vestry minutes
MS. 4835	Holy Trinity the Less Churchwardens' accounts
MS. 5019/1	St Pancras Soper Lane vestry minutes
MS. 9065	Depositions 1489–1516
MS. 9065A/2–9	Depositions 1594–1704
MS. 9189	Depositions 1622–1628
MS. 9532/1	Licences 1686–1700
MS. 9537/4–15	Visitations 1580–1700
MS. 9539A/1–3	Subscriptions 1627–1675
MS. 9585	Depositions 1581–1593
MS. 10116/1–13	Testimonials 1660–1700
MS. 12818/3–6	Christ's Hospital register

Hertfordshire Record Office (H.R.O.)

ASA/7/10	Act book
D/P/114–29/10	Walkern parish register
Qs. Misc. 912–917	Association oath rolls, 1696

House of Lords Record Office (H.L.R.O.)

Protestation returns
Petitions

Humberside Record Office

| PR 1958 | Cherry Burton covenant |

Lichfield Joint Record Office

Bishop Lloyd's surveys of Eccleshall

Merchant Taylors' Hall

MS. Nomina discipulorum, school admission register

Norfolk and Norwich Record Office (N.R.O.)

Case 13/62	Eaton parish covenant
Case 13/C	Test oath roll, 1673
DEP/17–60	Depositions 1579–1728
MLB/1–4	Marriage licences and bonds 1613–1694
REG/16	Visitations 1627
SUB/1–4	Subscription books 1637–1700
SUN/2, 4	Sundry documents 1582–1640
SUN/6	Marriage allegations 1661–1674
TES/1–8	Testimonials 1660–1700
VSC/1–4	Visitations 1604–1700
VIS/1–9	Visitations 1593–1699

Wills, consistory court 1633–1637

Great Yarmouth records:

C18/6	Council book
C19/21	Assembly Waste book
L3/13	Register of the Children's Hospital

PD 88/1   Hassingham parish register
PD 123/49   Little Plumstead parish register
PD 252/1   South Walsham parish register
Public Record Office (P.R.O.)
    C 213/1–476   Association oath rolls 1696
    SP 12/174   Instrument of Association, 1584
    SP 16/358   Essex ship-money account, 1637
Sidney Sussex College, Cambridge
    MS. Register, vol. 1 1598–1706
Somerset Record Office
    D/P/Winsh. 2/1/2   Winsham parish register
Suffolk Record Office (S.R.O.)
    FB 51/A3/1   Cretingham parish register
    FB 107/A1/1   St Stephen, Ipswich parish register
    FB 190/D1/1   Brantham parish register
    FBA 213/D/1   Harleston parish register
    FC 89/A1/1   Brundish parish register
    FC 124/D2/1   Friston parish register
    FC 193/D1/1   Linstead Parva parish register
    105/2/13   Quarter sessions order book 1695–1704
Trinity College, Cambridge
    Swineshead (Huntingdonshire) covenant
William Salt Library, Stafford
    Salt MS. 33   Transcript of 'Compton census'
Parish registers with incumbents
    Essex:
        Boxted, Hadleigh, East Hanningfield, Kelveden Hatch, Marks Tey,
        Prittlewell, Great Stambridge, Wormingford
    Norfolk:
        Breccles, East Rudham, Houghton-juxta-Harpley

Theses and unpublished papers

Benda, K. 'L'alphabétisation parmis les paysans de Hongrie a l'époque des
    Lumières', unpublished article, circulated at the Bad-Homburg col-
    loquium on 'Alphabétisation, changement social et développement',
    1979.
Cressy, David. 'Education and literacy in London and East Anglia, 1580–
    1700', Ph.D. thesis, University of Cambridge, 1973
Elliot, Vivien Brodsky. 'Mobility and marriage in pre-industrial England',
    Ph.D. thesis, University of Cambridge, 1978
Enright, B. J. 'Public petitions in the House of Commons', H.L.R.O., type-
    script, 1960
Evans, Nesta. 'The community of South Elmham, Suffolk', M.Phil. thesis,
    University of East Anglia, 1978
Finlay, R. A. P. 'The population of London, 1580–1650', Ph.D. thesis,
    University of Cambridge, 1976
Gremek, B. 'Remarks on literacy in Poland', unpublished communication to
    the Bad-Homburg colloquium on 'Alphabétisation, changement social
    et développement', 1979
Hull, Felix. 'Agriculture and rural society in Essex 1560–1640', Ph.D. thesis,
    University of London, 1950
Norwich Survey Unit, Report on probate inventories and book ownership,

circulated at conference on 'Books and book ownership in early modern England', University of East Anglia, March 1978
Overton, Mark. 'Probate inventories from the consistory court of the diocese of Norwich', unpublished transcriptions
Samaha, Joel. 'Notes on the examination books of Colchester, Essex, 1574—81', personal communication

Printed works: primary sources

Almanac for 1652—58. Huntington Library, ref. 429497
Arber, Edward, *A transcript of the registers of the company of stationers of London*, vols. 3 and 4 (1876—7)
Ascham, Roger, *The scholemaster, or plaine and perfite way of teachyng children to understand, write and speake the Latin tong* (1570)
The association, agreement and protestation of the counties of Cornwall and Devon (Oxford, 1643)
Bales, Peter, *The writing schoolemaster* (1590)
Ball, John, *A short treatise contayning all the principall grounds of Christian religion*, 9th impression (1633)
Baxter, Richard, *A Christian directory* (1673)
— *The poor husbandman's advocate* (1691), ed. Frederick J. Powicke (Manchester, 1926)
— *The poor man's family book* (1674)
— *Reliquiae Baxterianae* (1696)
— *Treatise of self-denyall* (1660)
Billingsley, Martin, *The pens excellencie: or the secretaries delighte* (1618)
Blagg, Thomas M., and L. Lloyd Simpson (eds.), *Derbyshire parish registers* (1914—17)
Blake, William J., 'Hooker's synopsis chorographical of Devonshire', *Report and Transactions of the Devonshire Association*, 47 (1915)
Bownde, Nicholas, *The doctrine of the sabbath* (1595)
Brears, Peter C. D. (ed.), 'Yorkshire probate inventories', *Yorkshire Archaeological Society Record Series*, 134 (1972)
Breton, Nicholas, *The court and country* (1618), in W. H. Dunham and S. Pargellis (eds.), *Complaint and reform in England 1436—1714* (New York, 1938)
Brinsley, John, *A consolation for our grammar schooles* (1622)
— *Ludus literarius, or the grammar schoole* (1612)
Brown, David, *The introduction to the true understanding of the whole arte of expedition in teaching to write* (1638)
— *The new invention intituled calligraphia* (St Andrews, 1622)
Bullard, J. V. (ed.), *Constitutions and canons ecclesiastical* (1934)
Bullokar, William, *A short introduction or guiding to print, write and read Inglish speech* (1580)
Bunyan, John, *Sighs from hell*, 2nd edn (1666?)
Calendar of State Papers, Domestic
Camden, William, *Britain* (1610)
Carter, Hector (ed.), 'The Surrey Protestation returns, 1641/2', *Surrey Archaeological Collections*, 59 (1962)
Cash, Margaret (ed.), 'Devon inventories of the sixteenth and seventeenth centuries', *Devon and Cornwall Record Society*, 11 (1966)

Cecil, William, 'A memorial for Thomas Cecil' (1561), in Louis B. Wright (ed.), *Advice to a son* (Ithaca, New York, 1962)
Chamberlayne, Edward, *Angliae notitia*, 3rd edn (1669)
Clement, F[rancis], *The petie schole* (1587)
Comenius, John Amos, *The great didactic* (1657), ed. M. W. Keating, 2nd edn (1910)
— *A reformation of schooles* (1642)
Conset, Henry, *The practice of the spiritual or ecclesiastical courts* (1685)
Constitutions and canons ecclesiastical . . . agreed 1603 (1612)
Coote, Edmund, *The English schoole-master* (1624 edn)
Defoe, Daniel, *A review of the state of the British nation* (1708)
Dick, Oliver Lawson (ed.), *Aubrey's brief lives* (1950)
Dobson, Christopher S. A. (ed.), 'Oxfordshire Protestation Returns 1641—2', *Oxfordshire Record Society*, 36 (1955)
Drucker, Lucy (ed.), 'Administrations in the archdeaconry of Northampton, 1667—1710', *British Record Society* (1947)
Dunham, W. H., and S. Pargellis (eds.), *Complaint and reform in England 1436—1714* (New York, 1938)
Dury, John, *The reformed school* (1649)
Dyer, A. D. (ed.), 'Probate inventories of Worcester tradesmen, 1545—1614', *Worcester Historical Society Miscellany*, 2 (1967)
Emmison, F. G. (ed.), *Bedfordshire parish registers* (Bedford, 1933)
— 'Jacobean household inventories', *Publications of the Bedfordshire Historical Record Society*, 20 (1938)
The English Reports (1903—8)
Favine, Andrew, *The theater of honour and knighthood* (1623)
Firth, C. H., and R. S. Rait (eds.), *Acts and ordinances of the interregnum, 1642—1660* (1911)
Frere, W. H. (ed.), *Visitation articles and injunctions of the period of the reformation* (1910)
Frith, Brian (ed.), *Gloucestershire marriage allegations 1637—1680* (Gloucester, 1954)
Fry, E. A. and G. S. (eds.), 'The Dorset Protestation returns, 1641—2', *Dorset Records*, 12 (1912)
Fuller, Thomas, *The holy state*, 2nd edn (Cambridge, 1648)
Gandy, Wallace (ed.), *The Association oath rolls of the British plantations* (1922)
— (ed.), *Lancashire Association oath rolls* (1921)
Gibson, Edmund, *Codex juris ecclesiastici Anglicani* (1713)
Gouge, William, *Of domesticall duties* (1622)
Harrison, William, *The description of England*, ed. Georges Edelen (Ithaca, New York, 1968)
Hart, John, *A methode or comfortable beginning for all unlearned to read English* (1570)
— *An orthographie* (1569)
Hartlib, Samuel, *Considerations tending to the happy accomplishment of England's reformation* (1647)
Havinden, M. A. (ed.), *Household and farm inventories of Oxfordshire, 1550—1590* (Historical Manuscripts Commission, 1965)
Hervey, S. H. A. (ed.), *Suffolk in 1524, being the return for a subsidy granted in 1523* (Woodbridge, 1910)
— (ed.), *Suffolk in 1674, being the hearth tax returns* (Woodbridge, 1905)
Hoole, Charles, *A new discovery of the old art of teaching schoole* (1660)

Howell, James, *Epistolae Ho-Elianae. The familiar letters of James Howell*, ed. Joseph Jacobs (1890—2)

Injunctions gyven by the auctoritie of the kynges highnes to the clergie (1536)

Inman, Francis, *A light unto the unlearned* (1622)

Jeaffreson, John Cordy (ed.), *Middlesex county records* (1887)

Jenkyns, Henry (ed.), *The remains of Thomas Cranmer* (1833)

Journals of the House of Commons, 1640—2

Journals of the House of Commons, 1642—4

Journals of the House of Lords, 1628—42

Kempe, William, *The education of children in learning* (1588)

Kennedy, P. A. (ed.), 'Nottinghamshire household inventories', *Thoroton Society Record Series*, 22 (1963)

Kennett, White, *The charity of schools for poor children* (1706)

Kenyon, G. H. 'Kirdford inventories, 1611 to 1776', *Sussex Archaeological Collections*, 93 (1955)

King, Gregory, 'A scheme of the income and expence of the several families of England, calculated for the year 1688', in Charles Davenant, *Political and commercial works*, ed. Sir C. Whitworth (1771)

Lambard, William, *Eirenarcha, or the office of the justices of the peace*, revised edition (1614)

LeHardy, William (ed.), *County of Middlesex, calendar to the sessions records*, new series, vol. 1 (1935)

— (ed.), *Hertfordshire county records, calendar to the sessions books* (Hertford, 1930)

Letters and papers, foreign and domestic, of the reign of Henry VIII.

Lye, Thomas, *A new spelling-book* (1677)

Macfarlane, Alan (ed.), *The diary of Ralph Josselin, 1616—1683* (1976)

Markham, Gervase, *The English husbandman* (1613)

Milles, Thomas, *The catalogue of honor, or tresury of true nobility peculiar and proper to the isle of Great Britaine* (1610)

Moore, John S. (ed.), *The goods and chattels of our forefathers. Frampton Cotterell and district probate inventories* (Chichester, 1976)

More, Thomas, *The apologye* (1533)

Mulcaster, Richard, *Positions . . . for the training up of children* (1581)

— *The first part of the elementarie* (1582)

Muller, James Arthur (ed.), *The letters of Stephen Gardiner* (Cambridge, 1933)

Nash, Thomas, *A pleasant comedie called Summers last will and testament* (1600)

Newcourt, Richard, *Repertorium ecclesiasticum parochiale Londinense* (1708—10)

Norden, John, *Speculi Britanniae pars: an historical and chorographical description of Essex* (1594), ed. Sir Henry Ellis (Camden Society, 1840)

— *Speculum Britanniae: an historical and chorographical description of Middlesex and Hartfordshire* [1593—8] (1723)

Nowell, Alexander, *A catechism, or first instruction and learning of Christian religion* (1571)

The office of Christian parents (Cambridge, 1616)

Osborne, Francis, *Advice to a son* (1656), ed. Louis B. Wright (Ithaca, New York, 1962)

Overton, Richard, *An appeale from the degenerate representative body* (1647)

Pank, W., *A most breefe, easie and plain receite for faire writing* (1591)

Piccope, G. J. (ed.), *Lancashire and Cheshire wills and inventories* (Chetham Society, 1857)

Proby, Granville (ed.), 'The Protestation returns for Huntingdonshire', *Trans. Cambridgeshire and Huntingdonshire Arch. Soc.*, 5 (1937)

Raine, James, William Greenwell, J. C. Hodgson and Herbert Maxwell Wood (eds.), 'Wills and inventories from the registry at Durham', *Surtees Society Publications*, 2 (1835), 38 (1860), 112 (1906), 142 (1929)

Rastell, John, *The grete abregement of the statutys* (1527)

Renshaw, Walter C., 'Witnesses from ecclesiastical deposition books, 1580– 1640', *Sussex Archaeological Collections*, 55 (1914)

Reyce, Robert, *The breviary of Suffolk, 1618*, ed. Lord Francis Hervey (1902)

Rice, R. Garraway (ed.), 'West Sussex Protestation returns', *Sussex Record Society*, 5 (1906)

Robinson, C. J. (ed.), *A register of the scholars admitted into Merchant Taylors' school, from a.d. 1562 to 1874* (Lewes, 1882–3)

Roper, John S., *Dudley probate inventories* (Dudley, 1965–6)

— *Sedgley probate inventories 1614–1787* (Dudley, 1960)

Sachse, William L. (ed.), *The diary of Roger Lowe* (1938)

Savage, Richard, and Edgar I. Fripp (eds.), *Minutes and accounts of the corporation of Stratford upon Avon* (Oxford, 1921–4)

Shakespeare, William, *Henry VI, Part 2*

Smith, Sir Thomas, *De republica anglorum* (1583)

Sparke, Michael, *Scintilla, or a light broken into darke warehouses* (1641)

Spedding, J. (ed.), *The letters and life of Francis Bacon*, vol. 4 (1868)

Starkey, Thomas, 'A dialogue between Cardinal Pole and Thomas Lupset', in Sidney J. Herrtage (ed.), *England in the reign of King Henry VIII* (1927)

Statutes of the Realm

Steele, Richard, *The husbandmans calling . . . being the substance of XII sermons preached to a country congregation*, 2nd edn (1672)

— *The religious tradesman* (1747)

— *The trades-man's calling* (1684)

Steer, Francis, W., *Farm and cottage inventories of mid-Essex 1635–1749*, 2nd edn (Chichester, 1969)

Steer, Francis W. (ed.), *Scriveners' company common paper . . . to 1678* (1968)

Stoate, T. L. (ed.), *The Cornwall Protestation returns* (Bristol, 1974)

Stoate, T. L., and A. J. Howard (eds.), *The Devon Protestation returns, 1641* (Bristol, 1973)

Stubbes, Phillip, *Anatomie of abuses* (1583)

Swinnock, George, *The Christian mans calling . . . the second part* (1663)

Tryon, Thomas, *Some memoirs of the life of Mr. Thomas Tryon . . . written by himself* (1705)

Turner, J. Horsfall (ed.), *The Rev. Oliver Heywood, B.A., 1630–1702; his autobiography, diaries, anecdotes and event books* (1882)

Vaisey, D. G., 'Probate inventories of Lichfield and district, 1568–1680', *Collections for a History of Staffordshire*, 5 (1969)

Wase, Christopher, *Considerations concerning free schools* (Oxford, 1678)

Willis, Arthur J. (ed.), *Winchester consistory court depositions, 1561–1602* (Lyminge, Kent, 1960)
Wilson, Thomas, *The state of England, anno dom. 1600*, ed. F. J. Fisher, *Camden Miscellany*, 16 (1936)
Wood, H. M. (ed.), 'Durham Protestations', *Surtees Society Publications*, 135 (1922)

Printed works: secondary sources

Adamson, J. W., *The illiterate Anglo-Saxon* (Cambridge, 1946)
Altick, Richard D., *The English common reader. A social history of the mass reading public, 1800–1900* (Chicago, 1957)
Axtell, James, *The school upon a hill; education and society in colonial New England* (New Haven, 1974)
Baldwin, T. W., *William Shakespere's petty school* (Urbana, 1943)
 — *William Shakespere's small Latine and lesse Greeke* (Urbana, 1941)
Beckingsale, D. W., 'The characteristics of the Tudor north', *Northern History*, 4 (1969)
Bennett, H. S. *English books and readers, 1475 to 1557* (Cambridge, 1969)
 — *English books and readers, 1558 to 1603* (Cambridge, 1965)
 — *English books and readers, 1603 to 1640* (Cambridge, 1970)
Bishop, Morris (ed.), *Letters from Petrarch* (Bloomington, Indiana, 1966)
Blagden, Cyprian, 'The distribution of almanacks in the second half of the seventeenth century', *Studies in Bibliography*, 11 (1958)
Blalock, H. M., *Social statistics* (New York, 1960)
Bond, Maurice F., *Guide to the records of parliament* (1971)
Brand, John, *Observations on popular antiquities*, ed. Henry Ellis (1813)
Bridenbaugh, Carl, *Vexed and troubled Englishmen, 1590–1642* (Oxford, 1968)
Brown, E. H. Phelps, and Sheila V. Hopkins, 'Seven centuries of the price of consumables, compared with builders' wage rates' *Economica*, 23 (1956)
Burn, Richard, *Ecclesiastical law* (1763)
Campbell, Mildred, *The English yeoman under Elizabeth and the early Stuarts* [1942] (1967)
Campbell, Oscar James, and Edward G. Quinn, *The reader's encyclopedia of Shakespeare* (New York, 1966)
Capp, Bernard S., *Astrology and the popular press, 1500–1800* (1979)
Carlisle, N., *A concise description of the endowed grammar schools in England and Wales* (1818)
Catalogue of the pamphlets, books, newspapers . . . collected by George Thomason, 1640–1661 (1908)
Charlton, Kenneth, *Education in Renaissance England* (1965)
Chartier, Roger, Dominique Julia and Marie-Madeleine Compère, *L'éducation en France du XVIe au XVIIIe siècle* (Paris, 1976)
Cipolla, Carlo M., *Literacy and development in the west* (1969)
Clark, Peter, *English provincial society* (Hassocks, Sussex, 1977)
 — 'The ownership of books in England, 1560–1640', in Lawrence Stone (ed.), *Schooling and society* (Baltimore, 1976)
Coate, Mary, *Cornwall in the great civil war . . . 1642–60* (Oxford, 1933).
Cornwall, Julian, 'Evidence of population mobility in the seventeenth century', *Bulletin of the Institute of Historical Research*, 40 (1967)

Cressy, David, *Education in Tudor and Stuart England* (1975)
- 'Educational opportunity in Tudor and Stuart England', *History of Education Quarterly*, 16 (1976)
- 'Describing the social order of Elizabethan and Stuart England', *History and Literature*, 3 (1976)
- 'Levels of illiteracy in England, 1530–1730', *Historical Journal*, 20 (1977)
- 'Occupations, migration and literacy in east London, 1580–1640', *Local Population Studies*, 5 (1970)
- 'School and college admission ages in seventeenth-century England', *History of Education*, 8 (1979)
- 'Social status and literacy in north-east England, 1560–1630', *Local Population Studies*, 21 (1978)
Davids, T. W., *Annals of evangelical nonconformity in the county of Essex* (1863)
Davies, Godfrey, *The early Stuarts*, 2nd edn (Oxford, 1959)
Doucet, Roger, *Les institutions de la France au XVIe siècle* (Paris, 1948)
Dugdale, Sir William, *The antiquities of Warwickshire*, 2nd edn (1730)
Dyer, Alan D., *The city of Worcester in the sixteenth century* (Leicester, 1973)
Edwards, L. W. Lawson, 'A checklist of printed Protestations', *Genealogists' Magazine*, 19 (1977)
Eisenstein, Elizabeth L., *The printing press as an agent of change: communications and cultural transformations in early modern Europe* (Cambridge and New York, 1978)
Elton, G. R., *Policy and police: the enforcement of the Reformation in the age of Thomas Cromwell* (Cambridge, 1972)
- *Reform and reformation, England 1509–1558* (1977)
- *Reform and renewal, Thomas Cromwell and the common weal* (Cambridge, 1973)
Emmison, F. G., *Elizabethan life: morals and the church courts* (Chelmsford, 1973)
Everitt, Alan, 'Farm labourers', in Joan Thirsk (ed.), *The agrarian history of England and Wales*, vol. 4 (Cambridge, 1967)
- 'The marketing of agricultural produce', in Joan Thirsk (ed.), *The agrarian history of England and Wales*, vol. 4 (Cambridge, 1967)
Fletcher, Anthony, *A county community in peace and war: Sussex 1600–1660* (1975)
Furet, François, and Jacques Ozouf, *Lire et écrire: l'alphabétisation des Français de Calvin à Jules Ferry* (Paris, 1977)
Furet, François, and Wladimir Sachs, 'La croissance de l'alphabétisation en France: XVIIIe–XIXe siècle', *Annales: E.S.C.*, 29 no. 3 (1974)
Gabel, Leona C., *Benefit of clergy in England in the later middle ages* (Northampton, Mass., 1928)
Gardiner, Dorothy, *English girlhood at school* (1929)
Gardiner, S. R., *History of England . . . 1603–1642* (1884)
Greg, W. W., 'Entrance, licence and publication', *The Library*, 25 (1944)
Guigue, M. G., *De l'origine de la signature et de son emploi au moyen age* (Paris, 1863)
Hart, Simon, 'Enige statistiche gegevens inzake analfabetisme te Amsterdam in de 17e en 18e eeuw', *Amstelodamum*, 55 (1968)

Heal, Ambrose, *The English writing-masters and their copy-books 1570–1800* (Cambridge, 1931)

Héricourt, Louis de, *Les loix ecclésiastiques de France* (Paris, 1756)

Hervey, John, Lord, *Some materials towards memoirs of the reign of king George II*, ed. Romney Sedgwick (1931)

Hey, David G., *An English rural community* (Leicester, 1974)

Hill, Christopher, *Economic problems of the church, from Archbishop Whitgift to the Long Parliament* (Oxford, 1956)

— 'Puritans and the "dark corners of the land" ', *Transactions of the Royal Historical Society*, 5, no. 13 (1963)

Hirst, Derek, *The representative of the people? Voters and voting in England under the early Stuarts* (Cambridge, 1975)

Hollingsworth, T. H., *Historical demography* (Ithaca, New York, 1969)

Holmes, Clive, *The Eastern Association in the English civil war* (Cambridge, 1974)

James, Mervyn, *Family, lineage and civil society. A study of society, politics and mentality in the Durham region, 1500–1640* (Oxford, 1974)

Jenkinson, Hilary, *The later court hands in England* (Cambridge, 1927)

Johansson, Egil, 'The history of literacy in Sweden in comparison with some other countries', *Educational Reports Umea*, 12 (1977)

Jones, M. G., *The charity school movement* [1938] (1964)

Jordan, W. K., *Philanthropy in England, 1480–1660* (1959)

Kenyon, G. H., 'Petworth town and trades 1610–1760, part 2', *Sussex Archaeological Collections*, 98 (1960)

Kingston, Alfred, *East Anglia and the great civil war* (1897)

— *Hertfordshire during the great civil war* (1894)

Laqueur, Thomas, 'The cultural origins of popular literacy in England, 1500–1850', *Oxford Review of Education*, 2 (1976)

Laslett, Peter, *The world we have lost*, 2nd edn (1971)

— 'The wrong way through the telescope: a note on literary evidence in sociology and historical sociology', *British Journal of Sociology*, 27 (1976)

Law, James T., *Forms of ecclesiastical law* (1831)

Lawson, John, and Harold Silver, *A social history of education in England* (1973)

Leach, A. F., *English schools at the reformation* (1896)

Lockridge, Kenneth A., *Literacy in colonial New England* (New York, 1974)

Macfarlane, Alan, *Reconstructing historical communities* (Cambridge, 1977)

McGrath, Patrick, 'Notes on the history of marriage licences', in Brian Frith (ed.), *Gloucestershire marriage allegations 1637–1680* (Gloucester, 1954)

McKenzie, D. F., *The London book trade in the later seventeenth century* (The Sandars Lectures, Cambridge (mimeograph) 1976)

Marchant, R. A., *The church under the law* (Cambridge, 1969)

Mason, Wilmer G., 'The annual output of Wing-listed titles 1649–1684', *The Library*, 29 (1974)

Morant, Philip, *The history and antiquities of the county of Essex* (1768)

Morrill, J. S., *Cheshire 1630–1660: county government and society during the English revolution* (Oxford, 1974)

Neuburg, Victor E., *Popular literature, a history and guide* (1977)

Nie, Norman H. *et al.*, *Statistical package for the social sciences*, 2nd edn (New York, 1975)

Notestein, Wallace, 'The English woman, 1580 to 1650', in J. H. Plumb (ed.), *Studies in social history* (1955)

O'Day, Rosemary, 'Church records and the history of education in early modern England, 1558–1642: a problem in methodology', *History of Education*, 2 (1973)

Oughton, Thomas, *Ordo judiciorum* (1738)

Outhwaite, R. B., 'Age at marriage in England from the late seventeenth to the nineteenth century', *Transactions of the Royal Historical Society*, 5, no. 23 (1973)

Patten, John, 'The hearth taxes, 1662–1689', *Local Population Studies*, 7 (1971)

Pilgrim, J. E., 'The rise of the new draperies in Essex', *University of Birmingham Historical Journal*, 7 (1958–9)

Roy, Ian, 'The English civil war and English society', in Brian Bond and Ian Roy (eds.), *War and society* (New York, 1975)

Royal Commission on Historical Manuscripts, *Fifth report* (1876)

Rylands, J. Paul, 'Merchants' marks and other medieval personal marks', *Transactions of the Historic Society of Lancashire and Cheshire*, 62 (1911)

Sanderson, Michael, 'Literacy and social mobility in the industrial revolution', *Past and Present*, 56 (1972)

Scheffer, J. De Hoop, *History of the free churchmen . . . 1581–1701* (Ithaca, New York, 1922)

Schlatter, Richard B., *The social ideas of religious leaders 1660–1688*, (Oxford, 1940)

Schoenbaum, S., *William Shakespeare, a documentary life* (New York, 1975).

Schofield, R. S., 'Dimensions of illiteracy, 1750–1850', *Explorations in Economic History*, 10 (1973)

— 'The measurement of literacy in pre-industrial England', in Jack Goody (ed.), *Literacy in traditional societies* (Cambridge, 1968)

— 'Sampling in historical research', in E. A. Wrigley (ed.), *Nineteenth-century society* (Cambridge, 1972)

Schools Inquiry Commission, Report, Appendix 4, *Parliamentary Papers*, 1867–8, vol. 28

Schulz, Herbert C., 'The teaching of handwriting in Tudor and Stuart times', *Huntington Library Quarterly*, 6 (1943)

Siegel, Sidney, *Nonparametric statistics for the behavioral sciences* (New York, 1956)

Simon, Joan, *Education and society in Tudor England* (Cambridge, 1967)

— 'Was there a charity school movement?', in Brian Simon (ed.), *Education in Leicestershire* (Leicester, 1968)

Sisson, Charles, 'Marks as signatures', *The Library*, 9 (1928)

Smith, Alan, 'Endowed schools in the diocese of Lichfield and Coventry, 1660–99', *History of Education*, 4 (1975)

Smith, Harold, *The ecclesiastical history of Essex under the Long Parliament and Commonwealth* (Colchester, 1932)

Smout, T. C., *A history of the Scottish people 1560–1830*, 2nd edn (1970)

Somerville, C. John, 'On the distribution of religious and occult literature in seventeenth-century England', *The Library*, 29 (1974)

— *Popular religion in Restoration England* (Gainesville, Florida, 1977)

Spufford, Margaret, *Contrasting communities, English villagers in the sixteenth and seventeenth centuries* (Cambridge, 1974)

— 'First steps in literacy: the reading and writing experiences of the humblest seventeenth-century spiritual autobiographers', *Social History*, 4, no. 3 (Oct. 1979), pp. 407–35

— 'Samuel Pepys' chapbook collection and the prosperity and stock of some of the chapbook publishers', forthcoming (*The Library*, 1981)

Steer, Francis W., 'Probate inventories', *History*, 47 (1962)

Stephens, W. B., 'Illiteracy and schooling in the provincial towns, 1640–1870: a comparative approach', in D. A. Reeder (ed.), *Urban education in the nineteenth century* (1977)

— 'Male and female adult illiteracy in seventeenth-century Cornwall', *Journal of Educational Administration and History*, 12 (1977)

— 'Male illiteracy in Devon on the eve of the civil war', *Devon Historian*, 11 (1975)

— *Sources for English local history* (Manchester, 1973)

Stone, Lawrence, 'Communication', *Past and Present*, 24 (1963)

— 'The educational revolution in England, 1560–1640', *Past and Present*, 28 (1964)

— 'Literacy and education in England, 1640–1900', *Past and Present*, 42 (1969)

— 'The size and composition of the Oxford student body 1580–1910', in Lawrence Stone (ed.), *The university in society* (Princeton, New Jersey, 1975)

Stone, Lawrence (ed.), *The university in society* (Princeton, New Jersey, 1974)

Stowe, A. Monroe, *English grammar schools in the reign of Queen Elizabeth* (New York, 1908)

Tate, W. E., *The parish chest*, 3rd edn (Cambridge, 1969)

Tawney, A. J. and R. H., 'An occupational census of the seventeenth century', *Economic History Review*, 5 (1934–5)

Thirsk, Joan (ed.), *The agrarian history of England and Wales*, vol. 4, 1500–1640 (Cambridge, 1967)

— 'Sources of information on population, 1500–1760', *The Amateur Historian*, 4 (1959)

Thomas, Keith, *Religion and the decline of magic* (1971)

— 'Women and the civil war sects', *Past and Present*, 13 (1958)

Thrupp, Sylvia L., *The merchant class of medieval London* (Chicago, 1948)

Urban, Waclaw, 'La connaissance de l'écriture en Petite-Pologne dans la seconde moitié du XVIe siècle', *Przeglad Historyczny*, 68 (1977)

Vann, Richard T., 'Literacy in seventeenth-century England: some hearth tax evidence', *Journal of Interdisciplinary History*, 5 (1974)

Victoria history of the counties of England

Vincent, W. A. L., *The state and school education 1640–1660* (1950)

— *The grammar schools: their continuing tradition, 1660–1714* (1969)

Waller, William Chapman, 'Ship-money in Essex, 1634–40', *Transactions of the Essex Archaeological Society*, n.s., 8 (1903)

Watson, Foster, *The English grammar schools to 1660* (1908)

Webster, Charles, *Samuel Hartlib and the advancement of learning* (Cambridge, 1970)

West, E. G., 'Literacy and the industrial revolution', *Economic History Review*, 2nd ser., 31, no. 3 (1978)

Wheatley, William, *The history of Edward Latymer and his foundations* (Hammersmith, 1953)

Withrington, Donald J., 'Lists of schoolmasters teaching Latin, 1690', *Scottish History Society, Miscellany*, 10 (1965)

Wright, Louis B., *Middle-class culture in Elizabethan England* (Chapel Hill, 1935)

Wright, Thomas, *The history and topography of the county of Essex* (1831–5)

Wrigley, E. A., 'A simple model of London's importance', *Past and Present*, 37 (1967)

Wyczanski, Andrzej, 'Alphabétisation et structure sociale en Pologne au XVIe siècle', *Annales, E.S.C.*, 29 (1974)

Zeller, Gaston, *Les institutions de la France au XVIe siècle* (Paris, 1948)

Index